ColdFusion 8 Developer Tutorial

An intense guide to creating professional ColdFusion web applications: get up to speed in ColdFusion and learn how to integrate with other web 2.0 technologies

John Farrar

BIRMINGHAM - MUMBAI

ColdFusion 8 Developer Tutorial

First published: June 2008

Production Reference: 1230608

Published by Packt Publishing Ltd.
32 Lincoln Road
Olton
Birmingham, B27 6PA, UK.

ISBN 978-1-847194-12-1

www.packtpub.com

Cover Image by Vinayak Chittar (vinayak.chittar@gmail.com)

Credits

Author

John Farrar

Reviewers

Rick Mason

Sean Corfield

Senior Acquisition Editor

Douglas Paterson

Development Editor

Ved Prakash Jha

Technical Editor

Shilpa Dube

Rasika Sathe

Copy Editor

Sumathi Sridhar

Editorial Team Leader

Mithil Kulkarni

Project Manager

Abhijeet Deobhakta

Project Coordinator

Lata Basantani

Indexer

Hemangini Bari

Proofreader

Chris Smith

Production Coordinator

Aparna Bhagat

Cover Work

Aparna Bhagat

About the Author

John Farrar started working with computer programming around 1977. He has had the opportunity to work on projects used by Apple, Blue Cross, Brunswick Recreation, Casio, GVSU, Johnson Controls, Sprint, and many others. This history covers over 30 years of knowledge and experience in the industry.

He started doing web development over ten years ago. In the early days of the Web, ColdFusion stood out to him not just as a way to make web pages into web applications but as a maturing solid platform good for the developer, site owner, and end users. He started at version 4.5 and has been enjoying every version upgrade more and more.

John owns a company called SOSensible. His company does work for large companies but has a special focus on also making sure technology is approachable beyond the enterprise. It has developed a number of Open Source solutions including COOP. COOP is a mix of "Custom Tags" and "CFCs" that provides structure while keeping development simpler. It demonstrates his love for the things that make ColdFusion/CFML a delightful language to build websites. COOP is a pet project of his that can allow upgrades of AJAX libraries and add in features as the libraries grow.

He has spoken at national and regional conferences, online meetings, and area user group meetings. He is also an Adobe User Group manager. John knows that community is a viable and productive tool to build developers and the companies they serve. He has learned much from great resources in the community including bloggers, books, conferences, and resources to great in number to mention here. He blogs them at `http://www.sosensible.com/index.cfm/blog/index/` and encourages others to join in and build the community with him.

Contact: `johnfarrar@sosensible.com`

Alternative Email: `sosensible@gmail.com`.

Thanks to Douglas Paterson, and the many staff members of Packt Publishing for helping me through my first published book. The guides and interaction were a great experience that helped me in numerous ways. There were a couple of community editors who helped review technical content. These assistants were Sean Corfield and Rick Mason and many of the suggestions made by them have been added to this book and are on file towards any revisions in the future. The efforts of the various people who work on Open Source and share their work with the community at large should be appreciated. Several were kind enough to work with me if there were any questions in writing this book and it is truly appreciated.

Also thanks to the love of my life, Jeanine, who enthusiastically motivated me to see the book through to completion.

About the Reviewers

Sean Corfield is the architect behind large-scale, high-availability websites for companies such as Macromedia, Toshiba, Oracle, Toyota, and Thomas Cook. He is a frequent speaker on software design within the ColdFusion community, at user groups and conferences across the world. Sean has championed and contributed to a number of ColdFusion frameworks and his passion for standards and software engineering led him to work on the C++ Standards Committee for eight years.

He is currently Chief Systems Architect and Vice President of Engineering at Broadchoice, Inc. based in the Bay Area, California.

Contact: sean@corfield.org

Rick Mason has been programming for over 20 years and has been a ColdFusion developer since 1999. He started SeedChoices.com, an ASP sales force automation solution for the farm seed industry seven years ago.

Mr. Mason is currently Senior Web Developer for SeeProgress.com. The Brighton, MI based firm lets consumers view progress of repairs online. They were honored in 2007 as one of the top 50 companies in the state to watch by the Edward Lowe foundation.

He also manages the Mid-Michigan ColdFusion Users Group, www.coldfusion.org, and is an active member of the ColdFusion community.

Contact: rmason@acd.net

Alternative Email: Rick@SeedChoices.com

I would like to thank my nieces, Danielle and Sarah Stone, for their continued inspiration.

Table of Contents

Preface   1

Chapter 1: Web Pages—Static to Dynamic   7
  Turning HTML into a Dynamic Web Page   7
  Understanding and Using Simple Variables   11
  Understanding Structures   16
  Let Us Get Interactive   18
  Setting Page Defaults   23
  Introduction to Lists and Loops   27
  Understanding Arrays   29
  Conditional Processing with If   32
  Conditional Processing with Switch   35
  Summary   36

Chapter 2: Basic CFCs and Database Interaction   37
  Our First CFC   38
  Our First Object   38
    Product (object)   38
  Using an Object Constructor   42
  Connecting to a Database   45
  Returning Data from the CFC   47
  Making Our Data Query Flexible   50
  The Basic Data Object Concept   53
  Object Method Access Control   56
  Summary   57

Chapter 3: Power CFCs and Web Forms   59
  The Practice of Protecting Access   60
  Web Forms Introduction   61
  Managing Our Product Data   64
  Getting Data to Our Edit Page   65

Saving Our Data	68
Improving Page Flow	71
Adding a New Record	72
Let Us Look Under the Hood	74
Summary	76
Chapter 4: Application, Session, and Request Scope	**77**
Life Span	77
Introducing the Application.cfc Object	79
Application Variables	82
The Start Methods	85
Application Start Method	85
Session Start Method	86
Request Start Method	87
The End Methods	87
Request End Method	88
Session End Method	88
Application End Method	88
On Error Method	89
Scope Visibility	89
Practical Application	92
Mappings per Application	93
Custom Tag Paths per Application	93
Summary	94
Chapter 5: Introduction to Custom Tags	**95**
Different Forms of Code Reuse	95
CFCs	96
Custom Tags	96
CFInclude	96
Our First Custom Tag	97
Custom Header/Footer Tags	98
Nested Tags	101
CFInclude from Custom Tags	106
Templates versus Skins	109
Managing Custom Tags	110
CFModule Approach	110
Tag Library Approach	111
Summary	111
Chapter 6: Better Interfaces for JavaScript Libraries	**113**
Thickbox Library HTML Style	114
ColdFusion-Powered Thickbox	116

Where Am I? (via Google Maps)	**121**
ColdFusion JavaScript	**127**
Multiple State Form Items	128
Inside the Fancy Form Tag	130
Summary	**132**
Chapter 7: Authentication and Permissions	**133**
How ColdFusion Recognizes Users	**133**
Custom Authentication (Additional Power)	**138**
Authentication Data Model	139
How to Use Advanced Authentication	142
Extra Notes	**146**
Summary	**146**
Chapter 8: CF AJAX User Interface	**147**
HTML-Based Websites	147
Server-Side Languages	148
Browser-Side Applications	148
Flash	148
JavaScript	148
ColdFusion AJAX	**149**
Layout	149
<cfdiv />	149
<cflayout />	151
<cfpod />	157
<cfwindow />	158
Menus and Tool Tips	163
<cfmenu />	163
<cftooltip />	166
Styling Notes	**168**
Tips	**168**
Summary	**169**
Chapter 9: CF AJAX Forms	**171**
Forms	**171**
<cfgrid />	172
Grid Paging	173
Grid Updates and Deletes	**176**
Linked Grids	**179**
<cfinput />	181
Binding Page Elements	**181**
Binding Immediately upon Load	182
The Date Requestor	**184**

The Autosuggest Box	**185**
<cfselect />	187
<cftextarea />	190
<cftree />	192
The Directory Tree	**194**
Summary	**197**
Chapter 10: CF AJAX Programming	**199**
Binding	**199**
On Page Binding	200
CFC Binding	200
JavaScript Binding	202
URL Binding	203
Bind with Event	**204**
Extra Binding Notes	**205**
Multiple Radio Buttons or Check Boxes and Multiple Select	**206**
Spry Binding	206
CFAJAXProxy	**206**
CFAJAX Proxy Binding	**207**
CFC Proxy Class Objects	**208**
Client Debugging	**213**
Firebug	**213**
Built-In Debugging	**215**
Logging Features	216
Customization	217
Automatically Wired AJAX Links	218
Execute JavaScript after Loading Content	219
Other Cool Commands	220
Post for CFAJAX Calls	221
Summary	**221**
Chapter 11: Working with PDF	**223**
Generating PDF Pages	**223**
Our First PDF Page Conversion	223
Splitting into Sections	224
Adding Headers and Footers and Variables	225
Adding Page Breaks and Variables	226
Adding Bookmarks	227
Saving PDF Documents	228
Printing from the Server	**228**
Working with PDF Forms	**230**
Populating PDF Forms with Data	**230**

Reading Data from PDF Forms	**233**
Manipulating PDF Documents	**234**
Merging Documents	234
Deleting Pages	235
Encrypting PDF Documents	**235**
Generating Thumbnails	**236**
Adding Watermarks	**237**
Final Thoughts	**238**
Summary	**239**
Chapter 12: Building Search Abilities	**241**
Database Searching	**241**
Verity Search Solutions	**241**
Built-In Search Engine	**242**
Creating a Collection	242
Indexing a Collection	244
Searching a Collection	245
The Search Form	246
The Results Page	246
Search Techniques	248
PDF Linking to Searches	250
Suggestions	251
Integrating Third-Party Searching	**252**
Google Details	**252**
Custom Search Engines (Google)	**253**
On-The-Fly Search Engine	253
Simple Search	256
Search Types	257
Site Restricted	259
Local Search	260
Summary	**261**
Chapter 13: Working with Files, Email, and Images	**263**
Working with Files	**263**
Uploading Files	263
Local File Control	266
Write File	268
Read File	268
Rename File	269
Append File	270
Read File via Loop	270
Working with Email	**270**
Working with Images	**274**
Image Information	**277**
Summary	**281**

Chapter 14: Feeds, REST Services, and Web Services   283
Collaboration   283
Flickr   283
Feeds   283
RSS   284
    CDF   288
    JSON   289
    SQL   292
Introduction to REST Services   292
SOAP Web Services   298
Summary   303

Chapter 15: Building Dynamic Reports   305
Traditional Web Page Reporting   305
Simple Report   305
Grouped Data   307
Drill-Down Reporting   309
Output Formats   311
PDF Output   312
Excel Output   313
CVS Output   315
XML Output   316
JSON Output   316
Using CFReport and Report Builder   317
Summary   325

Chapter 16: Dynamically Generated Web Presentations   327
Introduction to CFPresentation   327
Mixing in the Media   329
Caching the Contents   334
Dynamic Benefits   338
Scenario 1: Sales Force   338
Scenario 2: Client-Specific Presentations   339
Scenario 3: Live Audience Sensitive Content   339
Summary   340

Appendix A: Getting Your System Ready for Development   341
Tools   341
AJAX   344
Ant   345
Database Engines   345
Database Tools   347

Media Tools	**347**
Audio Software	348
Image Software	348
Video Software	349
Reporting	**350**
SVN	**350**
Unit Testing	**350**
Conclusions	**351**
Appendix B: Resources to Build Your Skills	**353**
Blogs	**353**
ColdFusion Conferences	**354**
Coding Frameworks	**355**
General ColdFusion Sites	**357**
Libraries and Tools	**358**
Aspect or IoC or DI	358
Content Handling/Generation	**359**
Database	**359**
JavaScript	**361**
Project Management	**363**
Script	**363**
Search	**364**
Site Integration APIs	**364**
Unit Testing or Debugging	**370**
XML Tools and Products	**371**
Other Notable Works	**373**
Index	**375**

Preface

Adobe ColdFusion is an application server, renowned for rapid development of dynamic websites, with a straightforward language (CFML), powerful methods for packaging and reusing your code, and AJAX support that will get developers deep into powerful web applications quickly.

This book is the most intense guide to creating professional ColdFusion applications available. Packed with example code, and written in a friendly, easy-to-read style, this book is just want you need if you are serious about ColdFusion.

This book will give you clear, concise and, of course, practical guidance to take you from the basics of ColdFusion 8 to the skills that will make you a ColdFusion developer to be reckoned with.

ColdFusion expert John Farrar will teach you about the basics of ColdFusion programming, application architecture, and object reuse, before showing you a range of topics including AJAX library integration, RESTful Web Services, PDF creation and manipulation, and dynamically generated presentation files that will make you the toast of your ColdFusion developer town.

This book digs deep with the basics, with real-world examples of the how and whys, to get more done faster with ColdFusion 8.

This book also covers the new features of ColdFusion 8 Update 1.

What This Book Covers

Chapter 1 describes how to enhance basic HTML pages with the power and simplicity of ColdFusion. It also explains the difference between static HTML pages and dynamic ColdFusion pages.

Chapter 2 describes how to create object classes and instantiate object instances. It also describes the object constructors. This chapter explains how to connect to a database through the internal methods of our objects.

Chapter 3 helps us in understanding how to manage multiple products through common forms for listing, editing, and adding data. This chapter explains integrating and streamlining the workflow of web forms and CFC database processing.

In *Chapter 4*, we will learn how to use the web server memory to create engaging and interactive web applications by using variable scopes. We will also learn how to share some information, and how to protect the rest of the information in a controlled manner.

In *Chapter 5,* we will learn about the basics of custom tags. We will also learn how to integrate `cfinclude` for libraries of segments. This chapter also includes skinning a website by using custom tags, the use of nested tags, and so on.

Chapter 6 includes wrapping of the ThickBox gallery functions into a custom tag for simple functional reuse and wrapping of a Google map library into our code with a custom tag for simplified interactive maps. This chapter helps us in understanding how to create a multi-state form list wrapped in a custom tag.

In *Chapter 7*, we will see how to use the authentication that comes standard with CF. This chapter explains how to control the site content based on current user permissions.

In *Chapter 8,* we will see how AJAX is different from HTML and regular server-oriented web pages. This chapter includes the comparison of HTML, server, and browser technology sites. It also explains about the ColdFusion widgets.

In *Chapter 9,* we will see the benefit received from the combined power of tag-based encapsulation with AJAX functionality.

Chapter 10 explains about binding, proxy connections, JSON features, Spry data integration, and debugging.

In *Chapter 11*, we will have a look at the different ways in which we can reorganize pages of PDF documents into a new PDF file from one or more separate PDF source documents.

Chapter 12 explains how to create Verity search collections, how to initialize the Verity indexes, how to interface with the indexes. This chapter also explains how to interface with PDF content for more control when calling documents.

Chapter 13 discusses files, emails, and images. This chapter helps in understanding how some of the common ColdFusion features empower developers to shift the web pages to web applications in many ways.

In *Chapter 14*, we will learn how to interact with other web servers and create features on our site that will allow others to interact with us.

Chapter 15 gives a broad introduction to ColdFusion's way of generating dynamic reports. This chapter also gives a brief introduction to the ColdFusion Report Builder tool.

Chapter 16 shows the unique presentation capabilities built into ColdFusion. It gives practical examples to help build custom presentations with dynamic content on demand.

Appendix A covers some important details of setting up a development environment. It also includes some important tips for better productivity.

Appendix B includes some links and resources that are aimed at giving us a good starting base of information. It also explains a group of libaries that prove to be very significant.

What You Need for This Book

For ColdFusion 8 Developer Tutorial, you will require the ColdFusion version 8. Updater 1. You will need an SQL server for creating the databases or phpMyAdmin site/SQL server will also do.

Who This Book Is For

This book is for web developers working with ColdFusion 8.

If your goal is to get a good grounding in the basics of the language as quickly as possible and put a site together quickly, this book is ideal for you. If you want to learn more about professional programming of ColdFusion, this book is definitely for you.

No prior knowledge of ColdFusion is expected, but basic knowledge of general web and software development skills is assumed.

Conventions

In this book, you will find a number of styles of text that distinguish between different kinds of information. Here are some examples of these styles, and an explanation of their meaning.

There are three styles for code. Code words in text are shown as follows: "You will also observe that there is an attribute called `access="public"` in many of the methods."

A block of code will be set as follows:

```
<cfscript>
 objProduct = createObject("component","product_1").init();
 objProduct.set_name(name="Egg Plant");
 result = objProduct.get_name();
</cfscript>
<!--- Content --->
<cfoutput>
 #result#
</cfoutput>
```

When we wish to draw your attention to a particular part of a code block, the relevant lines or items will be made bold:

```
<tr>
 <td>Description:</td>
 <td>
  <textArea name="description" id="idDescription"></textArea>
 </td>
</tr>
```

New terms and **important words** are introduced in a bold-type font. Words that you see on the screen, in menus or dialog boxes for example, appear in our text like this: "We could have your site link from **About Us** to a pop-up window rather than a whole separate page."

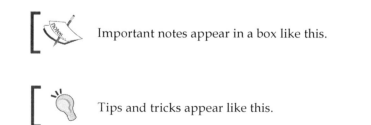

Important notes appear in a box like this.

Tips and tricks appear like this.

Reader Feedback

Feedback from our readers is always welcome. Let us know what you think about this book, what you liked or may have disliked. Reader feedback is important for us to develop titles that you really get the most out of.

To send us general feedback, simply drop an email to feedback@packtpub.com, making sure to mention the book title in the subject of your message.

If there is a book that you need and would like to see us publish, please send us a note in the **SUGGEST A TITLE** form on www.packtpub.com or email suggest@packtpub.com.

If there is a topic that you have expertise in and you are interested in either writing or contributing to a book, see our author guide on www.packtpub.com/authors.

Customer Support

Now that you are the proud owner of a Packt book, we have a number of things to help you to get the most from your purchase.

Downloading the Example Code for the Book

Visit http://www.packtpub.com/files/code/4121_Code.zip to directly downlad the example code.

The downloadable files contain instructions on how to use them.

Errata

Although we have taken every care to ensure the accuracy of our contents, mistakes do happen. If you find a mistake in one of our books—maybe a mistake in text or code—we would be grateful if you would report this to us. By doing this you can save other readers from frustration, and help to improve subsequent versions of this book. If you find any errata, report them by visiting http://www.packtpub.com/support, selecting your book, clicking on the **let us know** link, and entering the details of your errata. Once your errata are verified, your submission will be accepted and the errata added to the list of existing errata. The existing errata can be viewed by selecting your title from http://www.packtpub.com/support.

Questions

You can contact us at questions@packtpub.com if you are having a problem with some aspect of the book, and we will do our best to address it.

1
Web Pages—Static to Dynamic

In this chapter, you will learn how to enhance basic HTML pages with the power and simplicity of ColdFusion. This book demonstrates how to apply different techniques by building them into different real-world scenarios. In this chapter, we will apply what we learn about a prototype of a typical **FAQ** (Frequently Asked Questions) section of a website. We will cover the following skills in the process:

- Moving from HTML to dynamic web pages
- Simple and structured variables
- URL and CGI variable structures
- Setting default variables for pages
- Debugging and exception-handling techniques
- Working of lists and arrays in ColdFusion
- Repetition processes done with looping commands
- Conditional processing

Turning HTML into a Dynamic Web Page

Let us take a look at the differences between common HTML pages and the power of a server-side language. For now, we will leave the "pleasant side" of web pages. This is because we are going to focus our thinking on ColdFusion.

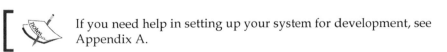 If you need help in setting up your system for development, see Appendix A.

Copy the "tutorial/chapter_1" directory to the "cfb/chapter_1" directory inside your server root. From your browser, enter http://localhost/cfb/chapter_1/1_1.htm in your address bar, and you will see a basic FAQ page. Open the "**view source option**" from the browser, and compare that with the code you will find when you open the file in an editor. You will find the same pages. Here, you will see that a normal server returns common HTML pages.

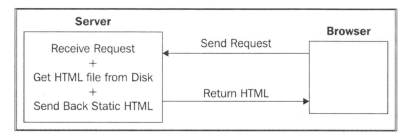

When ColdFusion is added, we have an extra step to how the pages are managed by the server. As a result, we are able to create pages that are made dynamic from the server side of the equation. This concept is the same for all server-side languages.

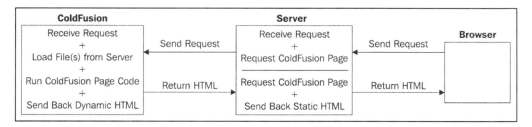

Now, let us get into a very basic introduction to ColdFusion. We will take one step at a time. Here is the code segment with common HTML. If you type the following code in an HTML page and load it into the browser, it will look the same as it does in the view source from the browser:

```
<!-- Example: 1_1.htm -->
<!-- HTML Comment -->
<div>
 <h3>Question: What is a variable?</h3>
  <p><strong>Answer:</strong></p>
  <p>     Variables are named storage containers inside programming
languages. Just think of variables as any type of named container
holding any type of stored content. You simply name the container and
store the content. Later you retrieve the content by using the same
name.</p>
  <p>12:53 PM</p>
</div>
```

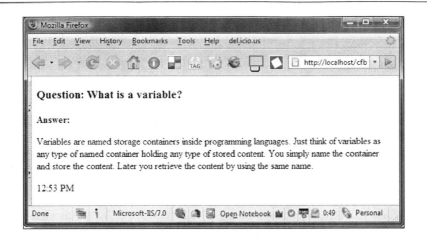

Now, we will look at a more dynamic version of the page by listing the required changes. You may be able to tell what is going on without any help, just by depending on your programming background.

Copy the file `1_1.htm` and save it as `1_2.cfm` in the same directory. Go back to the browser, and look for the web page, `http://localhost/cfb/chapter_1/1_2.cfm`. This page looks the same, and the code is basically the same if you use the browser page source view.

We are going to add the following two highlighted lines above the `<!-- HTML Comment -->`:

```
<!--- Processing --->
<!--- Content --->
<!-- HTML Comment -->
```

You will notice that the two new lines have three dashes instead of two. This is because they are "ColdFusion comments". If you go back to the browser and refresh the page, you will find something interesting when you view the source. The new comment lines, which you had added, are not shown on the page source since they are server-side ColdFusion comments. Remember to save the file before checking for the results.

First we have to create variables in ColdFusion. Add a line between the processing and content comments, and create the following two variables inside the `CFSet` tags. These variables are containers to store content for later use. Currently, we will be using them as text containers, and they will be known as "string variables".

```
<!--- Processing --->
<cfset myQuestion = "">
<cfset myAnswer = "">
<!--- Content --->
```

Cut the actual question out of the content section and paste it inside the quotes of the string variable, myQuestion. Now, cut the answer text out of the content section and paste it inside the quotes of the string variable, myAnswer. (The question and answer are the same as those specified in the previous example code.)

Now, we need to put the content, which we have moved to variables, back into the page. ColdFusion was the first to standardize server-side code tags. These look very much like HTML tags, but they add power and simplicity. We need to wrap our entire content section with CFOutput. Add the <cfoutput> opening tag right after the <--- Content ---> tag, and then put the </cfoutput> closing tag as the last line of the code page.

We have to place the variables in the content section of the code with some special ColdFusion output markers. ColdFusion uses the "pound" symbols on both sides of the dynamic content for markers. So put #myQuestion# in the place where you cut out the content section for the myQuestion variable.

Also, place #myAnswer# where you cut out the content section for the myAnswer variable. Save the file, and then run the page. (Check the following sample code for any issues to make sure that you typed things correctly. Then refresh the page again.)

We can output more variables. You can also replace the time with the function in the following code, at the end of the ColdFusion code sample. You can refresh the page over and over, and see that the time is being dynamically generated on the server:

```
<!--- Example: 1_2.cfm --->
<!--- Proccessing --->
<cfset myQuestion = "What is a variable?">
<cfset myAnswer = "Variables are named storage containers inside
programming languages. Just think of variables as any type of named
container holding any type of stored content. You simply name the
container and store the content. Later you retrieve the content by
using the same name.">
<!--- Content --->
<cfoutput>
 <div>
  <h3>Question: #myQuestion#</h3>
  <p><strong>Answer:</strong></p>
  <p>#myAnswer#  </p>
  <p>#timeFormat(now())#</p>
 </div>
</cfoutput>
```

The now() function in ColdFusion returns the current date or time. The timeFormat() function converts the output to display text with the time of its contents. If we update the screen, the current time will be displayed on each refresh.

Your first dynamic web page is created. If you do not know much, there is no need to worry. We will create web pages after this exercise. If you are new to this technology, then work through the examples and complete the chapter. Take a break, and then come back after going through the entire chapter, and repeat the exercises. You will be surprised by what you have learned.

> We will be removing the HTML standard wrappers from most of the examples in the book. Browsers do not need the markers to present the content. In your live site code, the markers should be included.

Understanding and Using Simple Variables

In this section, we will have a look at a couple of variable types with the help of which you will be getting an idea of how ColdFusion works with variables. We are going to look at the different types of simple variables.

There are four types of simple variables: string, numeric, Boolean, and date or time variables. Although a variable can have any name, there are a few basic guidelines for naming variables. They are as follows:

- A variable name must begin with a letter, which can be followed by any number of letters, numbers, and underscore characters.

- A variable name cannot contain spaces.

- Variable names are not case sensitive in ColdFusion. (`myVariable` is the same in ColdFusion as `Myvariable`.)

We will be covering two number classes, in this lesson. First, we will take a look at the integers. These are numbers with no decimal value. ColdFusion supports integers between - 2,147,483,648 and 2,147,483,647. It will also work with numbers outside this range, but the precision will not be exact.

In the first example given below, we will modify the code that we have been using to keep one of the string variables and add a numeric variable called `myAge`. The following two code examples are identical, so it is fine to do it either way. Proper indentation is key to either tag or the script-based code. (Run the code examples.)

```
<!--- Processing --->
<cfset myQuestion = "This is my question.">
<cfset myAge = 27>
<!--- Content --->
<cfoutput>
 myQuestion is (#myQuestion#)<br />
 myAge is (#myAge#)<br />
</cfoutput>

<!--- Processing --->
<cfscript>
 myQuestion = "This is my question.";
 myAge = 27;
</cfscript>
<!--- Content --->
<cfoutput>
 myQuestion is (#myQuestion#)<br />
 myAge is (#myAge#)<br />
</cfoutput>
```

You will notice that strings are declared with quotation marks. These can be either single or double quotation marks. Numbers do not use quotation marks. This would be the same in a variable declaration. In the preceding examples, it is in the form of an expression. Expressions are what we call code when we combine strings, or do math or some Boolean comparisons. Here, we will look at our first expression example by changing both the string and the numeric variables in our code. ColdFusion 8 added the += operator to the platform. This is a widely used notation to add the righthand value to the original value. Run the following example:

```
<!--- Example: 1_3.cfm --->
<!--- Processing --->
<cfscript>
 myQuestion = "This is my question.";
 myAge = 27;
 myQuestion = myQuestion & " Is this a string?";
 myAge += 1;
</cfscript>
<!--- Content --->
<cfoutput>
 myQuestion is (#myQuestion#)<br />
 myAge is (#myAge#)<br />
</cfoutput>
```

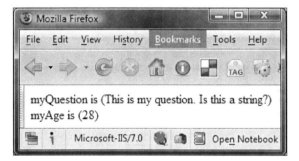

There is no requirement to write things in CFScript like the ones you will see in the book. Currently, JavaScript, AIR/Flash/Flex ActionScript, .Net, PHP, and JAVA use scripted code. These are the most common forms of coding.

Now, we will look at decimal-based numbers. We will modify the code to show some more things that you can do with numbers and to remove the string functions.

```
<!--- Example: 1_4.cfm --->
<!--- Processing --->
<cfscript>
 myAge = 27;
 halfAge = myAge/2;
</cfscript>
<!--- Content --->
<cfoutput>
 myAge is (#myAge#)<br />
 halfAge is (#halfAge#)<br />
 halfAge rounded is (#round(halfAge)#)<br />
 4.2 rounded is (#round(4.2)#)<br />
 4.2 ceiling is (#ceiling(4.2)#)<br />
</cfoutput>
```

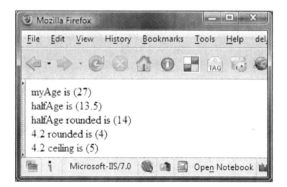

If you would like to have more information about the built-in functions, then you can download the manuals in Appendix A and go through the PDF documents. You will find that there are abundant built-in functions for application processing.

We have looked at creating a variable by using the value of another variable and by changing the values of variables. You will find everything from modulo functions to geometry functions for standard mathematical calculations. You will also find a rich number of string functions that can help you process your pages.

The following piece of code will help you find the additional types of things that you can do with strings:

```
<!--- Example: 1_5.cfm --->
<!--- Processing --->
<cfscript>
 myQuestion = "This is my question.";
 myQuestion = myQuestion & " Is THIS a string?";
 location = find("this",myQuestion);
```

```
</cfscript>
<!--- Content --->
<cfoutput>
 myQuestion is (#myQuestion#)<br />
 Location of "this" is (#location#) characters from the start of the
string.<br />
</cfoutput>
```

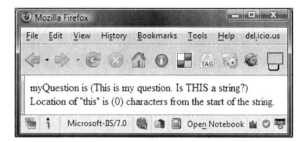

You might be curious to know why the value of the find returned zero rather than the actual position. You will notice that we changed the word "this" to "THIS". Computers see upper case letters differently from lower case letters. So THIS proved the point that strings are case sensitive. Let us see how we can find an alternative way with a ColdFusion's built-in function:

```
<!--- Example: 1_6.cfm --->
<!--- Processing --->
<cfscript>
 myQuestion = "This is my question.";
 myQuestion = myQuestion & " Is THIS a string?";
 location = findNoCase("this",myQuestion);
 location2 = findNoCase("this",myQuestion,location+1);
</cfscript>
<!--- Content --->
<cfoutput>
 myQuestion is (#myQuestion#)<br />
 Location of "this" is (#location#) characters from the start of the
string.<br />
 The second "this" is located at position (#location2#).<br />
</cfoutput>
```

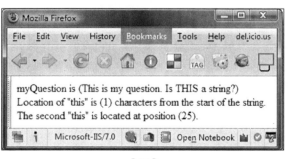

Here, we did a couple of things. First, we made our string search case insensitive. Then we added a second search to see if there were any more occurrences of the item being searched for in the string variable. We added +1 to the location in order to make sure that we skipped the first location in our search. It still returns the location based on the start of the string irrespective of an in-depth search. The following code shows the structure of the function that will help you understand the working of the function documentation:

```
FindNoCase(substring, string, [start])
```

The arguments of the functions are required unless they are wrapped in [ ]. This function searches for a `substring` inside `string`, optionally starting at `start` number of characters into the string.

Understanding Structures

Structures are one of the most powerful variables that we will be looking at in this book. An example is described that illustrates the working of the structure. Structures are like files and folders on a computer file system. Folders can be empty or they can contain multiple files or nested folders. Files may contain different types of content. Yet, you can never call a folder directly and retrieve the actual file content from a folder.

Structures in ColdFusion work along the same concepts. Your structures can be empty or they may contain both additional nested structures and variables holding data.

Let us look at our first built-in structure type called **CGI**. We will take a look at the most commonly used debugging tool for many developers. CGI is a collection of variables that gives details about things ranging from the current request, the browser of the requesting user, to information about the current running server. It does not tell us everything, but it does provide us with good information so that we may visit over and over again. All the structures start with a base structure element. The CGI structure starts with `cgi` followed by a dot (.) with the structure variable name:

```
cgi.structure_item_name
```

Let us look at an easy way to see what is available. If you do this yourself, you can scroll through and see how much information is offered. Here is the simple code. You will also note that the pound symbols surround the variable name. This is required for functions to work correctly. It may seem odd at first, but you will be able to grasp it quickly even if you do not get it at the first glance:

```
<!--- Example: 1_7.cfm --->
<!--- Processing --->
<!--- Content --->
<cfdump var="#cgi#">
```

The `<cfdump>` tag in ColdFusion takes any complex data type, and creates a grid or nested grid if there is a nested structure to display the contents of the variable. Dump allows us to see the state of a variable structure at a fixed point in the processing cycle of our web page. There are options for not expanding, and for giving a label to the dump for occasions when we may put more than one dump on a page during the programming cycle. We will not want to use this type of function on final production code because users might think that the system has crashed. When it comes to programmers, this is one of the greatest, and it has been one of the features of ColdFusion widely used by developers for many years. We will look at the end of the page where we can see the server port, if the port was secure, and that there were many other details with this dump.

You will see everything from the cookie variables to the remote address of the requesting user. If you were to access these directly in the code, you would have to do it as follows. You will notice that the structure 'cgi', contains a good number of variables. In this case, there are no nested structures but only variables. This makes for a better introduction to the structures:

```
<!--- Example: 1_8.cfm --->
<!--- Processing --->
<cfscript>
 requestedDomain = cgi.server_name;
 isSecure = cgi.server_port_secure;
</cfscript>
<!--- Content --->
<cfoutput>
 The requested domain was #requestedDomain#.<br />
 Was the current request secure (0 = No/1 = Yes) ? #isSecure# <br />
</cfoutput>
```

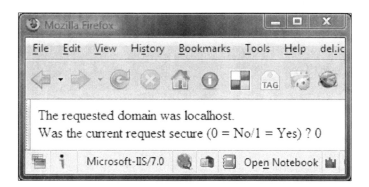

Let Us Get Interactive

We are going to get into a round trip interaction with web pages. This is the reason why web programming beginners will agree as to why these web pages are known as "Dynamic Web Pages."

We will be learning a new structure called "URL", and see one way to pass information from the user back to the server. We will start by calling the same page via the URL in order to understand this functionality. We will run the same code twice. For the first time we will not pass any URL variables.

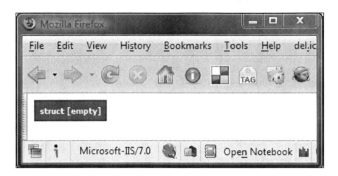

As seen on the screen, our first example returned an **empty** structure. For the second example run, you will see that we passed a URL variable called **NAME** with a value, **John**. You can actually pass in many URL variables at the same time. This structure works the same way as the CGI structure. We need to add name=John at the end of the URL to get the structure. Here is the URL:

http://localhost/cfb/code/chapter_1/1_9.cfm?name=John

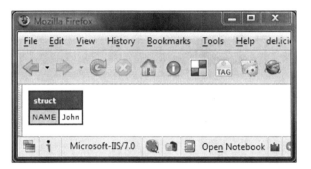

It does not contain any nested structure, so you could output the variable for name in content as follows:

```
<cfoutput>
  My name is #url.name#.
</cfoutput>
```

Many of the failed web pages come when we start getting interactive. In addition to having a look at the use of URL variables, we will take a brief look at how to catch missing variables with the use of the URL variables. This is known as **exception handling** in programming. Universally, the **try catch** method is used. This will be visible in script usage, and in tag usage. This will also be an opportunity for you to understand the concept of error or exception pages as you build ColdFusion applications and you find that things are not working as planned.

```
<!--- Example: 1_10.cfm --->
<!--- Processing --->
<!--- Content --->
<cfoutput>
 My name is #url.name#.<br />
</cfoutput>
```

We will start by running the page. In the URL type in the address followed by ?name=John. Type the URL precisely with the question mark. Here is the URL: http://localhost/cfb/code/chapter_1/1_10.cfm?name=John

Now, we will intentionally generate our first error. Remove the question mark from the end of the browser address box and the rest that follows it. Refresh the page.

Many times, you will see the detailed information on the screen, as shown in the earlier figure, when an error occurs. Not only did it tell us about the error but it also showed us the line of code where the error occurred. Do not count on this to happen all the time. By learning the use of the **try catch** block, the number of these issues will be reduced. In our next version of code, you will see how the **try catch** block can be used on the page to manage and help fix these errors:

```
<!--- Example: 1_11.cfm --->
<!--- Processing --->
<!--- Content --->
<cftry>
 <cfoutput>
  My name is #url.name#.<br />
 </cfoutput>
 <cfcatch>
  <cfdump var="#cfcatch#">
 </cfcatch>
</cftry>
```

Here, the information is presented in a different manner but it gets you to the same end. The exception is placed on the page using a `<cfdump>` tag. Most often, you will find that this is the most useful approach to debugging. You can also email the contents of the catch structure to an administrator. You may also note that the `StackTrace` and `objectType` structure elements have been minimized. You toggle elements in `CFDump` by clicking on the element text. This will hide all the nested information until you desire to see it again.

You might wonder why we included exception or error handling with CFDump. It is because the results of the catch are stored in a variable called `cfcatch` that contains a pleasant structure collection. Inside the structure, you will find a nested structure called `TagContext`. Let us modify our code so that just one subset of this structure is displayed on the screen. Change the `cfdump` to the following in your code:

```
<cfdump var="#cfcatch.TagContext#">
```

The structure allows us to drill down the pieces of information that we are interested in without pulling the rest of the details along with them. We have not covered arrays but you can drill down to the page where the problem occurred. We will learn how arrays work in ColdFusion. But now, let us change the line of code once again, and try:

```
<cfdump var="#cfcatch.TagContext[1].template#">
```

You will notice that the wrapper for our CFDump has disappeared. It has disappeared because we are now outputting a simple variable. If there is no structure or complex variable, then we get a simple variable where the CFDump is located on the page. In this case, as the code error occurred at the end of the line, it will start right from there, and this explains why it is on the same line as the web page content in the browser.

Setting Page Defaults

The information that you will obtain from here can be applied to more than page defaults. This is the most common place where you should use it. We will make a minor change in the code while creating a new page. We will use the `<cfparam>` tag to set the default values in the following code:

```
<!--- Example: 1_12.cfm --->
<!--- Processing --->
<cfparam name="url.name" default="( unknown user )">
<!--- Content --->
<cftry>
 <cfoutput>
  My name is #url.name#.<br />
 </cfoutput>
 <cfcatch>
  <cfdump var="#cfcatch#">
 </cfcatch>
</cftry>
```

Now, we have learned how to catch and handle exceptions. We have also learned how to solve such types of error in ColdFusion. We created a default value for this structure variable to prevent an error condition and handle it as a predictable exception. If we add the name back to the URL, it will still work as expected.

We have one more thing that can be done to understand the URL structure. We need to add some standard browser links on the page, and then click on them to see what happens. We will be creating two styles of links.

The first link will be a static link. This link will point back to our dynamic page to show one form of interaction through URL variables:

```
<!--- Example: 1_13.cfm --->
<!--- Processing --->
<cfparam name="url.name" default="( unknown user )">
<!--- Content --->
<cftry>
 <cfoutput>
  My name is #url.name#.<br />
  <a href="?name=Ted">Show this page with Ted for the name.</a><br />
  <a href="?name=Fred">Show this page with Fred for the name.</a>
  <br />
 </cfoutput>
 <cfcatch>
  <cfdump var="#cfcatch#">
 </cfcatch>
</cftry>
```

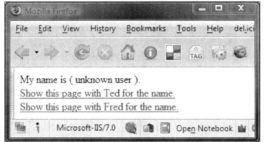

Click on either of the links on the screen, and you will see that the variable stored in the link is passed through the next time it loads from the server to the page. You will also note that the address bar will display the variables passed in when the URL requests to reload the pages. As displayed on the screen, we will click on **Fred** to try it.

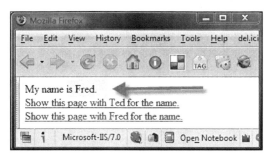

It will be clear that URL variables can come from more than one location. We have seen their existence in the address bar, and in web page links.

Our final use of URL variables will involve some processing that is actually based on the changes to the links that we click. Enter the following code:

```
<!--- Example: 1_14.cfm --->
<!--- Processing --->
<cfparam name="url.counter" default="10">
<cfparam name="url.calculate" default="0">
 <cfset url.counter +=  url.calculate>
<!--- Content --->
<cfoutput>
 I have #url.counter# cars.<br />
 <a href="?calculate=1&counter=#url.counter#">Add One.</a><br />
 <a href="?calculate=-1&counter=#url.counter#">Subtract One.</a><br />
</cfoutput>
```

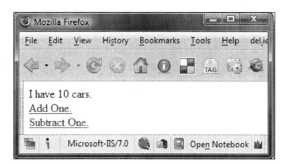

You can click on add and subtract as many times as you like to know if the page has become very interactive. The counter is passed back with the counter change based on the link that we click for the server from the web page. We had specified earlier that to use the variables to create the content, we must wrap them inside a CFOutput tag pair, and surround the variables with pound symbols.

This will be our last version of the script. It will be a bit more interesting than the other scripts. We are going to create some custom structure, and detect how to interact with that structure using what we have learned:

```
<!--- Example: 1_15.cfm --->
<!--- Processing --->
<cfparam name="url.speed" default="10">
<cfparam name="url.acceleration" default="0">
<cfscript>
 myCar = structNew();
 myCar.color = "blue";
 myCar.speed = url.speed + url.acceleration;
</cfscript>
<!--- Content --->
<cfoutput>
 <a href="?acceleration=-1&speed=#myCar.speed#">Slower</a> 
 <a href="?speed=#myCar.speed#">Cruise</a> 
 <a href="?acceleration=1&speed=#myCar.speed#">Faster</a><br />
 <cfdump var="#myCar#" label="My Car">
</cfoutput>
```

We have learned that creating a new structure is done by assigning a value to the variable using the function `structNew()`. You can nest structures inside the structures in addition to actual variable storage containers. It is the first step towards packaging your data inside the application. As applications grow, you will not want to do everything with simple variables setting at the root level of your variable structure. That would be impossible to maintain.

Another note is that we have persisted the values of the speed of the car by passing through the URL variables. We will learn many interesting ways of making our values exist from one page call to the next. We have learned how to use the structure, and gained an understanding of the URL variables.

Introduction to Lists and Loops

Lists are stored inside string variables. You can also have a list variable stored inside a structure. Lists have a "separator", which is commonly known as a **delimiter**, to divide the items, so the server can evaluate them. We are going to return to our FAQ application concept and build on what we have learned. Let us look at the code for lists.

```
<!--- Example: 1_16.cfm --->
<!--- Processing --->
<cfparam name="url.speed" default="10">
<cfparam name="url.acceleration" default="0">
<cfscript>
 questions = "What is the speed limit?,What is a car?,How much is
gas?";
</cfscript>
<!--- Content --->
<cfoutput>
 The second question is:<br />   
#listGetAt(questions,2)#
</cfoutput>
```

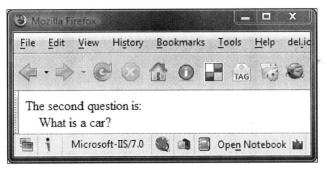

You can see that the list has three items in it. We have the content request the second item for display. The listGetAt() function is one of the simple powerful functions that make ColdFusion easy to program. You will find a number of astonishing list functions built into the language. We will combine lists and loops so you can see how things work together.

```
<!--- Example: 1_17.cfm --->
<!--- Processing --->
<cfparam name="url.question" default="What is the speed limit?">
<cfscript>
 questions = "What is the speed limit?,What is a car?,How much is
gas?";
```

```
   answers = "55,Depends who you ask!,more than before";
   myQuestion = listContains(questions,url.question);listContains(questi
ons,url.question);
</cfscript>
<!--- Content --->
<cfoutput>
   <strong>#listGetAt(questions,myQuestion)#</strong><br />Answer: 
#listGetAt(answers,myQuestion)#<br /><br />
</cfoutput>
All Questions<hr />
<cfloop list="#questions#" index="iQuestion">list="#questions#"
index="iQuestion">
  <cfoutput>
    <strong>Q</strong>: <a href="?question=#iQuestion#">#iQuestion#</
a><br />
  </cfoutput>
</cfloop>
```

We made two lists this time, one list for questions known as questions, and another for answers known as answers. When you build pairs of lists, check twice that they have the same number of items to prevent errors. This will keep us away from the debugging phase of development. If you look at where we assigned the numeric value of myQuestion, you will see that we are able to match the question asked in the list. If there is an exact match, then the number of that item in the list is returned. You will also observe that in the CFLoop list, the index variable contains the actual item stored in that position in the list.

Click on different questions, and see how things work. You will be able to see the variables being passed in the address bar.

 The `listContains()` function finds the accurate matches in a list. If you want to find the first item in a list with a partial match, then use `ListFind()`. Both of them have a NoCase version available.

We will continue to provide more information on loops as we get into arrays in the next section. There are several types of loops, and these are among the most preferred commands with ColdFusion developers.

Now, you have started to learn more about ColdFusion. Understand the finer points by applying your knowledge.

Understanding Arrays

An array is an interesting variable construct. It is a collection of commonly named variables with an index set. We will take the last code example and transfer it to arrays. Here we will change the back end, but the front end will run in exactly the same way, from a user's point of view. You will be able to see that we are now passing a variable from page to page in the following code rather than the whole questions as we did earlier.

```
<!--- Example: 1_18.cfm --->
<!--- Processing --->
<cfparam name="url.question" default="1">
<cfscript>
 question = arrayNew(1);
 question[1] = "What is the speed limit?";
 question[2] = "What is a car?";
 question[3] = "How much is gas?";
 answer = arrayNew(1);
 answer[1] = "55";
 answer[2] = "Depends who you ask!";
 answer[3] = "more than before";
</cfscript>
<!--- Content --->
<cfoutput>
 <strong>#question[url.question]#</strong><br />Answer: 
#answer[url.question]#<br /><br />
</cfoutput>
```

```
All Questions<hr />
<cfloop from="1" to="#arrayLen(question)#" index="iQuestion">
 <cfoutput>
   <strong>Q</strong>: <a href="?question=#iQuestion#">#question[iQuest
ion]#</a><br />
 </cfoutput>
</cfloop>
```

We now have two array variable constructs. Before you start assigning variables to an array, you need to declare the variable as an array type. Arrays can be multi-dimensional. We will focus on a single-dimensional array. If you forget to pass the number of dimensions when you declare an array, you will get an error when the code runs. So, do remember to declare the number of dimensions.

> The maximum number of dimensions in ColdFusion is three.
> A large multi-dimensional array can consume huge amounts of computer memory.

You will find a huge collection of array functions built into ColdFusion. You can use `arrayDeleteAt()` to remove an item in the middle of an array. There is also an `arrayInsertAt()` that does the reverse. The following three things are to be observed while using arrays:

- Items are not to be removed in the middle of an array list without using the built-in functions. This could result in a missing element and an error can occur when looping through the array collection.

- An item is not to be counted while it is in the indexed position. It may seem odd that we call the position of an index and think that the item can move. This is different because arrays are dynamic.

- The number of items in an array can change. The best way to do that is to use the function `arrayLen()`, as we did in the example code to obtain the current length of an array.

Now we will rewrite and run the same code as a multi-dimensional array. This is also known as an array of structures. Each dimension of the array has a structure. This allows for some unique layout of data within your application memory. We will add a CFDump at the end of the code, and view the structure created as follows:

```
<!--- Example: 1_19.cfm --->
<!--- Processing --->
<cfparam name="url.faq" default="1">
<cfscript>
 faq = arrayNew(1);
 faq[1] = structNew();
```

```
 faq[1].question = "What is the speed limit?";
 faq[1].answer = "55";
 faq[2] = structNew();
 faq[2].question = "What is a car?";
 faq[2].answer = "Depends who you ask!";
 faq[3] = structNew();
 faq[3].question = "How much is gas?";
 faq[3].answer = "more than before";
</cfscript>
<!--- Content --->
<cfoutput>
 <strong>#faq[url.faq].question#</strong><br />Answer:  #faq[url.
faq].answer#<br /><br />
</cfoutput>
All Questions<hr />
<cfloop from="1" to="#arrayLen(faq)#" index="iFAQ">
 <cfoutput>
 <strong>Q</strong>: <a href="?faq=#iFAQ#">#faq[iFAQ].question#</a><br
/>
 </cfoutput>
</cfloop>
<cfdump var="#faq#">
```

We have gone through what you can do with structures, arrays, and loops. ColdFusion experts find creative uses for them. They are quite simple to use and very flexible to implement.

Conditional Processing with If

Now, we have reached the last section of our quick introduction to ColdFusion. We would be remiss if we were to forget conditional processing. There are two tags that make the bulk of conditional processing in ColdFusion.

The first tag is `<cfIf>`. If you are familiar with any other programming language, you will find this function as you expect. While coding with tags, the language should be able to differentiate between tag braces, and greater than and lesser than logic. In ColdFusion, this is done by replacing the greater than symbol with GT and the lesser than symbol with LT. We use GTE for greater than or equal to, and LTE for lesser than or equal to. If something is equal, we can either use IS or EQ.

Now, let us look at something related to the code. What can we do to make sure that someone does not play tricks with the URL, and make our page fail by changing the URL variables? Let us put in some conditional processing to perform business logic in the processing section:

```
<!--- Example: 1_20.cfm --->
<!--- Processing --->
<cfparam name="url.faq" default="1">
<cfscript>
 faq = arrayNew(1);
 faq[1] = structNew();
 faq[1].question = "What is the speed limit?";
 faq[1].answer = "55";
 faq[2] = structNew();
 faq[2].question = "What is a car?";
 faq[2].answer = "Depends who you ask!";
 faq[3] = structNew();
 faq[3].question = "How much is gas?";
 faq[3].answer = "more than before";
</cfscript>
<cfif NOT isNumeric(url.faq)>
 <cfset url.faq = 1>
<cfelse>
 <cfset url.faq = round(url.faq)>
 <cfif url.faq LT 1>
  <cfset url.faq = 1>
 <cfelseif url.faq GT arrayLen(faq)>
```

```
   <cfset url.faq = arrayLen(faq)>
  </cfif>
 </cfif>
 <!--- Content --->
 <cfoutput>
  <strong>#faq[url.faq].question#</strong><br />Answer:  #faq[url.
 faq].answer#<br /><br />
 </cfoutput>
 All Questions<hr />
 <cfloop from="1" to="#arrayLen(faq)#" index="iFAQ">
  <cfoutput>
   <strong>Q</strong>: <a href="?faq=#iFAQ#">#faq[iFAQ].question#
   </a><br />
  </cfoutput>
 </cfloop>
```

We will skip the screenshot because there is no change as to how the user sees the page. The only difference is in the processing logic needed to prevent someone from messing with the stability of the page. This will lay the foundation for protecting things such as commerce pages.

Earlier, we forgot about the Boolean variable type. The conditional statements inside the "if" statements evaluate to either true or false. These are the Boolean values. You will also find that you can use either a zero, or a non-zero number to represent a Boolean logical evaluation. Therefore, any expression that evaluates either to zero or false has the same results. The other non-zero numbers and values such as true, yes, and no are valid Boolean conditions. You can just take the same code and assign it to a variable. Then you could use the variable inside the "if" statement instead of evaluating the logic inside the statement. Normally, place it inside the <cfIf> statement, which is more meaningful.

```
    <cfset myBoolean = NOT isNumeric(url.faq)>
```

We examine to make sure that the variable is a number. You are advised to change the value in the address bar to text in order to prevent page breaks. You will find that it selects the first item because the input in the URL variable is invalid. This is done by using the logical condition NOT. The NOT condition takes the result of the test and reverses it. You will notice that if this is not the condition used, then an alternative set of code is processed:

```
    <cfif NOT isNumeric(url.faq)>
```

We will attempt to break it by entering in a negative number, since there are no items at that location in the array index, which would have led to page break. We have prevented it with our conditional logic by resetting the value when any basic type of hacking occurs.

Let us take another look at the code with all the processing logic inside the CFScript. The best part of the platform is that it is flexible; it can be done both ways:

```
<!--- Example: 1_21.cfm --->
<!--- Processing --->
<cfparam name="url.faq" default="1">
<cfscript>
faq = arrayNew(1);
faq[1] = structNew();
faq[1].question = "What is the speed limit?";
faq[1].answer = "55";
faq[2] = structNew();
faq[2].question = "What is a car?";
faq[2].answer = "Depends who you ask!";
faq[3] = structNew();
faq[3].question = "How much is gas?";
faq[3].answer = "more than before";
if(! isNumeric(url.faq))
{
 url.faq = 1;
}
else
{
 url.faq = round(url.faq);
 if(url.faq < 1)
 {
  url.faq = 1;
 }
 else if(url.faq > arrayLen(faq))
 {
  url.faq = arrayLen(faq);
 }
}
</cfscript>
```

We only show the top half of the code here, because the content section of the code is identical to the previous example. You may notice that you can use some more traditional script-style logic symbols while coding in script. Both these should help in evaluating between syntax for the script and the syntax for the tag-based logic.

Conditional Processing with Switch

You can achieve contextual selection of code segments with the `<cfIf>` tag, but the `<cfSwitch>` tag has a unique style that will become a conditional processing favorite in certain scenarios. In this section, we will restructure the FAQ example using the switch statement logic. This is the best use of a switch statement, but it will help you understand how the logic works. You will not see any difference when you look at the browser from the user side.

```
<!--- Example: 1_22.cfm --->
<!--- Processing --->
<cfparam name="url.faq" default="">
<cfscript>
 faq = arrayNew(1);
 faq[1] = structNew();
 faq[1].question = "What is the speed limit?";
 faq[1].answer = "55";
 faq[1].id = 'a';
 faq[2] = structNew();
 faq[2].question = "What is a car?";
 faq[2].answer = "Depends who you ask!";
 faq[2].id = 'b';
 faq[3] = structNew();
 faq[3].question = "How much is gas?";
 faq[3].answer = "more than before";
 faq[3].id = 'c';
</cfscript>
<cfswitch expression="#url.faq#">
 <cfcase value="b">
  <cfset question = faq[2].question>
  <cfset answer = faq[2].answer>
 </cfcase>
 <cfcase value="c">
  <cfset question = faq[3].question>
  <cfset answer = faq[3].answer>
 </cfcase>
 <cfdefaultcase>
  <cfset question = faq[1].question>
  <cfset answer = faq[1].answer>
 </cfdefaultcase>
</cfswitch>
<!--- Content --->
<cfoutput>
 <strong>#question#</strong><br />Answer:  #answer#<br /><br />
```

```
</cfoutput>
All Questions<hr />
<cfloop from="1" to="#arrayLen(faq)#" index="iFAQ">
<cfoutput>
 <strong>Q</strong>: <a href="?faq=#faq[iFAQ].id#">#faq[iFAQ].
question#</a><br />
</cfoutput>
</cfloop>
```

In the above example, we added an extra structure element for each array item to work well, and have illustrated the switch condition. The hyperlink reference passed to the browser is based on the value of the id in each structure element. If the url. faq contains no value, then the default value will be empty. This is because we are illustrating how to use the cfdefaultcase when there is no other match. We were able to eliminate all the protection logic that we had in the previous example. The page has been made simpler in this example.

In the cfswitch statement, the value of the expression is stored for comparison with each case until a match is found. If no match is found, it will check for a default case. If the default case exists, then that code segment will be executed. Test the code and visualize your understanding of what we have accomplished with this code.

Summary

We have learned the following in this chapter, on dynamic web development:

- The difference between static HTML pages and dynamic ColdFusion pages
- Simple variables (String or Text, Numeric and Boolean)
- Structured variables such as URL and CGI
- Setting default variable values for pages
- Simple techniques to assist in debugging our code
- Use of try and Catch exception handling
- Use of lists stored in a simple string variable
- Ways to use arrays and how they can contain a data collection for easier management
- Use of loops with the help of lists and arrays
- Building conditional logic into your code with CFIF and CFSWITCH statements

2
Basic CFCs and Database Interaction

All the major software platforms have different types of objects. These are known as CFCs or ColdFusion Components. CFCs allow us to bundle and re-use the code in many ways that will make development much easier. Our approach in this book will be to learn by doing. In this chapter, we will learn by building the start of a simple shopping system. We will also learn to work with databases. Let us start learning the easier way to write software with CFCs. Here is a list of the contents that will be covered in this chapter:

- The ColdFusion object called CFC
- Making our objects or CFCs come alive with methods
- The difference between a class and the objects created from the CFC
- An object constructor and its use
- Protecting inner characteristics of objects with getter and setter methods
- Connecting to a database through the internal methods of our objects or CFCs
- A new variable structure called a "query", which is used to hold recordset queries
- Controlling the different types of variables returned from methods
- Keeping our object or CFC thread safe, when multiple users are running the same code segments

Our First CFC

Create a file with an extension `.cfc` when creating CFCs. Non-CFC files are created with an extension `.cfm`.

Each CFC is wrapped with a set of tags and contains one or more functions, which are also referred to as methods. We will also be creating an object to continue with the CFCs. There are different types of objects, and CFC is normally used in ColdFusion. Look at this empty code for CFC:

```
<cfcomponent>
 <cffunction>
 </cffunction>
</cfcomponent>
```

Certainly, we cannot do much with this segment of code. This is just for us to get a first glimpse of CFC code. Here, you can view a `cfcomponent` tag that encloses the CFC. You can add additional attributes, but for now, we are going to keep it as simple as possible and try to learn how to write CFCs without getting bogged down by details. We have also included a function inside the CFC. This is known as a method.

Let us begin by understanding the qualities of our first object. Most of objects can be considered as a computer model of a real world object. This will help us in understanding the concept of objects.

Our First Object

Our first object is a generic model of a product. There are things that different products have in common. This object will be a reflection of the common attributes and methods that we will use to model a product (object). Our product (object) has attributes and methods. Let us work through this whole chapter again before you form an opinion of CFCs in code:

Product (object)

- Attributes
  - name
  - description
  - price

- Methods
  - set_name
  - get_name
  - set_description
  - get_description
  - set_price
  - get_price

As we work through these examples, we will also continue to refine this in order to make it even better. The following is an example given in code:

```
<cfcomponent>
 <cffunction name="init">
  <cfscript>
   variables.attributes = structNew();
   variables.attributes.name = "";
   variables.attributes.description = "";
   variables.attributes.price = "";
  </cfscript>
 <cfreturn this>
 </cffunction>
</cfcomponent>
```

The above code helps us to begin with a constructor. This concept is common to most objects that you will see in any language. Here, you can see that we have stored the name, description, and price attributes inside the object. You will also learn that things stored inside the variables of a CFC cannot be accessed outside a CFC. We first call the constructor to construct the object.

It should be noted that the `variables` scope persists from one call of a CFC object to another. When we use variables that should exist only for the current function call in a CFC, all the non-persistent variables should be declared with a `var` before the variable. This is not a `var` with period but a `var` with a space to declare it as a local temporary variable.

We now have the object started and we will be adding the getter and setter methods. As the name implies, they get and set the attributes of an object. There are other ways to build objects that have dangerous issues. We are providing you with knowledge for a safe and professional way, right from the beginning. Now, let us look at some more code. We will be adding this right after the `init` function or method. You will also note that we have added a ColdFusion comment to the page if you read through the code. If you are not writing multiple lines of code, the `<cfset>` tag is cleaner than wrapping stuff inside a `<cfscript> </cfscript>` tag pair.

> Save the CFC file as `product_1.cfc` in the directory in which you are working.

```
<cfcomponent>
 <cffunction name="init">
  <cfscript>
   variables.attributes = structNew();
   variables.attributes.name = "";
   variables.attributes.description = "";
   variables.attributes.price = "";
  </cfscript>
  <cfreturn this>
 </cffunction>
 <!--- get/set attribute:name --->
 <cffunction name="get_name">
  <cfreturn variables.attributes.name>
 </cffunction>
 <cffunction name="set_name">
  <cfargument name="name">
  <cfset variables.attributes.name = arguments.name>
 </cffunction>
</cfcomponent>
```

Setter and getter methods are used to create **encapsulated variables**. It takes a lot of experience before developers start to identify the simple things that cause errors in code. This technique helps to reduce the issue. We should take a look at the code in action before we get into telling what it does. Save the file in a new directory for this chapter, in a file called `product_1.cfc`.

Now, we will create a standard ColdFusion page. Create a file called `2_1.cfm` and enter the following code. Later, you can place your objects in a different file. But, for now, all the files for Chapter 2 should be in the same directory, on your web server. You should refer to the filename without the `.cfc` extension while creating the object instance. This is because when we set the component argument in the creation function, it assumes that on its own. Refer to the following example:

```
<!--- Example: 2_1.cfm --->
<!--- Processing --->
<cfscript>
 objProduct = createObject("component","product_1");
</cfscript>
<!--- Content --->
<cfdump var="#objProduct#">
```

Here, we have a page that creates an instance of the object class. Assume the CFC is stored on the server as a pattern. These patterns are called **classes**. ColdFusion uses this class to create an instance of the class. You can name the objects and we will prefix them with `obj` to help us remember them as objects. Then we will output it to the screen so we can have a brief look at what we are developing.

Here, we can see many defaults that are created for objects even if they are not declared. Most of them are empty. The values passed into a method are called **arguments**. Now, our object has three methods. We will write an intentional bug into our software so that you can view the type of error that occurs for future reference. We will enhance our previous code and remove the `<cfdump>` tag:

```
<!--- Example: 2_2.cfm --->
<!--- Processing --->
<cfscript>
 objProduct = createObject("component","product_1");
 result = objProduct.get_name();
</cfscript>
<!--- Content --->
<cfoutput>
 #result#
</cfoutput>
```

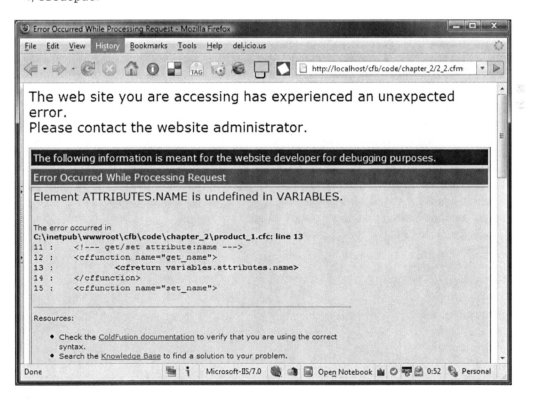

Here, you will find that the error messages do not always direct to the actual problem. The error message displayed in the above screen explains that the **variables.attributes.name** does not exist in the CFC.

This is because we did not call our constructor when we created our object instance. Here, we will explain it in detail. If the error is not as detailed, go to the **ColdFusion Administrator**, click **Debugging & Logging | Debug Output Settings**, and select the **Enable Robust Exception Information** option. Save and reload the page.

Using an Object Constructor

We will modify our code to correct the deletions. Modify the line by adding the `.init()` method at the end, as shown in the following highlighted line. You will discover that you can tack on a method that has to be called when you create an object on the same line. This is a commonly used method. When you use a constructor, you should always return the "this" variable to the user. It will correctly pass the object back when you place the constructor at the end of the creation of the object. If you visualize the `init()` method in the CFC, you will find that we include it with the `<cfreturn this>` tag:

```
<!--- Example: 2_2b.cfm --->
<!--- Processing --->
<cfscript>
 objProduct = createObject("component","product_1").init();
```

You will observe that we are handling the value of the `name` attribute of our product object with the `get_name()` method. The values passed into a method are called **arguments**. By adding the above highlighted code, you will view a blank page as the output. This does not display any error, but one more thing is missing to complete our first test of our `object` attribute name:

```
<cfscript>
 objProduct = createObject("component","product_1").init();
 objProduct.set_name(name="Egg Plant");
 result = objProduct.get_name();
</cfscript>
<!--- Content --->
<cfoutput>
 #result#
</cfoutput>
```

Add the highlighted line to the code, and then run the page. You can also change the name of the product according to your choice.

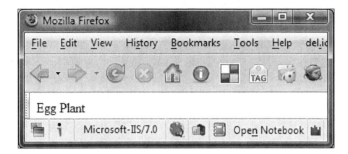

Now, we can add other attributes and we will have our first CFC completed. We need to add the getter and setter methods for the object class's description and price attributes. One of the things that using the variables does is to allow the values set inside our object to persist from one method call to the next. There are many ways to have both temporary and permanent values of the object. We will be discussing them later in the chapter. Add the following highlighted lines to the `.cfc` and `.cfc` pages:

```
<cfcomponent>
… <!--- get/set attribute:description --->
 <cffunction name="get_description">
  <cfreturn variables.attributes.description>
 </cffunction>
 <cffunction name="set_description">
  <cfargument name="description">
  <cfset variables.attributes.description = arguments.description>
 </cffunction>
 <!--- get/set attribute:price --->
 <cffunction name="get_price">
  <cfreturn variables.attributes.price>
 </cffunction>
 <cffunction name="set_price">
  <cfargument name="price">
  <cfset variables.attributes.price = arguments.price>
 </cffunction>
</cfcomponent>
```

We will make some changes to the following code. We will be setting the values of all the object attributes through the methods. We will also be handling outputting the variables with one change. Rather than set the variables, we will use the object to put the values directly in the content section.

```
<!--- Example: 2_3.cfm --->
<!--- Processing --->
<cfscript>
 objProduct = createObject("component","product_1").init();
 objProduct.set_name(name="Egg Plant");
 objProduct.set_description(description="A plant with egg like
                                        fruit.");
 objProduct.set_price(price="2.57");
</cfscript>
<!--- Content --->
<cfoutput>
 Name: #objProduct.get_name()#<br />
 Description: #objProduct.get_description()#<br />
 Price: #objProduct.get_price()#<br />
</cfoutput>
```

Now, if you compare the following results with the code, you will be able to see one of the benefits of developing code with objects. We are dealing with our data in a conceptual way that is like thinking more about a real-world object.

This does not mean that we will not work with a database. It does mean that we can start to separate more of our processing from our presentation. We can use the same object for both processing and presenting. We saw the following in action:

- Objects can be created from class files called CFCs.
- Objects have a constructor that is run when an object is created.
- Methods can have arguments to pass data into the object.
- When methods are called, they can return a value to the user, which can be assigned to another variable, or can be used for output.

Connecting to a Database

Earlier ColdFusion developers used to display the data and presentation on the same page. There was no "data layer" for developing software. It was all combined on the same page. This made the pages much longer, and there was much more to work through to figure out bugs, or page enhancements. It was very close to what we call "information overload". CFCs change that by encapsulating the data as a separate layer. The interface serves as an easy way to force and handle data, to and from your database.

First, view Appendix A to set up your database and then set up your environment for this section. If you are not skilled with databases, then we have suggestions in Appendix B. You will not need that as we write the ones you need in the code examples for this book.

Here, we will create another version of our object class, `product.cfc`. Let us name it `product_2.cfc`, so we can keep things separate, in case you want to go back and compare them later. Let us take a look at the starting version of this data-oriented object. If you are using DreamWeaver, or CFEclipse, then there are tools for creating CFCs and data-based CFCs. We suggest you to start here for better understanding. This also makes it easier for you to move from one developer coding tool to another:

```
<cfcomponent output="false">
 <cffunction name="init" access="public" output="false">
  cfscript>
  variables.attributes = structNew();
  variables.attributes.name = "";
  variables.attributes.description = "";
  variables.attributes.price = 0;
  </cfscript>
  <cfreturn this />
 </cffunction>
 <!--- Getter and Setter Methods --->
 <cffunction name="get_name" access="public" output="false">
  <cfreturn variables.attributes.name />
 </cffunction>
 <cffunction name="set_name" access="public" output="false">
  <cfargument name="name" type="any" required="true" />
  <cfset variables.attributes.name = arguments.name />
  <cfreturn />
 </cffunction>
 <cffunction name="get_description" access="public" output="false">
  <cfreturn variables.attributes.description />
 </cffunction>
 <cffunction name="set_description" access="public" output="false">
```

```
    <cfargument name="description" type="any" required="true" />
    <cfset variables.attributes.description = arguments.description />
    <cfreturn />
</cffunction>
<cffunction name="get_price" access="public" output="false">
    <cfreturn variables.attributes.price />
</cffunction>
<cffunction name="set_price" access="public" output="false">
    <cfargument name="price" required="true" />
    <cfset variables.attributes.price = arguments.price />
    <cfreturn />
</cffunction>
<!--- Data Methods --->
<cffunction name="getRecordset" access="public" output="false">
    <cfargument name="where" required="false" />
    <!--- TODO: Implement Method --->
    <cfreturn />
</cffunction>
<cffunction name="getRecord" access="public" output="false">
    <cfargument name="id" required="false" />
    <!--- TODO: Implement Method --->
    <cfreturn />
</cffunction>
</cfcomponent>
```

You should be able to tell that the setter and getter methods of this object class are the same as those of the first one that we built. While building CFCs, we should take common functions within an object class, and group them together. It is always smart to organize your code. So, we have the same `init` function and the same getter and setter methods. At the bottom of the CFC code, you will notice a section for data management. We are going to begin with the `getRecordset()` method. Note the name of the data source. (See Appendix A, if you have not set this up yet.) We are using a DSN, data source name, called `cfb`. We are adding the highlighted section of the code to this method.

```
<cffunction name="getRecordset" access="public" output="false">
    <cfargument name="where" default="" />
    <cfscript>
    var rsReturn = "";
    </cfscript>
    <cfquery datasource="cfb" name="rsReturn">SELECT id, name,
                                description, price FROM product
    </cfquery>
    <cfreturn rsReturn/>
    <cfreturn />
</cffunction>
```

We will step through these additions one at a time. First, we will look at the rsReturn variable. It could be declared in a <cfset>, or inside a <cfscript> </cfscript> code segment. We will discuss the scope in detail, later. When we create any variable inside a CFC method, you should add the word var and a space between var and the variable that you are declaring. If this is not done you will get errors when the method or variable is used multiple times within the CFC. So again, you must add var to your variables to create what are called **thread safe variables**.

> We are using the variable rsReturn to store the recordset returned by the query. To be a thread-safe variable, rsReturn must be declared with var but we do not need to specify it as a query.

Next, we are introduced to our first database tag in ColdFusion. This approach to connect to the data source in ColdFusion is quite simple. This is one area wherein the other platforms have still not matched ColdFusion. The select SQL statement is used to pull back any records found in that request. This can be a single or a cross selection of multiple related tables. See Appendix B for suggestions to extend your knowledge of SQL, later. Right now, just use the queries that we have prewritten for you. You should list the fields, which you have stored in the select section of the SQL statement as seen in the previous example. Use the attribute datasource to name the database data source name created on your system. The name attribute is where the recordset will be stored. This is referred to as a query set in ColdFusion. We will be using the universal term of recordset, for simplicity.

Returning Data from the CFC

Finally, we return the variable rsReturn to the user. This has changed the variable type to a ColdFusion query, which is the name for the returned recordset from the <cfquery> tag.

Now, we need to create a calling page. We have to see what is returning from the database and how it appears inside ColdFusion. The following is the code of our calling page:

```
<!--- Example: 2_4.cfm --->
<!--- Processing --->
<cfscript>
objProduct = createObject("component","product_2").init();
rsProducts = objProduct.getRecordset();
</cfscript>
<!--- Content --->
<cfdump var="#rsProducts#">
```

We are viewing something new in the recordset dump for ColdFusion version 8. This version includes the attributes for cached, execution time, and the SQL that was run to produce the query. These can be very helpful for development, debugging, and logging. You will also see that the result set displays each row in a table. Each of the fields returned from the database is columns in the recordset. The number on the left of the table is the row of the recordset that is returned. Note that it is not the index of the database. Database tables should always have a primary index key to refer to an individual record later. You will find that we use a field called ID in the database table. We have five records in our database.

Now, we should be able to use this recordset in more places than the `<cfdump>` tag. Let us take a look at how this is done. We will use a number of examples to show how to retrieve data from your recordset. The first example will be using the `<cfoutput>` tag and displaying the results in an unordered list. We will add an attribute called `query`, and set it equal to the recordset that we retrieved from our object instance. The following is the code for the example:

```
<!--- Example: 2_5.cfm --->
<!--- Processing --->
<cfscript>
 objProduct = createObject("component","product_2").init();
 rsProducts = objProduct.getRecordset();
</cfscript>
```

```
<!--- Content --->
<ul><cfoutput query="rsProducts">
 <li>#rsProducts.name#</li></cfoutput>
</ul>
```

We are going to modify the code so that it gets linked back, and we can return an individual record. We will place them on the same page, but how you do this would depend on what you are doing. Let us look at the modified code of the example. This time, we will change the code with example 2_5. Add or modify the highlighted rows to the following code:

```
<!--- Example: 2_5.cfm --->
<!--- Processing --->
<cfparam name="url.id" default="">
<cfscript>
 objProduct = createObject("component","product_2").init();
 rsProducts = objProduct.getRecordset();
 rsProduct = objProduct.getRecordset(where = "id = #url.id#");
</cfscript>
<!--- Content --->
<ul><cfoutput query="rsProducts">
 <li><a href="?id=#rsProducts.id#">#rsProducts.name#</a>
 </li>
</cfoutput></ul>
<cfif rsProduct.recordCount EQ 1>
 <cfoutput><table>
  <tr>
   <th>Product</th>
   <td>#rsProduct.name#</td>
```

```
    </tr>
    <tr>
     <th>Description</th>
     <td>#rsProduct.description#</td>
    </tr>
    <tr>
     <th>Price</th>
     <td>#dollarFormat(rsProduct.price)#</td>
    </tr>
   </table></cfoutput>
 </cfif>
```

Making Our Data Query Flexible

We set the default value so that the page does not fail if there is no value passed in for the id variable. We added the singular getProduct variable. The only difference is that this will return a single record after the CFC is modified. At present, CFC does not handle the argument, where, even though it is a part of the method. We have to build in the functionality. Change the highlighted lines to make this method work correctly. Since we are not adding the query type to the <cfoutput> tag, it will not loop through the query. It will only return the first record in the recordset. In this instance, there is only one record that will be same. Thus the following code displays only one row on our webpage:

```
<cfquery datasource="cfb" name="rsReturn">SELECT id, name,
description, price FROM product<cfif arguments.where NEQ ""> WHERE 1=1
AND #arguments.where#</cfif>
</cfquery>
<cfreturn rsReturn/>
</cffunction>
```

This is the SQL query for the where statement. This is why we called the argument where. Some users prefer to call this argument filter. Now, you can pass in any legal value. If you review the calling page, you will see that we are passing in the 'url'.id now. This means that if there is no value, it will not find any match to it, and we will obtain an **empty recordset**. If you pass in an id that matches a record in the database, then you will obtain that record back, and it will return only one row. It is very beneficial to put our query values in a <cfqueryparam> wrapper to prevent SQL injection attacks. At present, we are learning basic code. So, this is safe unless we are planning to hack ourselves!

The last thing we did in our page was to add a table section that displayed the values of the requested record only if a match was found. This is the result that is displayed when you click on one of the links. The individual record is shown below the unordered list. Click through the different items, and you will see the products that are retrieved from the database.

Now, we will take a moment to view some of the advantages of using CFCs. Let us consider what we would have done if these were two pages, and we were adding the <cfquery> tag section of code to the existing pages. You would have queries on both pages. Now, we will begin to look at the actual use of an object. The page is much simpler. There is still work to do though. We need to take this example just a little further. First, we will modify the getRecord part of our code, and re-run the page to show that we are actually getting the same results. Again you will see that the rows that were replaced have been highlighted. We remembered to add a var to our method to ensure that it is a thread-safe variable. You also observed that we are calling one of the methods inside the same object without naming any object. When you call a method in the same object, you can address it like a regular built-in function of ColdFusion. Finally, we take the results, which were returned from getRecordset, and store them briefly in the method's myReturn variable. You can name this variable. We are using this name because it is descriptive of the variable's purpose:

```
<cffunction name="getRecord" access="public" output="false">
 <cfargument name="id" required="false" />
 <cfset var myReturn = getRecordset(where = "id = #arguments.id#")>
 <cfreturn myReturn />
</cffunction>
```

Now, we have to modify the code again in the calling page. The following is the only line of code that we need to change. Find the line with the rsRecord on it and replace it with the following line:

```
rsProduct = objProduct.getRecord(url.id);
```

When you run the page, you will observe no difference. Yes, functionally, there is nothing much different. It was easy to call the method because we placed the where clause into the getRecordset function. What we want to do for our object, though, is to load the current record into the protected attributes of the object. Change the name of getRecord to load. Then, we will loop assign the values returned in the recordset to the protected attributes of the object instance. If an empty record is returned, we will set all the variables to a default value. We could do this in the same function, but we will create another function to handle this:

```
<cffunction name="load" access="public" output="false">
  <cfargument name="id" required="false" />
  <cfscript>
   var myReturn = getRecordset(where = "id = #arguments.id#");
   setAttributes(myReturn);
  </cfscript>
  <cfreturn myReturn />
</cffunction>
<cffunction name="setAttributes" access="public" output="false">
  <cfargument name="record" required="true" />
  <cfscript>
   if(arguments.record.recordCount == 0)
   {
    variables.attributes.page = "";
    variables.attributes.description = "";
    variables.attributes.price = 0;
   }
   else
   {
    variables.attributes.name = arguments.record.name;
    variables.attributes.description = arguments.record.description;
    variables.attributes.price = arguments.record.price;
   }
  </cfscript>
</cffunction>
```

After we have changed the function to `load`, we place the internal part of that function into a script. It is worth noting that we must do certain things in order, or we will get an error while creating methods. First, you must declare all your arguments that can be passed into our methods. Next, we must create `var` variables to make sure that they are thread safe.

You should also observe that we used script to show you that we can be more like the global standard for script usage, as of CF8. Conditional processing in tags should use the EQ and GT type testing. In CF8, there are functions that work in a manner similar to what you either know from JS and other platforms, or may use in the future.

The Basic Data Object Concept

Here, we create the function for assigning the encapsulated variables of the object, when it is created. We are now ready to write the next form of the calling page. We are only going to change two things on that page. We will change the line where we were creating another recordset to call a method for assigning the internal variable values in the object. Then, we will change our content section of the code to use the object by using the getter method to pull the encapsulated variable values. The highlighted rows are the ones that are modified, as displayed in the following code:

```
<!--- Example: 2_6.cfm --->
<!--- Processing --->
<cfparam name="url.id" default="0">
<cfscript>
objProduct = createObject("component","product_2").init();
rsProducts = objProduct.getRecordset();
objProduct.load(url.id);
</cfscript>
<!--- Content --->
<ul><cfoutput query="rsProducts">
 <li><a href="?id=#rsProducts.id#">#rsProducts.name#</a></li></
cfoutput>
</ul>
<cfif objProduct.get_name() NEQ "">
 <cfoutput>
  <table>
   <tr>
    <th>Product</th>
    <td>#objProduct.get_name()#</td>
   </tr>
   <tr>
```

```
        <th>Description</th>
        <td>#objProduct.get_description()#</td>
       </tr>
       <tr>
        <th>Price</th>
        <td>#dollarFormat(objProduct.get_price())#</td>
       </tr>
      </table>
     </cfoutput>
    </cfif>
```

We are doing an excellent job by making it easier to separate processing from markup. We are using the same object to do our processing and our output to the markup content section of the page. This is a good way of re-using things.

One of the goals of objects is to maximize the re-use of things. We will be "refactoring" our object. We are going to take what we have and make it simpler. Now, we have a bunch of getters and setters. Every new "data focused" object is going to have unique getters and setters. This means that the interface on this object is not as portable as on other objects. The following are the procedures for building a shopping cart. The item object will have an interface different from the product item. It is not always possible to match the interfaces, so that they have common methods and arguments. Yet, practically it is better to do things that way.

Let us take all our getters and setters, and transfer them to a single getter and setter method. The getter can retrieve all the hidden attributes, and the setter would be able to do the same thing. Since, we are not setting any values at present, we will discuss them later. The principle is the same. We will remove all the getter functions, and save the new CFC as `product_3.cfm`. Add the new `get()` method at the top of the getter and setter section. In our code, we can see that we use the `arguments.attribute` to check if a variable exists, and if so, pull it. If a `false` field is requested, then we return an empty field, rather than throwing an error:

```
    <!--- Getter and Setter Methods --->
    <cffunction name="get" access="public" output="false">
     <cfargument name="attribute" required="true">
     <cfset var myReturn = "">
     <cfif structKeyExists(variables.attributes,arguments.attribute)>
      <cfreturn variables.attributes[arguments.attribute] />
     <cfelse>
      <cfreturn "">
     </cfif>
    </cffunction>
```

We need to modify or create another version of the calling page. Do not forget, we have just created a new object, so we need to confirm that the calling page is creating an instance of the correct object class. Now, change that class to `product_3`. Then, change the variable methods from the current getters such as `#objProduct.get_name()#` to `#objProduct.get('name')#`. This shows a minor difference, but the portability of this object has increased significantly. We can still have protected variables, but currently we have many more versatile object classes. Again, this is just the beginning of how much power we can build in:

```
<!--- Example: 2_7.cfm --->
<!--- Processing --->
<cfparam name="url.id" default="0">
<cfscript>
objProduct = createObject("component","product_3").init();
rsProducts = objProduct.getRecordset();
objProduct.load(url.id);
</cfscript>
<!--- Content --->
<ul><cfoutput query="rsProducts">
 <li>
<a href="?id=#rsProducts.id#">#rsProducts.name#</a>
</li></cfoutput>
</ul>
<cfif objProduct.get('name') NEQ "">
 <cfoutput>
  <table>
   <tr>
    <th>Product</th>
    <td>#objProduct.get('name')#</td>
   </tr>
   <tr>
    <th>Description</th>
    <td>#objProduct.get('description')#</td>
   </tr>
   <tr>
    <th>Price</th>
    <td>#dollarFormat(objProduct.get('price'))#</td>
   </tr>
  </table>
 </cfoutput>
</cfif>
```

Now, we have achieved an object as simple as we need, to show different aspects of working with objects.

Object Method Access Control

Objects are not intended to create output other than returning the actual variables. That is why the attributes `output="false"` have been added all over the CFC code. You will also observe that there is an attribute called `access="public"` in many of the methods. There are actually a number of settings for this. This tells us where the calling code must be for the method to run. Here is a list of settings and definitions for each one of them:

- **Public**—This is the most common, default setting, if it has not been already declared. It means that any code on the server can call the object method and run it.

- **Private**—In this case, the method can be called only from within the CFC. We would have taken the method `setAttribute()` and made it private. This method would be called from within the present CFC, and not from outside the CFC.

- **Package**—This is the condition when only code in the same directory can call the method. The term package comes from the object-oriented world, and it is an interesting way to protect code integrity.

- **Remote**—This is one of the most powerful aspects of ColdFusion. This is actually what is called a web service. Setting this makes the object visible to the outside world.

Summary

One of the biggest advantages of CFCs is the ability to encapsulate logic. This means that we can use the same code repeatedly without rewriting it. This makes initial development better. It also makes debugging and updates much more manageable. In this chapter, you have been introduced to the power of objects. We will be using objects often throughout the book. This chapter is built as a foundation to understand the following:

- Creating object classes and instantiate object instances.
- Creating methods, and using the method and method arguments to interact with objects.
- Using object constructors for setting object information at the time of creation.
- Using getter or setter methods to control securely the information inside an object. We also learned that with these, you can do more than just getting and setting the values at the same time, with validation logic or other processing.
- Connecting to a database to gain information back through an object.
- Using a new variable structure called query to store data recordsets.
- Returning multiple types of variables back from object methods.
- Declaring all internal method variables that are specific to a method with a leading `var`. This is key to making sure our processing remains thread safe.

Power CFCs and Web Forms

3

In this chapter, we will learn to move forward from making our code work to making it interesting to write and re-use. We could call this a "power CFC". Power is doing away with the old practice of copying and pasting code again and again with some minor edits in the pasted code. Here, we will learn to re-use the CFC code to make it much simpler.

There used to be long pages of what we called "spaghetti code", because the page would go on and on. You had to follow the conditional logic by going through the page up and down, and then had to understand how things worked. This made writing, updating, and debugging a difficult task even for the highly skilled developers. CFCs allow you to encapsulate some part of the logic of a page inside an object. CFCs are the object packaging method used in ColdFusion.

Database interaction is quite universally wrapped in CFCs. We will look at it as our primary example of power CFCs in the context of working with "web forms". If you are new to development, then these concepts will make it easier for you. Here is the overview of what this chapter contains:

- The practice of protecting access to CFC methods
- The working of web forms
- Managing multiple products through common forms for listing, editing, and adding data
- Improving the page flow, also known as work flow
- Returning messages to the user to know things are working
- Learning the power of inheritance
- Simplifying by passing entire collections, rather than manual line-by-line passing of the variable values

The Practice of Protecting Access

In CFC methods, there is an attribute called "access". The access methods are explained in Chapter 2. Some methods within a CFC are more examples of reuse. We have updated the sample code for _product.cfc in addition to what you had in the previous chapter. It is an example of a power CFC. There is a method inside the CFC called setDefault().

```
<cffunction name="setDefaults" access="private" output="false">
 <cfset var iAttr = 0>
  <cfloop list="#listLen(variables.field.names)#" index="iAttr">
  <cfscript>
   variables.attribute[#listGetAt(variables.field.names,iAttr)#] =
setDefault(variables.field.names,iAttr);
  </cfscript>

 </cfloop>
</cffunction>
```

The logic for this would actually be used in more than one place inside the object. When you create the object on first run, it would call this method and set the defaults. When you use the load method to insert another record inside the CFC, it will run this method. This will become simpler as you use CFCs and methods more often. There is a concept called **refactoring**, where we take common features and wrap them for reuse. This takes place even inside a CFC. Again, we repeat that the setDefault() function above is another method inside the same CFC.

Now, we look at the access in the code and note that it is set to private. This means that only this object can call the method. One of the things that can make CFCs work is keeping them simpler to the outside world. The interface to the outside world of the CFC is its methods. We can make a method hide from the outside world, and also protect access to the method by setting the access attribute to private. If you want to make sure that only CFCs in the same directory can access these CFCs' methods, then you will have to set the attribute to package. This is a value that is rarely used.

The default value for the access is public, if you do not set it. This means that any code running on the server can access the CFC. (Shared hosting companies block one account from being able to see the other accounts on the same server. If you are concerned about your hosting company, then you should either ask them about this issue or move to a dedicated or virtual hosting server.)

The remaining value is `remote`. This is actually how you create a number of "cool power" uses of the CFC. There is a technology on the Web called web services. Setting the CFC to `remote` allows you to access the CFC as a web service. You can also connect to this CFC through Flash applications, Flex, or AIR using this remote access. This method also allows the CFC to respond to AJAX calls. Now, we will learn to use more of the local power features.

Web Forms Introduction

Here, we will discuss web forms along with CFCs.

Let us view our web form page. Web forms are the same in ColdFusion as they are in any other HTML scenario. You might even note that there is a very little use for web forms until you have a server side technology such as ColdFusion. This is because when the form is posted, you need some sort of program to handle the data posted back to the server.

```
<!--- Example: 3_1.cfm --->
<!--- Processing --->
<!--- Content --->
<form action="3_1.cfm" method="post">
 <table>
  <tr>
   <td>Name:</td>
   <td><input type="text" name="name" id="idName" value="" /></td>
  </tr>
  <tr>
   <td>Description:</td>
   <td><input type="text" name="description" id="idDescription"
value="" /></td>
  </tr>
  <tr>
   <td>Price:</td>
   <td><input type="text" name="price" id="idPrice" value="" /></td>
  </tr>
  <tr>
   <td> </td>
   <td><input type="submit" name="submit" value="submit" /></td>
  </tr>
 </table>
</form>
```

First, you should notice that all the information on the page is in the content section. Anything that goes from the server to the browser is considered as content. You can fill in and submit the form, and you will observe that all the form fields get cleared out. This is not because this form posts back to the same page. Self-posting forms are a valid method of handling page flow on websites. The reason why nothing seems to be happening is because the server is not doing anything with the data being sent back from the browser. Let us add `<cfdump var="#form#"/>` to the bottom of the content below the form tag and observe what we get when we post the form.

We have seen another common structure in ColdFusion. It is known as the form structure. There are two types of common structures that send data to the server. The first one is called **get** and the second one is called **post**. If you see the code, you will notice that the method of the form is post. Post is the same as form in ColdFusion.

You should also observe that there is one extra field in the form structure that is not shown in the URL structure variable. It is the **FIELDNAMES** variable. It returns a simple list of the field names that were returned with the form. Let us edit the code and change the form tag attribute to "get". Then, refresh the page and click the **submit** button with the new information.

From the above screenshot, it is evident that the browser looks at the 'get' or 'post' value of the form, and sends a 'get' or 'post' back to the server. 'Post' is a "form method" belonging to the past and this is why ColdFusion translates posted variables to the form structure. Let us change the dump tag to "url" and observe what we get. Fill out the form and submit again with the new change. This displays the values in our structure as we would expect. This means you can either send url type data back to the server, or form type data with forms.

The advantage of sending form data is that form data can handle a larger volume of data being sent back to the server as compared to 'get' or url request. So the method of choice for forms is 'post'. Change both the method of the form attribute and the value of the `cfdump var` to form again.

The **Description box** is not ideal for entering product descriptions. So, we are going to use a text area in its place. This is how we change our line of code to accommodate a text area box. You can change the size of forms' objects using the attributes and styles:

```
<tr>
 <td>Description:</td>
 <td>
  <textArea name="description" id="idDescription"></textArea>
 </td>
</tr>
```

Here, we see our form looking different. If you fill up the description with more content than the box can hold, it shows the scroll bars appropriately.

Managing Our Product Data

Currently, we have a form that can be used for two purposes. It can be used to enter a new product as well as an existing one. We are going to re-use this form. Reuse is the fastest path to make things easier. But, we must not think that it is the only way to do things. What we should think is that not re-using something requires a reason for doing it differently.

In order to edit an existing product, we will have to create a page that shows the existing product records. Let us create the page.

```
<!--- Example: product_list.cfm --->
<!--- Processing --->
<cfscript>
 objProduct = createObject("component","product").init(dsn="cfb");
 rsProducts = objProduct.getRecordset();
</cfscript>
<!--- Content --->
<h3>Select a product to edit.</h3>
<ul>
 <cfoutput query="rsProducts">
  <li><a href="product_edit.cfm?id=#rsProducts.id#">#rsProducts.
name#</li>
 </cfoutput>
</ul>
```

There is no new code here. This is the browser view that we get when we run this page. Here, we will 'post' our edit page. Before you run the code, take the code from 3_1.cfm that we wrote at the beginning of the chapter and save a copy as product_edit.cfm to make the page work correctly when someone clicks on any of the products.

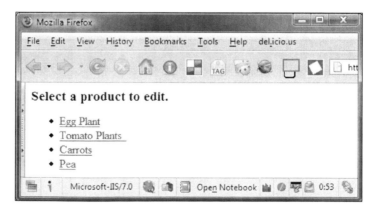

Now, we will click on a product. Let us manage the **watermelon** for now and observe what happens on the next page.

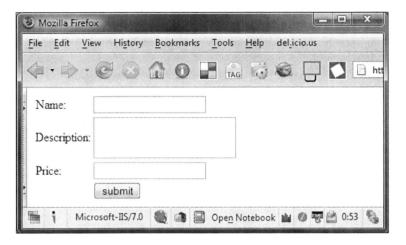

This is our edit page, and we will modify it so that it can get the data when we click through from our list page.

Getting Data to Our Edit Page

The current page looks similar to the page where we put the form. To get the data from our database onto the page, we need to do a few things here. First, let us change the action of the form tag to `product_edit.cfm`. We can modify the processing section of the page first, which will make things simpler. Add the following code to your `product_edit.cfm` page:

```
<!--- Processing --->
<cfparam name="url.id" default="0">
<cfscript>
 objProduct = createObject("component","product").init(dsn="cfb");
 objProduct.load(url.id);
</cfscript>
```

We need the default value set so that we do not receive an error message if the page is called without an `id`. After we set our default, we will see that we have created an object from our CFC object class. This time, we are passing the **Data Source Name** `dsn` into the object through the constructor method. This makes our code more portable, and ready for reuse. Once we have an instance, we set the current record using the load method and passing the `id` of the data record to the method. Let us look at the minor changes that we will make to the content section. We will add the values of the object's protected attributes.

```
<!--- Content --->
<cfoutput>
<form action="product_edit.cfm" method="post">
 <table>
  <tr>
   <td>Name:</td>
   <td>
    <input type="text" name="name" id="idName" value="#objProduct.
get('name')#" />
   </td>
  </tr>
  <tr>
   <td>Description:</td>
   <td>
    <textArea name="description" id="idDescription">#objProduct.
get('description')#</textArea>
   </td>
  </tr>
  <tr>
   <td>Price:</td>
   <td>
    <input type="text" name="price" id="idPrice" value="#objProduct.
get('price')#" />
   </td>
  </tr>
  <tr>
   <td> </td>
   <td>
    <input type="submit" name="submit"  value="submit" />
   </td>
  </tr>
 </table>
</form>
</cfoutput>
```

Now, we will refresh the form and see if we get different results.

Doesn't this look better? We can go back to the list page and call up an existing product in the edit form.

If we **submit** back to the same form, it will empty out the form. It should not do that, but the form is not posting the ID of the record back to the server. This can lead to a problem because, if we do not send the ID of the record back, the database will have no idea as to which record's details should be changed. Let us solve these issues first, and then we will learn to use a new tag called the `<cfinclude>` tag along the way.

The first problem that we are going to solve is a problem where we are calling the page with the ID value in the URL structure; then, if we post the page we will be calling the page with the ID in the form structure. We are going to use a technique that has been used and re-used for years in the ColdFusion community. We are going to combine the two scopes into a new common structure. We will create a structure called **attributes**. First we will check if it exists. If it does not, then we will create the structure. After that, we will merge the URL structure, and then the form structure into the attributes structure. We will put that code in a common page called `request_attributes.cfm`, so we can include it on any page we want, re-using the code. Do remember that the form and URL scope always exist.

```
<!--- request_attributes.cfm --->
<cfscript>
if(NOT isDefined("attributes"))
{
 attributes = structNew();
}
structAppend(attributes,url);
structAppend(attributes,form);
</cfscript>
```

Let us modify our edit page in order to take care of a couple of issues. We need to include our script that we have just created. We will modify our edit page in the processing section as highlighted here:

```
<!--- Processing --->
<cfinclude template="request_attributes.cfm">
<cfparam name="attributes.id" default="0">
<cfscript>
  objProduct = createObject("component","product").init(dsn="cfb");
  objProduct.load(attributes.id);
</cfscript>
```

There is only one more thing we need now. We need our form to store the id value of the record that is being managed. We could just put it in a text box like the other fields but the user does not need to know that information. Let us use a hidden input field and add it after our form tag.

```
<!--- Content --->
<cfoutput>
<form action="product_edit.cfm" method="post">
  <input type="hidden" name="id" value="#objProduct.get('id')#">
```

Refresh the screen, and it will work when we push the form around, or when we choose an item from the product list page. We have now created our edit or add page.

Saving Our Data

Now if we could get our data to save, that would be great. We will be using the same database that we used in the last chapter. We can see the appendix if we need to set up this database for practice. Let us look at the two ways in which a record is saved in ColdFusion. The first is how we would save a new record. This is called an INSERT query:

```
<cfquery datasource="cfb"name="qryInsert">
  INSERT INTO product( name , description , price)VALUES( <cfqueryparam
value="#form.name#"> , <cfqueryparam value="#form.description#"> ,
<cfqueryparam value="#form.price#">)
</cfquery>
```

Here, we see the basic code structure of an insert query. We can see that the one thing different from the standard queries here in the values section. We have a new ColdFusion tag. The query param tag is used to help to make sure that SQL **injection** is not used to attack your server. There are some more things that you can do with this tag. We just have to know that for all insert and update queries, we should always perform this to protect our data. The `queryParam` tag is a great tool to block **SQL injection** attacks. It also automates passing either text or non-text types to SQL for us. That brings us to our update query:

```
<cfquery datasource="cfb" name="qryUpdate">UPDATE product
SET name = <cfqueryparam value="#form.name#"> , description =
<cfqueryparam value="#form.description#"> , price = <cfqueryparam
value="#form.price#">WHERE ID = <cfqueryparam value="#form.id#">
</cfquery>
```

There are a few obvious differences between the two queries beyond what they accomplish. We see an additional item on this query called WHERE. Without this, you would not be able to update all the records in your query. So it is important to get it right. You never updated the ID field of a record either. This means we do not put the ID in the set end of the query.

We also need to take note that we use the `<queryparam>` tag to protect our data integrity. We need to do one more thing, so that our page knows which is the correct query to execute, on any given page call. We need to have our page first, and check if a form was sent. We will do that by looking for submit in the attributes. We do not look into the form value because there can be times you set the method to 'get'. In this case, the values will show up in ColdFusion as URL variables. Here again, we save time by not having to write a whole bunch of extra page logic to handle how information comes to our page. It is another case of admiring code reuse in action.

```
<cfif structKeyExists(attributes,"submit")>
</cfif>
```

Now, we need to know if we should be inserting or updating the record. We are using another one of those simpler techniques here. We set the ID field inside the data object to zero if it is a new record. Therefore, if ID equals zero, we will insert the record into our database. Otherwise, we will update the record with a matching ID value. Here is our modified logic to go in the middle of the above conditional statement. It goes in the middle because we only want it to run if the page was submitted from a form. If you are doing this, do not forget to include a form button, and name the button by inserting submit for the name attribute of the input tag as in our following example. We could name it something else, but we have to remember to name the submit button and check for matching attributes:

```
<cfif structKeyExists(attributes,"submit")>
 <cfif attributes.id EQ 0>
  <!--- REPLACE WITH INSERT --->
 <cfelse>
  <!--- REPLACE WITH UPDATE --->
 </cfif>
</cfif>
```

Let us take a look at the processing part of our page.

```
<!--- Example: product_edit.cfm --->
<!--- Processing --->
<cfinclude template="request_attributes.cfm">
<cfparam name="attributes.id" default="0">
<cfscript>
 objProduct = createObject("component","product").init(dsn="cfb");
 objProduct.load(attributes.id);
</cfscript>
<cfif structKeyExists(attributes,"submit")>
 <cfif attributes.id EQ 0>
  <cfquery datasource="cfb" name="qryInsert">
INSERT INTO product( name , description , price) VALUES( <cfqueryparam
value="#attributes.name#"> , <cfqueryparam value="#attributes.
description#"> , <cfqueryparam value="#attributes.price#">)
  </cfquery>
 <cfelse>
  <cfquery datasource="cfb" name="qryUpdate">
UPDATE product SET name = <cfqueryparam value="# attributes.name#"> ,
description = <cfqueryparam value="# attributes.description#"> , price
= <cfqueryparam value="# attributes.price#"> WHERE ID = <cfqueryparam
value="# attributes.id#">
  </cfquery>
 </cfif>
</cfif>
```

We can see that the page has become much larger. Now, it is time to see it working. Let us modify some data and submit the form back to the server. Let us modify the description to say 'and sweetest member' and click on the **submit** button.

Improving Page Flow

The page got refreshed and showed us an update. But it might not be obvious that an update was made. There is also an issue that it does not appear as if the data was updated because we pulled the data object details before the update was made. Also when we store our edit, it would be nice if we were sent back to the list page. Let us take a look at the redirect tag in ColdFusion. After an insert or update, the browser will be returned back to the list page. We will also pass a message to the page so that the user will get the updates. First, we will create a message in each of our insert and action code segments. Then, we will push the page back to the list page by passing the message with it:

```
if structKeyExists(attributes,"submit")>
 <cfif attributes.id EQ 0>
  <cfquery datasource="cfb" name="qryInsert">
INSERT INTO product( name , description , price ) VALUES(
<cfqueryparam value="#attributes.name#"> , <cfqueryparam
value="#attributes.description#"> , <cfqueryparam value="#attributes.
price#"> )
  </cfquery>
  <cfset returnMessage = "Your product has been added.">
 <cfelse>
  <cfquery datasource="cfb" name="qryUpdate">
UPDATE product SET name = <cfqueryparam value="#attributes.name#"> ,
description = <cfqueryparam value="#attributes.description#"> , price
= <cfqueryparam value="#attributes.price#"> WHERE ID = <cfqueryparam
value="#attributes.id#">
  </cfquery>
  <cfset returnMessage = "Your product (#attributes.name#) has been
updated.">
 </cfif>
 <cflocation url="product_list.cfm?message=#returnMessage#">
</cfif>
```

You can see that we tacked the message onto the end location of our target page. We need to add a <cfparam> tag to the calling page, so it will be able to handle calls where the URL variable is not available. Then we can add a little section of the page to show the messages, when they exist. Let us edit the product_list.cfm page as shown here:

```
<!--- Example: product_list.cfm --->
<!--- Processing --->
<cfparam name="url.message" default="">
<cfscript>
 objProduct = createObject("component","product").init(dsn="cfb");
 rsProducts = objProduct.getRecordset();
```

```
</cfscript>
<!--- Content --->
<cfif url.message NEQ "">
 <div>
  <cfoutput>#url.message#</cfoutput>
  <hr />
 </div>
</cfif>
<h3>Select a product to edit.</h3>
<ul><cfoutput query="rsProducts">
 <li><a href="product_edit.cfm?id=#rsProducts.id#">#rsProducts.name#</
li></cfoutput>
</ul>
```

This is how the page looks, when we submit our form.

Adding a New Record

We have seen the update function work. But, we have not seen the working of our insert function yet. We will modify the code so that we can add a new record. We will have to modify the content section of the `product_list.cfm` page to complete this function. The previous page is already set up to run.

```
<!--- Content --->
<cfif url.message NEQ "">
 <div>
  <cfoutput>#url.message#</cfoutput>
  <hr />
 </div>
</cfif>
```

```
<h3>Select a product to edit.</h3>
<ul>
 <li><a href="product_edit.cfm">+ New Product</li>
 <cfoutput query="rsProducts">
 <li><a href="product_edit.cfm?id=#rsProducts.id#">#rsProducts.name#</
li></cfoutput>
</ul>
```

Now, let us observe the page again. Once the page is loaded, and we click refresh, we will see the following page:

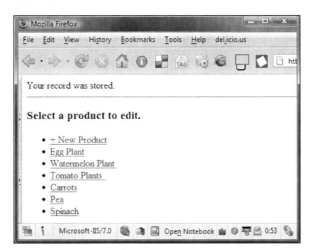

Let us click the **+ New Product** link, and observe what we get. We receive a new form to fill in the details. Let us enter some information and see how a new record is being added.

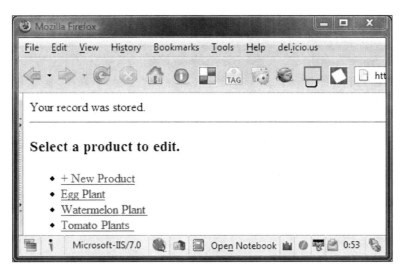

In the above screenshot, we can see that the record has been stored. Now, we are able to fully manage database table by using the editing functions that we have built into our pages.

Let Us Look Under the Hood

Well, since we are focusing on re-using and learning CFCs, it would be great if we could move our logic from our page into the CFC. You can have a look at Chapter 2 if you want to see the CFC that we were building for the product table. A constructor is used to get a CFC set up for use. Some CFCs do not require it, while others do. Obviously, this one has a dsn. So, it requires a constructor. We have the following:

```
<cfcomponent output="false" extends="_sdo">
 <!--- Constructor Methods --->
 <cffunction name="init" access="public" output="false">
  <cfargument name="dsn" required="true">
  <cfargument name="id" default="0">
  <cfscript>
   variables.field.name = "id,name,description,price";
   variables.field.defaults = "0,'','',0";
   variables.field.allowNull = "0,0,0,0";
   variables.table = "product";
   variables.pKeyField = "id";
   variables.pKeyNew = 0;
   variables.pKeyType = "autoInteger";
   variables.dsn = arguments.dsn;
   setDefaults();
```

```
    </ctscript>
    <cfreturn this />
  </cffunction>
</cfcomponent>
```

We can observe that all the extra methods that are being used are actually inside a parent CFC called `_sdo.cfc`. We are inheriting the methods of the parent CFC. By refactoring our common logic into a common CFC, we can have simpler CFCs for our data objects. This CFC is known as a Simple Data Object. Refer to `http://genesisrecords.riaforge.org`.

There is an 'untapped power' under the hood of our `_sdo.cfc`. It also has a `save()` method and a `saveStruct()` method. If you are manually setting the protected attributes, one at a time, then the `save()` method will store the data for you. If you are taking a form or URL structure that has the values that we would want to store, then use the `saveStruct()` method. This will be similar to the variable names with the fields in your simple data object. Now, store them by passing in one structure variable collection. Let us make some changes in our edit page.

First, we need to remove the last set of query sections that we had added previously and then put some simpler code onto our page. Then, we will move the logic for saving records so that it works with our power CFC. We will then check if a message exists and redirect to the new page once the form is submitted.

```
<!--- Processing --->
<cfinclude template="request_attributes.cfm">
<cfparam name="attributes.id" default="0">
<cfscript>
 myRedirect = "";
 objProduct = createObject("component","product").init(dsn="cfb");
 if(structKeyExists(attributes,"submit"))
 {
  result = objProduct.saveStruct(attributes);
  myRedirect = "product_list.cfm?message=#result.message#";
 }
 else
 {
  objProduct.load(attributes.id);
 }
</cfscript>
<cfif myRedirect NEQ "">
 <cflocation url="#myRedirect#">
</cfif>
```

Summary

We have reduced the size of our 'page down'. Also, if we want to set up a function to edit another table, we can use the techniques that have been discussed in this chapter. We can create a simple data object, and child along with a few parameters that we have seen in `product.cfc`. This is known as **Object Relational Management (ORM)** by the development community. It is a very simple example to get started. Now, we can clearly see that when it comes to reuse, this is a much better way to write our code. The following is a summary of our discussion in this chapter:

- We implemented access permissions on CFC methods.
- We learned to integrate and streamline the workflow of web forms and CFC database processing.
- We learned to add and edit data through CFCs and web forms.
- We discovered the power of code reuse through inheritance.
- We learned to interact with method arguments by using simple variables.

4
Application, Session, and Request Scope

There is a huge difference between a web application and a dynamic webpage. Web applications persist basic information, so we can create things such as shopping carts, let users log in and out, and much more. HTML helps us to click through pages with links. In this chapter, we will learn how we can use web server memory to create engaging and interactive web applications by using variable scopes.

Further, we are going to discover the differences between application, session, and request scopes. We will learn how to share some information, and how to protect the rest of the information in a controlled manner. In this chapter, we will have a look at the following:

- The life expectancy types of information. This affects the system memory and the place where different information is stored.
- The `Application.cfc` object class, the cornerstone of ColdFusion applications.
- The special standard method events, which ColdFusion calls in the `Application.cfc` object.
- Custom tag paths and mapping settings inside the object, the two special functions of the `Application.cfc` object.

Life Span

Each of our shared scopes has a **life span**. They come into existence at a given point, and cease to exist at a predictable point. Learning to recognize these points is very important. It is also the first aspect of "Scope".

The 'request scope' is created when a request is made to your ColdFusion server from any source. This could either be a web browser, or any type of web application that can make an HTTP request reach your server. Any variable placed into the request structure will persist until the request processing is complete.

Persistence is the property of data remaining available for a period of time. Without persistence, the only way to make information last would be to pass all the information from one webpage to another, in all forms and in all links. You may have heard people say that webpages are stateless. If you passed all the information in the browser, they would be closer to stateful applications, but would be difficult to manage. We will learn how to do things in a simpler fashion. Here is a chart of the "life spans" of the key scopes.

Scope	Begins	Ends
Request	Begins when a server receives a request from any source. Created before any session or an application is created.	Ends when the processing for this request is complete. Ending has nothing to do with the end of application or sessions.
Application	Begins before session but after request. Begins only when an `application.cfc` is run, or when the `<application>` tag is called.	Ends when the amount of time since a request is greater than the expiration time set for the application.
Session	Begins after an application is created. Created inside the same sources as the application.	Ends when the amount of time since a request is greater than the expiration time set for the session.

We will be discussing the scopes in more detail later in this chapter.

All the scopes expire if you shut down your server. When we close our browser window or reboot the client side, a session does not come to an end, but our connectivity to that particular session scope ends. The information and resources for storing that session are held until the session expires. Then we are either able to start a new session, or we are unable to reconnect to that session.

Introducing the Application.cfc Object

The first thing we need to do is to understand how this application page is called. When a .cfm or .cfc file is called, the server seeks for an Application.cfc file in that directory. It also looks for an Application.cfm file. We do not create application or session scope with the .cfm version because .cfc is much more powerful. It provides for better encapsulation and code reuse. If the file is found, ColdFusion runs it. If the file is not found, then it moves up one directory towards the sever root directory in order to search for an Application.cfc file. The search stops either when a file is found, or once it reaches the root directory and a file is not found.

There are several methods in the Application.cfc file. The following table gives the method names and the details as to when those methods are called.

Method Name	When Method is Called
onApplicationEnd	The application ends; the application times out
onApplicationStart	The application first starts: the first request for a page is processed or the first CFC method is invoked by an event gateway instance, a web service, or Macromedia Flash Remoting CFC
onError	An exception occurs that is not caught by a try or catch block
onRequest	The onRequestStart method finishes (this method can filter request contents)
onRequestEnd	All pages in the request have been processed
onRequestStart	A request starts
onSessionEnd	A session ends
onSessionStart	A session starts

When the `Application.cfc` file is run for the first time, these methods are called in the order as shown in the screenshot below. The request variable scope is available at all times. Yet, to make the code flow right, the designers of this object made sure of the order in which the server runs the code. You will also find that for technical reasons, there are some issues that arise when we use the `onRequest()` method. Therefore, we will not be using this method.

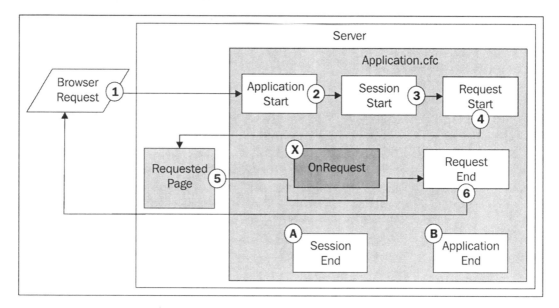

1→ The browser sends a request to the server. The server passes processing to the `Application.cfc` file, if it exists. It skips the step if it does not exist. The `application.cfc` has methods that execute if they too exist. The first method is `onApplicationStart()`. This executes on the basis of the application name. If the unique named application is not currently running on the server, then this method is called.

2→ The next thing that `Application.cfc` does is to check if the request to the server is a 'pre-existing session'. If the request is a new request, then it calls the `onSessionStart()` method, if it exists.

3→ On every request to the server, if the `onRequestStart()` method exists, then it is called at this particular point in the processing.

4→ Now, the actual page requested is called and processed.

5→ After the requested page is processed, the control is passed back to the `onRequestEnd()` method, if it exists in `Application.cfc`.

6→This is the point when ColdFusion has completed its work of processing information to respond to the browser request. At this point, you could either send HTML to the browser, a redirect, or any other response.

X→This step normally occurs after the `onRequestStart()` method. If the onRequest method was used, then by default it prevents calling of CFCs. We do not say that it is always wrong to use this method. We will avoid it altogether just for the sake of learning ColdFusion. This only affects remote calls.

A→The `onSessionEnd()` method is called if it exists when the time since the user has last made a request to the server is greater than the time for the session timeout.

B→The `onApplicationEnd()` method is called if it exists when the time since the last request was received by the server is greater than the timeout for the application.

Once the application is created and other requests are made to the server, these methods are called. The application and session already exist so the server does not start them again.

- `onRequestStart()`
- `onRequest()`
- `onRequestEnd()`

Here is a representation of the complete process that is less granular. We can see that the application behaves just as it did in the earlier illustration; we just do not go into much detail about every method that is called internally. We also see that the requested page can call additional code segments. These code segments can be a CFC, a custom tag, or an included page. Those pages can also include other pages, so that they create a proper hierarchy of functionality. Always try to make sure that functionality is layered, so the separation of layers provides simpler creation, maintenance, and long-term support for your web applications.

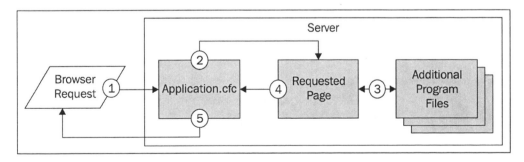

The variables set in `Application.cfc` can be modified before the requested page is called, and even after that. Let us say, you want to record the time at which the session was last hit. You could choose to set a variable, `<cfset session._stat. lasthit = now()>`. This could be set either at the beginning of a request, or at the end. Here, the question is where you would put this function. At first, you might think that you would add this function to the `OnSessionStart()` method or `OnSessionEnd()` method. This would cause an issue because these two methods are only called when a session has begun or when it has come to an end. You would actually put the code into the `OnRequestStart()` or `OnRequestEnd()` code segment of the `Application.cfc` for the correct function. The request methods are called with every server request. We will have a complete `Application.cfc` to use as a model for creating our own variations in the future project. Remember to place the code in the right place and validate using CFDump, or by some other means to make sure it works when creating changes.

Application Variables

There are some application variables that determine the behavior of an application. Inside the application, all the variables are stored inside `this` scope. This scope refers to the `.cfc` file where it is found. Generally, this is not considered a good practice because the variables are not protected from outside the object. In `Application.cfc`, this is not an issue because there is no code to create an instance of the object for reuse.

Variable	Default	Description
name	no name	This is the application name. If you do not set this variable, or set it to the empty string, your CFC applies to the unnamed application scope, which is the ColdFusion MX J2EE servlet context. For more information on unnamed scopes, see "Sharing data between ColdFusion pages and JSP pages or servlets" in the *ColdFusion Developer's Guide*.
applicationTimeout	Administrator value	Life span, as the actual number of days of the application, including all Application scope variables. Use the CFML `CreateTimeSpan` function to generate this variable's value.
clientManagement	Administrator value	Checks whether the application supports Client scope variables.
clientStorage	Administrator value	Where Client variables are stored; Client variables can be cookie, registry, or the name of a data source.

Variable	Default	Description
loginStorage	Cookie	Whether to store login information in the Cookie scope, or the Session scope.
sessionManagement	no	Checks whether the application supports Session scope variables.
sessionTimeout	Administrator value	Life span, as the actual number of days, of the user session, including all session variables. Use the CFML CreateTimeSpan function to generate this variable's value.
setClientCookies	True	Whether to send CFID and CFTOKEN cookies to the client browser.
setDomainCookies	False	Whether to set CFID and CFTOKEN cookies for a domain (not just for a host).
scriptProtect	Administrator value	Whether to protect variables from cross-site scripting attacks.
secureJSON	Administrator value	A Boolean value that specifies whether to add a security prefix to a value that the ColdFusion function returns in JSON-format, in response to a remote call.
		The default value is the value of the Prefix serialized JSON setting in the **Administrator Server Settings | Settings page** (which defaults to `false`). You can override this value in the `cffunction` tag. For more information see "Improving Security" in the *ColdFusion Developer's Guide*.
secureJSONPrefix	Administrator value	The security prefix to the value that a ColdFusion function returns in JSON-format, in response to a remote call, if the `secureJSON` setting is `true`.
		The default value is the value of the Prefix serialized JSON setting in the **Administrator Server Settings | Settings page** (which defaults to `//`, the JavaScript comment character).
		For more information see "Improving Security" in the *ColdFusion Developer's Guide*.

Variable	Default	Description
welcomeFileList		A comma-delimited list of names of the files. It tells ColdFusion not to call the onMissingTemplate() method if the files are not found. Use this variable to prevent ColdFusion from invoking the onMissingTemplate handler if all of the following items are true.
		Your web server (for example, web.xml file) has a welcome file list with the CFML pages such as index.cfm that it tries to run if an URL specifies the path ending in a directory.
		The web server sends a request for CFML pages; it is the welcome list to ColdFusion without determining that the page exists.
		You have to support "directory browsing" in directories that do not have any of the files on the welcome file list.
		You specify this variable only if the Application.cfc file specifies an onMissingTemplate handler. It should contain the same list of files as your web.xml welcome file list.
		Note: You do not need to use the welcomeFileList variable with web servers, such as Apache. You also need to use the welcomeFileList variable with the most integrated web and application servers, such as integrated ColdFusion or JRun web server.

```
<cfscript>
  this.name = "ApplicationName1";
  this.applicationTimeout = createTimeSpan(0,2,0,0);
  this.clientManagement = true;
  this.clientStorage = "cookie;
  this.loginStorage = "session";
  this.sessionManagement = true;
  this.sessionTimeout = createTimeSpan(0,0,20,0);
  this.setClientCookies = true;
  this.setDomainCookies = false;
  this.scriptProtect = false;
</cfscript>
```

This is just an example as to how we could set these variables. There is no special way to do this always. For each site, we should consider how we want these settings to be. The type of work done by some people may mean that they end up using the same setting all the time. That is also fine, as long as, we remember to think about getting the settings right.

The Start Methods

We will have a look at the 'start methods' and make some observations now. Each method has its own set of arguments. All `Application.cfc` methods return a Boolean value of `true` or `false` to declare if they completed correctly or not. Any code you place inside the method will execute when the event occurs. These are the events that match with the name of the method. We will also include some basic code that will help you build an application core that is good for reuse and talk about what those features provide.

Application Start Method

The following is the code structure of the application start method. You could actually place these methods in any order in the CFC, as the order does not matter. Code that uses CFCs only require the methods to exist. If they exist then it will call them. We place them in our code so that it helps us to read and understand the structure.

```
<cffunction name="onApplicationStart" output="false">
 <cfscript>
 // create default stat structure and pre-request values
  application._stat = structNew();
  application._stat.started = now();
  application._stat.thisHit = now();
  application._stat.hits = 0;
  application._stat.sessions = 0;
 </cfscript>
</cffunction>
```

We have no arguments for the `onApplicationStart()` method. We have included some extra code to show you something that can be done in this function. Please note that if we change the code in this method, it will only run at the very first time when an application running in ColdFusion is hit. To hit it again, we need to either change the application name or restart the ColdFusion server. The above section explained how to change the application's name under *Application Variables*.

From the start methods, we can see that we can access the variable scopes that allow persistence of key information. We will understand the power of this object by creating some statistics that can be used in most situations. We could use them for debugging, logging, or in any other appropriate use case. Again, we have to be aware that this only gets hit the very first time a request is made to a ColdFusion server, where the application name in the variable settings does not exist at that time. We will be updating many of our statistics in the request methods. We will also be updating one of our variables in the session end method.

Session Start Method

The session start method only gets called when a request is made for a new session. It is good that ColdFusion can keep track of these things. The following is example code that allows us to keep a record of the session-based statistics that is similar to the application-based statistics:

```
<cffunction name="onSessionStart" output="false">
 <cfscript>
 // create default session stat structure and pre-request values
  session._stat.started = now();
  session._stat.thisHit = now();
  session._stat.hits = 0;
  // at start of each session update count for application stat
  application._stat.sessions += 1;
 </cfscript>
</cffunction>
```

You might have noticed in the previous code for ColdFusion 8, where we used '+='. In the former versions of ColdFusion, you had to type that particular line differently. The following two examples are the same in function:

Example 1: `myTotal = myTotal +3`

Example 2: `myTotal += 3`

This is common in JavaScript, ActionScript, and many other languages. It is new in version 8 of ColdFusion. We change the application-based setting because sessions cannot see each other. Therefore, we use the application either to count or to add a count every time a new session starts.

Request Start Method

This is one of the longest methods in the chapter. The first thing you will notice is that the script that is called is passed to the method by ColdFusion. The variation is that any scripts starting with an underscore will be blocked from execution. This means that you can start any .cfm page or .cfc page with an underscore, and this protects it from being called outside the local server.

```
<cffunction name="onRequestStart" output="false">
 <cfargument name="thePage" type="string" required="true">
  <cfscript>
   var myReturn = true;
   // fancy code to block pages that start with underscore
   if(left(listLast(arguments.thePage,"/"),1) EQ "_")
   {
    myReturn = false;
   }
   // update application stat on each request
   application._stat.lastHit = application._stat.thisHit;
   application._stat.thisHit = now();
   application._stat.hits += 1;
   // update session stat on each request
   session._stat.lastHit = session._stat.thisHit;
   session._stat.thisHit = now();
   session._stat.hits += 1;
  </cfscript>
 <cfreturn myReturn>
</cffunction>
```

The next sections are to update all the application and session statistics variables that need to be updated with each request. You should also notice that we are recording the last time the application or session was requested.

The End Methods

Previously, some of the methods in this object were impossible to achieve with the earlier versions of ColdFusion. It was possible to do an end request function, but only a few users made use of it. We find that by using this object many more people are taking advantage of these features, than did in the earlier version of ColdFusion.

The new methods that have added have the ability to run code specifically when a session ends, and when an application ends. This allows us to do things that we could not do previously. We can keep a record of how long a user is online without having to hit the database every time. When the session starts, you can store it in the session scope. When the session ends, you can take all that information and store it in the session log table.

Request End Method

We are not going to use every method that is available to us. As we have the concept from the other sections, this would be redundant. The concepts of this method are very similar to the `onRequestStart()` method with the exception that it occurs after the requested page has been called. If you create content in this method and set the output attribute to `true`, then it will be sent back to browser requests. Here you can place the code that logs information about our requests.

```
<cffunction name="onRequestEnd" returnType="void" output="false">
 <cfargument name="thePage" type="string" required="true">
</cffunction>
```

Session End Method

In the session end method, we can perform logging functions that are specific to the end of a session. You need to use the argument's scope variables to read both the application and session variables. If you are changing application variables as in our example code, then you must use the argument's scope for that.

```
<cffunction name="onSessionEnd" returnType="void" output="false">
 <cfargument name="SessionScope" type="struct" required="true">
 <cfargument name="ApplicationScope" type="struct" required="false">
 <cfscript>
 // NOTE: You must use the variable scope below to access the
//application structure inside this method.
  arguments.ApplicationScope._stat.sessions -= 1;
 </cfscript>
</cffunction>
```

Application End Method

This is our end method for applications. Here you can do the logging activity. As in the session method, you need to use the argument's scope in order to read variables for the application. It is also good to note that at this point, you can no longer access the session scope.

```
<cffunction name="onApplicationEnd" returnType="void" output="false">
 <cfargument name="applicationScope" required="true">
</cffunction>
```

On Error Method

The following code demonstrates how we can be flexible in managing errors sent to this method. If the error comes from `Application.cfc`, then the event (or method that had an issue) will be the value of the `arguments.eventname` variable. Otherwise, it will be an empty string. In our code, we change the `label` on our dump statement, so that it is a bit more obvious where it was generated.

```
<cffunction name="onError" returnType="void" output="true">
 <cfargument name="exception" required="true">
 <cfargument name="eventname" type="string" required="true">
 <cfif arguments.eventName NEQ "">
  <cfdump var="#arguments.exception#" label="Application core
exception">
 <cfelse>
  <cfdump var="#arguments.exception#" label="Application exception">
 </cfif>
</cffunction>
```

Scope Visibility

There are some places where variable scopes can be seen from other code, and others where they cannot. In this chapter, the creation and management of several aspects of these variables will be explained just by referring to the code. Scope just means where something is visible. Each variable type listed in the following table has a specific range of code that can see the variable's structure for each of the scopes.

Variable Scope	Visibility (Ability to interact with it)
Application	To all ColdFusion code in this unique application while it persists
Request	To all the ColdFusion code within the same request
Session	To all the ColdFusion code in this unique application while the unique session persists and only to the connections that identify themselves to the server as that session

There are a few other scopes that are available. These include the client scope and the server scope. These are usually avoided, but may be of use in certain unique circumstances. You will also find that there are a few applications that have not found everything they need in the scope. The client scope has a number of limitations. The server scope is a very bad idea on shared hosting servers because people who share your server can read and write to the same values as you. Therefore, in this scenario, it is bad practice to use the server scope.

Let us create a set of example pages to exercise our knowledge that we have just gathered. First, we will look at our `Application.cfc` file:

```
<cfcomponent output="false">
 <cfscript>
  this.name = "ApplicationName1";
  this.applicationTimeout = createTimeSpan(0,2,0,0);
  this.clientManagement = ;false;
  this.clientStorage = "";"cookie";
  this.loginStorage = "session";
  this.sessionManagement = true;
  this.sessionTimeout = createTimeSpan(0,0,0,20);
  this.setClientCookies = true;
  this.setDomainCookies = false;
  this.scriptProtect = false;
 </cfscript>
 <cffunction name="onApplicationStart" output="false">
  <cfscript>
  // create default stat structure and pre-request values
   application._stat = structNew();
   application._stat.started = now();
   application._stat.thisHit = now();
   application._stat.hits = 0;
   application._stat.sessions = 0;
  </cfscript>
 </cffunction>
 <cffunction name="onSessionStart" output="false">
  <cfscript>
  // create default session stat structure and pre-request values
   session._stat.started = now();
   session._stat.thisHit = now();
   session._stat.hits = 0;
   // at start of each session update count for application stat
   application._stat.sessions += 1;
  </cfscript>
 </cffunction>
 <cffunction name="onRequestStart" output="false">
  <cfargument name="thePage" type="string" required="true">
  <cfscript>
   var myReturn = true;
   // fancy code to block pages that start with underscore
   if(left(listLast(arguments.thePage,"/"),1) EQ "_")
   {
    myReturn = false;
```

```
    }
    // update application stat on each request
    application._stat.lastHit = application._stat.thisHit;
    application._stat.thisHit = now();
    application._stat.hits += 1;
    // update session stat on each request
    session._stat.lastHit = session._stat.thisHit;
    session._stat.thisHit = now();
    session._stat.hits += 1;
  </cfscript>
  <cfreturn myReturn>
 </cffunction>
 <!--- *** This is generally not used *** 
 <cffunction name="onRequest" returnType="void">
  <cfargument name="thePage" type="string" required="true">
  <cfinclude template="#arguments.thePage#">
 </cffunction>
 <cffunction name="onRequestEnd" returnType="void" output="false">
  <cfargument name="thePage" type="string" required="true">
 </cffunction>
 <cffunction name="onApplicationEnd" returnType="void" output="false">
  <cfargument name="applicationScope" required="true">
 </cffunction>
 <cffunction name="onSessionEnd" returnType="void" output="false">
  <cfargument name="SessionScope" type="struct" required="true">
  <cfargument name="ApplicationScope" type="struct" required="false">
  <cfscript>
  // NOTE: You must use the variable scope below to access the
//application structure inside this method.
    arguments.ApplicationScope._stat.sessions -= 1;
  </cfscript>
 </cffunction>
 <cffunction name="onError" returnType="void" output="true">
  <cfargument name="exception" required="true">
  <cfargument name="eventname" type="string" required="true">
  <cfif arguments.eventName NEQ "2">
   <cfdump var="#arguments.exception#" label="Application core
exception">
  <cfelse>
   <cfdump var="#arguments.exception#" label="Application exception">
  </cfif>
 </cffunction>
</cfcomponent>
```

Now, we will create (or use the example file for) a page called index.cfm.

Practical Application

We are not going to cover every application in detail. We are going to discuss a couple of variations on where and how to use scoped persistence. This means by using one of the scopes listed earlier, we can have a variable or CFC object last for the entire visibility period in the table.

Let us say we created a CFC called `user.cfc`, and then inside the `Application.cfc` `onSessionStart()` method, we created an instance of the class. We would want our object to last for the full life of our session. We would create code similar to this to enhance our former code for the `sessionStart` method. If we check out the example code on the site, the `user.cfc` file has already been created. Here is the modified version. The modified code is an example of how we would create a persistent object for the user. It would last until the session expires. One of the good things about application, session, and request scoped variables and objects is that they exist until that scope expires and the server takes care of clearing them up for us. When we say they no longer exist, it is because the server removes them from the computer memory resources.

```
<cffunction name="onSessionStart" output="false">
 <cfscript>
 // create default session stat structure and pre-request values
  session._stat.started = now();
  session._stat.thisHit = now();
  session._stat.hits = 0;
  // at start of each session update count for application stat
  application._stat.sessions += 1;
  // create an instance of the user class
  session._user = createObject("component","user").init();
 </cfscript>
</cffunction>
```

Now, any features that are in this object can be called from the request start or end methods. It could also be called from the actual pages requested. This is fantastic because we have now automated the creation of the user object outside our general page code. With time, we will get into the practice of packaging up more and more information into CFC classes. It would be good if we did the same thing with our statistics. If we look close enough, we will see that in reality, the application and the session statistics are the same. We could create an extended version of the `stat` base class for any changes, and then all of the code would be in a single file and ready for reuse.

Mappings per Application

In ColdFusion 8, there is a setting in Admin that allows the `Application.cfc` file to set custom application mappings. These are not the global mappings that existed previously. It is a great feature. Previously, these needed to be set from the ColdFusion Administrator. But now we can set these ourselves from the application itself. Here are the instructions on how to allow them to work:

- Check the **Enable Per App Settings** option on the **Settings** page of the ColdFusion Administrator. (Or ask the hosting provider or web administrator for the site to do so.)

- Include code similar to that given below in your `Application.cfc` file:

```
<cfset this.mappings["/myPDFs"] = "c:\inetpub\myPDFs\"> or
<cfset structInsert( this.mappings, "/myPDFs", "c:\inetpub\myP-
DFs\")>
```
(Make sure, if you are using the `structInsert` approach, that you first create the structure).

Custom Tag Paths per Application

Here is some good news for those using shared hosting providers. This will enable the use of custom tag path mappings set in `Application.cfc` similar to the mappings above.

- Check the **Enable Per App Settings** option on the **Settings** page of the ColdFusion Administrator. (Or, ask the hosting provider or web administrator for the site to do so.)

- Include code similar to that given below in your `Application.cfc` file.

```
<cfset customtagpaths = "c:\mapped1,c:\mapped2">
<cfset customtagpaths = ListAppend(customtagpaths,"c:\
mapped3")>
<cfset This.customtagpaths = customtagpaths>
```

Summary

This chapter included information on application, session, and request scope management in ColdFusion.

You may also find it practical to do logging, closing connections, and more in the end methods of `Application.cfc`. Here is a list of what was covered in this chapter:

- `Application.cfc`
- The concept of variable scope
- The various methods of the `Application.cfc` class
- Setting per application mappings and custom tag paths
- Use of the `OnRequest()` method
- Modification of our persistent application and session items in `onRequestStart()` and `onRequestEnd()`
- Creating persistent variables and packaging them up into classes wherever possible.

Introduction to Custom Tags

5

Reuse makes coding easier, faster, and maintainable. We find that the same benefits are possible with the browser side of building websites. In this chapter, we will learn about the basics of custom tags through an example of skinning websites. Skins give us the ability to change the appearance of a website without the need to touch the application code running on the site. We will learn how to create and manage the look-and-feel of our website by combining CSS and content containers—technology that has become the most popular standard. We will also learn how to write and understand custom tags in ColdFusion. Custom tags have some advantages that CFC objects do not have. In this chapter, we will cover the following:

- Varying forms of code reuse in ColdFusion
- Passing information to a custom tag
- Reuse of concepts such as skins with custom tags
- Different methods of storing and accessing tags and tag libraries

Different Forms of Code Reuse

There are unique benefits to each of these technologies. Let us discuss them in brief here and see how to use them together in the development of websites. This will help us in knowing how to encapsulate our program code for the best reuse. We will also have a look at 'include' files.

Now, we will be using our tags to 'skin' a site. This is a term that means something similar to the behavior of a chameleon. The chameleon changes the color of its skin to show a different personality. Our sites can be upgraded much faster and more easily if we create skinned sites. This chapter will help us move in that direction much more easily. Custom tags are the easiest way to skin sites.

CFCs

ColdFusion components are typically used for two purposes. The first purpose is data access and interaction. The second is packaging business logic. Packaging them into object classes is a great way to simplify pages that use the objects.

CFCs also provide the ability to inherit the design of other CFCs. This feature can revolutionize software development.

Another very unique aspect of CFCs is that they can be 'stateful'. This means that you can create them and access them repeatedly during the time the instantiated object class is in existence. The two things that persist in ColdFusion are variables and objects. You should always consider moving your variable persistence into a CFC. Caching a data record or a recordset for persistence in a CFC is also good practice.

CFCs can also be used to work as Web Services. It is the easiest way to code a Web Service on any platform. You just set the access attribute to remote.

Custom Tags

We will discuss the advantages and the various uses of custom tags. We choose skinning because it is the best example of the power and techniques of custom tag creation and its benefits.

- Custom tags can wrap a block of code and conditionally execute that code
- Custom tags can process logic based on both start and end tags
- Custom tags can have parent-child functionality
- Custom tags can read and set calling code variables
- Custom tags can return multiple variables

CFInclude

This built-in tag is a great way to raise development. However, there are a couple of things missing from 'includes' that are good features of CFCs and custom tags. They are the use of interfaces and putting variables inside a separate area. This means that anything that happens on an included code segment is just like it was part of the page that originally called it. This is not always bad, and you will find us using some 'includes' for our skinning tags also. We suggest that you consider only using 'includes' as a library of code extensions for the page that called them. This was not the case before CF6. ColdFusion version 6 added CFCs. With the combined power of CFCs and custom tags this is the best way to maintain and develop sites.

Our First Custom Tag

We are going to start with a simple page and look at changing it into a combined page that calls custom tags. We should also note that some of the fancy non-generic layout is being delivered via a CSS file included through the HTML. First let us look at the original code of our page.

```
<!DOCTYPE html PUBLIC "-//W3C//DTD XHTML 1.0 Transitional//EN"
"http://www.w3.org/TR/xhtml1/DTD/xhtml1-transitional.dtd">
<html xmlns="http://www.w3.org/1999/xhtml">
<head>
    <meta http-equiv="Content-Type" content="text/html; charset=iso-
8859-1" />
    <title>ColdFusion Site - Creating Custom Tags</title>
    <link rel="stylesheet" href="right.css" type="text/css" />
</head>
<body>
<div id="header">
  <h1 id="siteName">ColdFusion Site</h1>
  <div id="globalNav"> <a href="#">Home</a> | <a href="#">AboutUs</a>
| <a href="#">Shop</a> | <a href="#">Forum</a> | <a href="#">FAQ</a> |
<a href="#">Links</a> | <a href="#">Contact Us </a> </div>
</div>

<div id="content">
  <h2 id="pageName">Creating Custom Tags</h2>
  <div class="story">
    <h3>Power Markup via Custom Tags </h3>
    <p> Custom tags are one powerful method of making HTML sites
easier to build, manage and update. If you have never learned the
power of custom tags you should get a copy of ColdFusion Bootcamp and
read all about it! </p>
  </div>
</div>
<div id="sideBar">
  <div class="relatedLinks">
    <h3>Custom Tags</h3>
    <ul>
      <li><a href="#">Page</a></li>
      <li><a href="#">Sidebar</a></li>
      <li><a href="#">Header</a></li>
      <li><a href="#">Footer</a></li>
    </ul>
  </div>
  <div class="relatedLinks">
    <h3>CFCs</h3>
    <ul>
```

```
        <li><a href="#">Database</a></li>
        <li><a href="#">Business Logic</a></li>
        <li><a href="#">Inheritance</a></li>
      </ul>
   </div>
</div>
<div id="footer"><a href="#">About Us</a> | <a href="#">Site Map</
a> | <a href="#">Privacy Policy</a> | <a href="#">Contact Us</a> |
&copy;2008 Our Copywrite </div>
<br />
</body>
</html>
```

This is a standard CSS-based HTML site. The first thing we are going to do is to separate the visible header and footer sections of the page. We will start by creating files called `header.cfm` and `footer.cfm` in the same directory for now. Here is how the page will appear:

Custom Header/Footer Tags

Now, we will look at our first tag. This is the header tag.

```
<cfif thisTag.ExecutionMode EQ "start">
<div id="header">
```

```
    <h1 id="siteName">ColdFusion Site</h1>
    <div id="globalNav"> <a href="#">Home</a> | <a href="#">AboutUs</a>
 | <a href="#">Shop</a> | <a href="#">Forum</a> | <a href="#">FAQ</a> |
<a href="#">Links</a> | <a href="#">Contact Us </a> </div>
</div>
</cfif>
```

We could actually just skip the start tag and end tag, but that would help someone in using the tag incorrectly. Look at the two styles of coding our new custom tag and you will see the difference.

```
<cf_header>
```

versus

```
<cf_header />
```

Just as in HTML, there are some tags that do not need a closing tag, but there are other tags that do use a closing tag. The modern standards suggest that for HTML, we close all HTML tags. Since we are focusing on doing markup interaction, and these are tags that are going to be used by the designers who are working on ColdFusion sites, we suggest that you build all your tags in such a way that designers can use them without much effort.

Look at the code and you will find a new scope that is available inside the custom tags. The new scope is called `thisTag`. The `thisTag` scope has the following variables:

thisTag variable	description
hasEndTag	This is a Boolean value signifying that the calling page has an end tag that is used for calling the tag. The end tag can be a separate end tag or a /> at the end of the start tag.
executionMode	There are two modes, 'Start' and 'End'. If you put an end tag at the back of the start tag, then the tag will be executed twice, once with each mode.
generatedContent	There can be content generated in three places. During the execution of code in the start tag, it can generate content. If you have separate start and end tags, and there is content generated between the tags, then it will be added to the generated content. Lastly, if you generate content during the end tag call to the custom tag, that too will be added.
assocAttribs	This variable is used for nested tags in parent-child relationships. It allows you to make data visible between the parent/child tags.

Here is the new footer custom tag code for our `footer.cfm` file. The traditional way to call a custom tag is by using `<cf_` before the name of your CFM file, and it calls that code as a custom tag. The results seem good because you gain the ability to update your header and footer for all pages by using these custom tags in one place. This means that if you had fifty or five hundred web pages using these custom tags, you could update them in one place, and all files would instantly use the headers and footers. Thus, custom tags are powerful tools that can be reused.

```
<cfif thisTag.ExecutionMode EQ "start">
<div id="footer"><a href="#">About Us</a> | <a href="#">Site Map</
a> | <a href="#">Privacy Policy</a> | <a href="#">Contact Us</a> |
&copy;2008 Our Copywrite </div>
<br />
</cfif>
```

Now, let us look at our updated file. The highlighted sections show where we moved the code from our page to our custom tags. If you are using the example files, this file is called `one.cfm` in the examples folder.

```
<!DOCTYPE html PUBLIC "-//W3C//DTD XHTML 1.0 Transitional//EN"
"http://www.w3.org/TR/xhtml1/DTD/xhtml1-transitional.dtd">
<html xmlns="http://www.w3.org/1999/xhtml">
<head>
   <meta http-equiv="Content-Type" content="text/html; charset=iso-
8859-1" />
   <title>ColdFusion Site - Creating Custom Tags</title>
   <link rel="stylesheet" href="right.css" type="text/css" />
</head>
<body>
<cf_header />
<div id="content">
  <h2 id="pageName">Creating Custom Tags</h2>
  <div class="story">
    <h3>Power Markup via Custom Tags </h3>
    <p> Custom tags are one powerful method of making HTML sites
easier to build, manage and update. If you have never learned the
power of custom tags you should get a copy of ColdFusion Bootcamp and
read all about it! </p>
  </div>
</div>
<div id="sideBar">
  <div class="relatedLinks">
    <h3>Custom Tags</h3>
    <ul>
      <li><a href="#">Page</a></li>
      <li><a href="#">Sidebar</a></li>
```

```
    <li><a href="#">Header</a></li>
    <li><a href="#">Footer</a></li>
  </ul>
  </div>
  <div class="relatedLinks">
    <h3>CFCs</h3>
    <ul>
      <li><a href="#">Database</a></li>
      <li><a href="#">Business Logic</a></li>
      <li><a href="#">Inheritance</a></li>
    </ul>
  </div>
</div>
<cf_footer />
</body>
</html>
```

Nested Tags

Let us have a look at how we can create a nested custom tag. Our parent will be the sidebar tag and the child tags will be sidebar_section and sidebar_item. We will learn how it allows us to separate content from containers. This type of coding helps us to send AJAX, FLEX, and other content in the future. In this chapter, we will be concentrating on HTML.

First, we will create a single sidebar tag in a similar way to how we created the custom tags for the header and the footer. It will give us a chance to see how we use our thisTag.executionMode = "end" logic. To learn more, we are going to use the conditional switch logic. You can either use switch or if logic.

```
<cfswitch expression="#thisTag.executionMode#">

   <cfcase value="start">
        <!--- No code here at this time.  --->
   </cfcase>
   <cfcase value="end">
      <cfoutput>
<div id="sideBar">
  <div class="relatedLinks">
    <h3>Custom Tags</h3>
    <ul>
      <li><a href="##">Page</a></li>
      <li><a href="##">Sidebar</a></li>
      <li><a href="##">Header</a></li>
      <li><a href="##">Footer</a></li>
    </ul>
```

```
    </div>
    <div class="relatedLinks">
      <h3>CFCs</h3>
      <ul>
        <li><a href="##">Database</a></li>
        <li><a href="##">Business Logic</a></li>
        <li><a href="##">Inheritance</a></li>
      </ul>
    </div>
  </div>
      </cfoutput>
    </cfcase>

</cfswitch>
```

Note that inside the `<cfoutput>` tag, we are using double # (pound) signs. If you do not follow this, you will face some issues. Putting a double pair allows the browser to receive a single pound sign. You can see that this time we put the content into a section of code that runs during the end call of the tag.

If you are working in the current version, the file is placed in the 'examples' folder as `two.cfm`. We are keeping them as two seperate tags because we will be adding the nested child tags to it as we continue.

```
<cf_sidebar>
</cf_sidebar>
```

We will continue to build our example and then we will run the completed code. This time we are going to build the `sidebar_section` tag. We will use the `switch` conditional logic as we did in the parent sidebar tag. First, we call the list of `AncestorTags` with the following line of code:

```
<cfset AncestorTags = getBaseTagList()>
```

This gives us a list of all the parent tags. The list starts with the current tag and ends with the outermost custom tag. Then we will apply some logic to make sure that the tag is nested inside the correct parent. This helps to provide exception handling for the people who are using the custom tags. We did not list it as a reason but it is another advantage of custom tags over 'includes'. Detailed exception messages are very helpful while building applications. We check for the condition where the parent tag is not in the list and if such a situation exists, we throw an error message. Refer to the following code.

```
<cfif NOT listFindNoCase(AncestorTags,"cf_sidebar")>
  <cfthrow
    type="customTag.skin"
```

```
        detail="You must nest this tag (sidebar_section) inside a sidebar
    tag."
        message="Improperly nested tag.">
    </cfif>
```

We will now include a link that allows us to look at the base tag data of the outer parent of a nested association. This data will hold access to the base tag attributes and to the base tag caller scope. This could be very useful in some situations.

We will also set the attribute of the current tag to a default of empty, if no title for the section has been passed in. In this way, we will not get errors from a missing variable. Here is the code for the attribute and the association with base tag data.

```
    <cfset baseTagData = getBaseTagData("cf_sidebar")>
    <cfparam name="attributes.title"name="title" default="">
```

This is the logic that is needed for the start of our tag. Now, let us move to the end of our tag.

```
    <cfcase value="end">
      <cfoutput>
      <div class="relatedLinks">
        <h3>#attributes.title#</h3>
        <ul>
    #thisTag.generatedContent#
        </ul>
      </div>
      </cfoutput>
      <cfset thisTag.generatedContent = "">
    </cfcase>
```

We are using the generated content as in any other cfoutput. The difference is that when we use this content inside our tag, we need to set it to an empty string so that it does not get passed back outside our tag. We will also modify our base sidebar tag to do a similar thing. Then, we will create a sidebar_item tag that follows the same principles. Here is the code for all the three tags.

```
    <!--- sidebar base tag --->
    <cfswitch expression="#thisTag.executionMode#">
       <cfcase value="start">
    <!--- No code here at this time.  --->
       </cfcase>
       <cfcase value="end">
          <cfoutput>
    <div id="sideBar">
    #thisTag.generatedContent#
    </div>
```

```
        </cfoutput>
      <cfset thisTag.generatedContent = "">
      </cfcase>

  </cfswitch>

  <!--- sidebar_section tag --->
  <cfswitch expression="#thisTag.executionMode#">

    <cfcase value="start">
      <cfset AncestorTags = getBaseTagList()>
      <cfif NOT listFindNoCase(AncestorTags,"cf_sidebar")>
        <cfthrow
          type="customTag.skin"
          detail="You must nest this tag (sidebar_section) inside a
  sidebar tag."
          message="Improperly nested tag.">
      </cfif>
      <cfset baseTagData = getBaseTagData("cf_sidebar")>
      <cfparam name="attributes.title"name="title" default="">
    </cfcase>

    <cfcase value="end">
      <cfoutput>
      <div class="relatedLinks">
        <h3>#attributes.title#</h3>
        <ul>
   #thisTag.generatedContent#
        </ul>
      </div>
        </cfoutput>
      <cfset thisTag.generatedContent = "">
      </cfcase>

  </cfswitch>

  <!--- sidebar_item tag --->
  <cfswitch expression="#thisTag.executionMode#">

    <cfcase value="start">
      <cfset AncestorTags = getBaseTagList()>
      <cfif NOT listFindNoCase(AncestorTags,"cf_sidebar_section")>
        <cfthrow
          type="customTag.skin"
          detail="You must nest this tag (sidebar_item) inside a
  sidebar_section tag."
          message="Improperly nested tag.">
      </cfif>
      <cfparam name="attributes.link"name="link" default="">
```

```
    </cfcase>
    <cfcase value="end">
       <cfoutput><cfif attributes.link NEQ "">
      <li><a href="#attributes.link#">#thisTag.generatedContent#</a></
li>
       <cfelse>
      <li>#thisTag.generatedContent#</li>
      </cfif>
      </cfoutput>
      <cfset thisTag.generatedContent = "">
    </cfcase>
</cfswitch>
```

Now, let us look at the calling page to summarize our achievements.

```
<!DOCTYPE html PUBLIC "-//W3C//DTD XHTML 1.0 Transitional//EN"
"http://www.w3.org/TR/xhtml1/DTD/xhtml1-transitional.dtd">
<html xmlns="http://www.w3.org/1999/xhtml">
<head>
    <meta http-equiv="Content-Type" content="text/html; charset=iso-
8859-1" />
    <title>ColdFusion Site - Creating Custom Tags</title>
    <link rel="stylesheet" href="right.css" type="text/css" />
</head>
<body>
<cf_header />
<div id="content">
  <h2 id="pageName">Creating Custom Tags</h2>
  <div class="story">
    <h3>Power Markup via Custom Tags </h3>
    <p> Custom tags are one powerful method of making HTML sites
easier to build, manage and update. If you have never learned the
power of custom tags you should get a copy of ColdFusion Bootcamp and
read all about it! </p>
  </div>
</div>
<cf_sidebar>
  <cf_sidebar_section title="Custom Tags">
     <cf_sidebar_item link="##">Page</cf_sidebar_item>
     <cf_sidebar_item link="##">Sidebar</cf_sidebar_item>
     <cf_sidebar_item link="##">Header</cf_sidebar_item>
     <cf_sidebar_item link="##">Footer</cf_sidebar_item>
  </cf_sidebar_section>
  <cf_sidebar_section title="CFCs">
     <cf_sidebar_item link="##">Database</cf_sidebar_item>
```

```
        <cf_sidebar_item link="##">Business Logic</cf_sidebar_item>
        <cf_sidebar_item link="##">Inheritance</cf_sidebar_item>
    </cf_sidebar_section>
</cf_sidebar>

<cf_footer />

</body>
</html>
```

The highlighted sections have replaced the HTML. At first, this may seem like it takes too long to bring a good return on investment. Yet, when you write a site that has 500 pages and need to change this code, it can result in great savings. Further, if you move a copy of this application to a new client, then you can update the skin tags rather than going to every page of a customer site, when your containers do not allow you to interact with CSS.

CFInclude from Custom Tags

Now, let us feature out the rest of the common page code. We will be creating a custom tag named 'page' this time. Here we will see how to combine our CFInclude with our custom tags. We are going to dynamically select different layouts to 'include' based on the content of the custom tag. By placing some part of the logic in the custom tag, we avoided having to copy and paste the common information appearing on every page. We also made the custom tag more versatile since it includes different layouts. This is different from just including it in the original page in certain important ways. We can have defaults and business logic built into the custom tags without pasting them onto each page in the site. This also means that if an update is needed, the tag can be updated and the whole site is updated with one tag as against updating every page where the template is included. Here is the new custom tag.

```
<!--- page custom tag --->
<cfswitch expression="#thisTag.executionMode#">

    <cfcase value="start">
        <cfparam name="attributes.layout" default="default">
        <cfparam name="attributes.title" default="">
        <cfparam name="attributes.author" default="">
        <cfparam name="attributes.description" default="">
        <cfparam name="attributes.keywords" default="">
        <cfparam name="attributes.generator" default="ColdFusion
Custom Skin Tags">
    </cfcase>

    <cfcase value="end">
        <cfinclude template="layout_#attributes.layout#.cfm">
```

```
      <cfset thisTag.generatedContent = "">
    </cfcase>

</cfswitch>
```

Here is the modified page. It is stored as `three.cfm` in our 'examples' folder. Now, when we look at a page, we see the content section of the page wrapped in a custom tag named 'page'. So, from where are we getting the rest of the look and feel? It is coming from the template. If you look at the preceding code for the `page.cfm` custom tag, you will find a `CFInclude` that uses the `attributes.layout` to know which page needs to be pulled. It pulls a file called `layout_default.cfm` if there is no file that is named. Otherwise, it substitutes the name of the layout that has been requested.

```
<cf_page
  title="ColdFusion Site - Creating Custom Tags"
  keywords="learn,CF,Coldfusion"
  description="This is the third page from the learning custom tags
chapter.">
  <h2 id="pageName">Creating Custom Tags</h2>
  <div class="story">
    <h3>Power Markup via Custom Tags </h3>
    <p> Custom tags are one powerful method of making HTML sites
easier to build, manage and update. If you have never learned the
power of custom tags you should get a copy of ColdFusion Bootcamp and
read all about it! </p>
  </div>
</cf_page>
```

If you view the source, you will see the following in the header section of the HTML. The attributes pass the information into the custom tag and the template puts this content back out with the HTML.

```
<head>
  <meta http-equiv="Content-Type" content="text/html; charset=iso-
8859-1" />
  <title>ColdFusion Site - Creating Custom Tags</title>
    <meta name="description">
    <meta name="generator">
    <meta name="keywords">
    <link rel="stylesheet" href="right.css" type="text/css" />
</head>
```

We have now taken our pages to the point where the page is basically about itself and not about the HTML containers and templates that are stuffed in for the browser. If you are running the example code, then add an attribute to the `<cf_Page >` tag called `layout` and set it to `reverse`. Refer to the screenshot below. Now, the sidebar has moved to the other side of the page with the help of CSS. Yet, it was done without having to know the name of the CSS file. This means that you can create a basic set of layouts that can be re-used. The layout page called by our skin system has the sidebar on the other side of the main content body.

If we want to create a gallery or an application that does not use the sidebar, we can create another layout called `layout_noSideBar.cfm`. The following screen appears if we change the name of the layout in our `<cf_Page >` tag to `noSideBar`.

Now, let us say that we want to create special templates for different sections of the site. This is a great way to minimize the processes. If we want a template for an FAQ section of a site, we just need to go and create a template called `layout_faq.cfm` and then change the template name in the `page` tag. We will now get a new sidebar, but obviously not a matching page. We allowed it to remain that way because it shows that any layout can hold the content of the page.

Templates versus Skins

If we want to achieve a static website with templates, we can change our basic template and have a tool such as DreamWeaver rewrite every page that used that template. Then, we can upload all the modified pages to the site. Perhaps, the difference there would not be much. Let us say that you were going to have a special sale that would last for three days. You need your site to appear three days prior to the sale and revert at the end. Well, doing it as a template-based site will involve a lot of work. On the other hand, if you skin the site, it could be much simpler.

We have design-time templates and run-time templates. Skinning a site involves server-side templates. This allows us to write dynamic applications and move the application to another customer site. Imagine that each time we build another customer site we have to change all the templates. Then imagine that we change some basic function shared by an application that involves many customers. All we have to do is to examine those customers' applications and update the code one at a time. On the other hand, if we are skinning the site, we can just take that page and update all the sites by installing the new files. This will save all the manual code updates on those sites that had different templates embedded directly on the page.

Now, you can reverse the concept and create custom tags for the content of every page and then have a look at its apperance. Managing your site should be done by separating your content from your presentation in code just as much as separating your content from presentation in the browser with CSS. You may come across other ways to do this apart from custom tags. Till now, we have focused on the importance of skinning dynamic websites and we have learned how to create the custom tags and use them simultaneously.

Managing Custom Tags

One of the issues that you will face is the issue of where to store your custom tags. In this section, we are going to talk about the common use of custom tags and how to store them. Shortly, we will discuss two alternative methods of using custom tags.

The custom tags can be stored in your system custom tag directory or the current folder where the tags are called. In Chapter 4, we discussed how you could set application mappings for custom tags. This can be done in the ColdFusion Administration but do not let the custom tags be set at the server level if you are doing shared hosting as shared hosting rarely provides administration access.

CFModule Approach

You can use this custom command in ColdFusion to call the custom tags. It works similarly to directly calling a custom tag. Let us say you are going to call the page item we were working with by using the CFModule tag. This is how your page will appear. You can also find this page in the examples folder as four.cfm.

```
<cfmodule template="page.cfm"
  layout="faq"
  title="ColdFusion Site - Creating Custom Tags"
  keywords="learn,CF,Coldfusion"
  description="This is the third page from the learning custom tags
chapter.">
  <h2 id="pageName">Creating Custom Tags</h2>
  <div class="story">
    <h3>Power Markup via Custom Tags </h3>
    <p> Custom tags are one powerful method of making HTML sites
easier to build, manage and update. If you have never learned the
power of custom tags you should get a copy of ColdFusion Bootcamp and
read all about it! </p>
  </div>
</cfmodule>
```

If we were calling the custom tag in a different directory on the web server, we would just include the path from the root of the server as we would on any other web page.

Tag Library Approach

This is a unique way of using custom tags that makes the pages easier to read. When we have tag libraries, we prefix the tag with the library name and a colon rather than the traditional CF_ prefix. While creating tag libraries, you need to know the path of the files in your library. They should be in one directory. You must create a library call on every page that uses the library form of call. Here is sample code for creating a library. We should always try to put it at the top of the page.

```
<cfimport prefix="skin" taglib="/share/tags/skin">
<skin:page …>
Page content
</skin:page>
```

This would run similarly to our `<cf_page>` tag call but it is declared in the code that we are using the skin library. Normally, any of these libraries are stored together. So, a common practice is to use the tag library approach. This does not require the use of the application settings. The only challenge is that any code using this will require the custom tags to be present in the same location, or that every page that is using the library should be edited so as to accommodate the location of the tags. You cannot use a dynamic variable on this tag. It must be hard-coded.

Summary

In this chapter, we have created a number of custom tags in order to understand each of these concepts. We have custom tags for the page, head, header, footer, sidebar, and sidebar_item. We have explained how to create a number of them. The other tags are built in a similar manner. We also learned how to integrate cfinclude for libraries of segments. This should be avoided in CFCs due to thread safety issues. This is another area where custom tags work better.

We have covered the following in this chapter:

- Custom tags
- Passing attributes into a custom tag
- Using nested tags
- Skinning a website by using custom tags
- Different methods of calling custom tags
    - `<cf_ >`
    - `<cfmodule >`
    - `<cfimport >`

6
Better Interfaces for JavaScript Libraries

There may be different ways to deal with things that do not require any other technology besides ColdFusion. Yet, by including libraries outside ColdFusion, you can do a lot more. The AJAX revolution, Flex, AIR, and Web Services are all examples of the external uses of ColdFusion.

We are going to look at integrating some external solutions through ColdFusion custom tags. You will find all the JavaScript libraries included in the code for this book. We will be integrating ThickBox, which is a jQuery-based widget. We will look at the differences between a typical HTML approach and dealing with things in a server-side approach. This will involve a lot of work. However, the work that it will save over time through reuse will prove to be profitable over time. In this chapter, we will cover the following:

- Wrapping the ThickBox gallery functions into a custom tag for simple functional reuse
- Wrapping a Google map library into our code with a custom tag for simplified interactive maps
- Creating a multi-state form list wrapped in a custom tag

Thickbox Library HTML Style

Thickbox masks out the background page for us, so we can concentrate on the information being shown. Here is an example of the page before we click on an image.

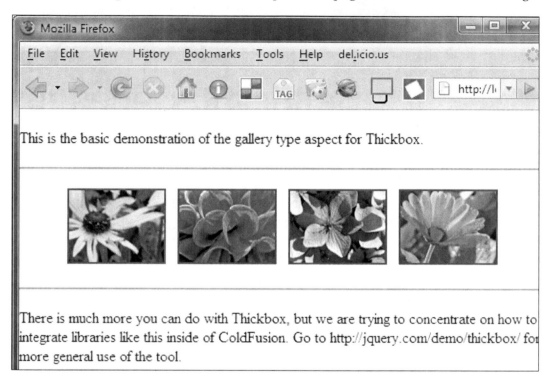

Now, when we click on any image, the following screen will appear. If you look carefully, the area around the image is the same as above but it is greyed out. We can also move through the images without going back to the smaller images on the other page. This can be used in a number of ways. We could use it for any small image or a set of images on a page.

Here is the HTML we will use for this page.

```
<html>
<head>
<script type="text/javascript" src="jquery.js"></script>
<script type="text/javascript" src="thickbox.js"></script>
<link rel="stylesheet" href="thickbox.css" type="text/css"
media="screen" />
</head>
<body>

<br />
This is the basic demonstration of the gallery type aspect for
Thickbox.
<br /><br /><hr /><br />
<div style="text-align:center">
<a href="images/plant1.jpg" title="This is our yellow flower."
class="thickbox" rel="gallery-plants"><img src="images/plant1_t.jpg"
alt="Plant 1" /></a>
```

```
 
<a href="images/plant2.jpg" title="This is our red flower."
class="thickbox" rel="gallery-plants"><img src="images/plant2_t.jpg"
alt="Plant 2" /></a>
 
<a href="images/plant3.jpg" title="This is our blue flower."
class="thickbox" rel="gallery-plants"><img src="images/plant3_t.jpg"
alt="Plant 3" /></a>
 
<a href="images/plant4.jpg" title="This is our orange flower."
class="thickbox" rel="gallery-plants"><img src="images/plant4_t.jpg"
alt="Plant 4" /></a>
</div>

<br /><hr /><br />
There is much more you can do with Thickbox, but we are trying
to concentrate on how to integrate libraries like this inside of
ColdFusion.
Go to http://jquery.com/demo/thickbox/ for more general use of the
tool.
</body>
</html>
```

ColdFusion-Powered Thickbox

Now, if you are familiar with HTML, you will notice that it has become a much simpler page. Yet, when we work with data inside ColdFusion, we rarely hard-code data onto the page as you see here. This is how the data will look when it goes to the browser, but it is not the best method of putting information back out. Rather than doing a loop right here on the page, we are going to use one of those powerful custom tags. We will write it to encapsulate our logic and make the page appear better. We will note that it is a more pleasant experience to reuse a custom tag than to retype or paste and adapt our code to every use.

Now, we are going to build our custom tag to handle this functionality in a more elegant way. The designer does not care about the data and does not want to merge this page with loops and conditional statements. If we do not separate the processing and markup into different code files, then separating the processing to the top of the code will make a clean separation thereby preventing many bugs in our pages. The developers will find many ways to generate or acquire our data. Here is the tag that will be used to add some elegance to the markup section of the page.

```
<cfswitch expression="#thistag.ExecutionMode#">
   <cfcase value="start">
       <cfparam name="attributes.class" default="thickGallery">
       <cfparam name="attributes.set"
        default="gallery_#createUUID()#">
```

```
            <cfparam name="attributes.id" default="#attributes.set#">
            <cfparam name="attributes.picture" default="picture">
            <cfparam name="attributes.title" default="title">
            <cfparam name="attributes.thumb" default="thumb">
            <cfparam name="attributes.alt" default="alt">
    </cfcase>
    <cfcase value="end">
    <cfoutput>
    <div class="#attributes.class#" id="#attributes.id#"
                            align="center">
        <cfloop from="1" to="#arrayLen(attributes.pictures)#"
                    index="iNumber">
 <a href="#attributes.pictures[iNumber][attributes.picture]#"
title="#attributes.pictures[iNumber][attributes.title]#"
class="thickbox" rel="#attributes.set#"><img src="#attributes.pictures
[iNumber][attributes.thumb]#" alt="#attributes.pictures[iNumber][attri
butes.alt]#" /></a>
        </cfloop>
      <cfif thisTag.GeneratedContent NEQ "">
          <div align="center">
              #thisTag.GeneratedContent#
          </div>
      </cfif>
        </div>
    </cfoutput>
    <cfset thisTag.generatedContent = "">
    </cfcase>
</cfswitch>
```

We will not be required to pass in all these attributes to use the custom tag. These extra attributes are just there so that you can choose to set some extra attributes to override the default names, if your data structure is different. Firstly, we will look at using the integration custom tag with minimal code. We will be using the tag twice. For the second time, we will add a caption to the gallery. You will also note that you can set the name of the gallery if you choose and the ID of the tag that contains the gallery for doing additional JavaScript DOM interaction. (We also added the new update feature code for doing array and structured variable creation. CF8 allows us to do this, but it does not have the ability to do this nested. We can also see that we can add comments while using CFScript.)

```
<cfscript>
/* This is the old school for comparison.
pictures = arrayNew(1);
photo = structNew();
photo.picture = "images/plant1.jpg";
```

```
photo.title = "This is our yellow flower.";
photo.thumb = "images/plant1_t.jpg";
photo.alt = "Plant 1";
arrayAppend(pictures,photo);
photo = structNew();
photo.picture = "images/plant2.jpg";
photo.title = "This is our red flower.";
photo.thumb = "images/plant2_t.jpg";
photo.alt = "Plant 2";
arrayAppend(pictures,photo);
photo = structNew();
photo.picture = "images/plant3.jpg";
photo.title = "This is our blue flower.";
photo.thumb = "images/plant3_t.jpg";
photo.alt = "Plant 3";
arrayAppend(pictures,photo);
photo = structNew();
photo.picture = "images/plant4.jpg";
photo.title = "This is our orange flower.";
photo.thumb = "images/plant4_t.jpg";
photo.alt = "Plant 4";
arrayAppend(pictures,photo);
*/
pictures = [ // array
   { // structure
         picture = "images/plant1.jpg",
         title = "This is our yellow flower.",
         thumb = "images/plant1_t.jpg",
    alt = "Plant 1"
   },
   { // structure
         picture = "images/plant2.jpg",
         title = "This is our red flower.",
         thumb = "images/plant2_t.jpg",
    alt = "Plant 2"
   },
   { // structure
         picture = "images/plant3.jpg",
         title = "This is our blue flower.",
         thumb = "images/plant3_t.jpg",
    alt = "Plant 3"
   },
   { // structure
         picture = "images/plant4.jpg",
```

```
        title = "This is our orange flower.",
        thumb = "images/plant4_t.jpg",
    alt = "Plant 4"
    }
];
</cfscript>
<html>
<head>

<script type="text/javascript" src="jquery.js"></script>
<script type="text/javascript" src="thickbox.js"></script>

<link rel="stylesheet" href="thickbox.css" type="text/css"
media="screen" />

</head>
<body>

<br />
This is the basic demonstration of the gallery type aspect for
Thickbox.
<br /><br /><hr /><br />
    <cf_thickGallery
        pictures="#pictures#" />
<hr><br />
    <cf_thickGallery
        pictures="#pictures#">
    This is a second gallery set with a caption.
    </cf_thickGallery>

<br /><hr /><br />
There is much more you can do with Thickbox, but we are trying to
concentrate on how to integrate libraries like this inside ColdFusion.
Go to http://jquery.com/demo/thickbox/ for more details on the general
use of the tool.
</body>
</html>
```

The start of the page is much longer but whenever you interact with data rather than the code, that particular section will be as long as it is either way. In general, the advantage for custom tags is completely in the markup. If you want to make the data sections of the page more elegant, you should move that portion of logic into a CFC. The data can be pulled from a query rather than an array of structures.

Dynamic pages are dependent on the data from which they are pulled. If you look at the markup section of the page, you will be amazed by how short and powerful it has become. If it was a real-world tag, we would build in automated checking in order to vary the logic after knowing whether the data was an array of structures or a query recordset. One good thing about this is that it does not require any looping or conditional logic to occur outside the thickGallery custom tag. This makes the designers happier. There are many developers who can enjoy this benefit. Here is the new page. Note the caption under the second example.

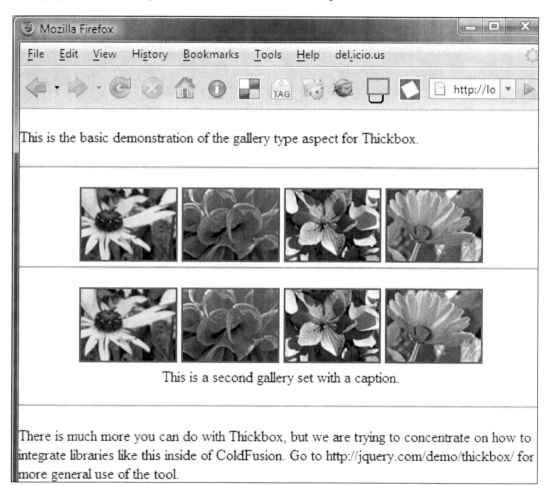

It would be much simpler if we did not have to revisit all the features of ThickBox every time we use it. Wrapping up logic like this goes a long way. If we are looping and doing conditional processing in the midst of our markup, then we can improve our code by wrapping up the common display code in a custom tag.

Where Am I? (via Google Maps)

Here we are going to have a look at maps. First, we need to figure out where we are currently located. We need to find out the longitude as well as the latitude position. Once we have that information, we can use maps.

This is the geocode location for where this book was written:

Longitude: -86.51531

Latitude: 42.043423

This is the global position based on the world standards. We should be able to go to any popular search engine and find the same type of information. You will find the information about this library at `http://jquery.com/plugins/project/jQMaps`. But you will have to go to the demonstration to get the JavaScript, if it is updated from that in the 'examples' directory. Refer to the following screenshot:

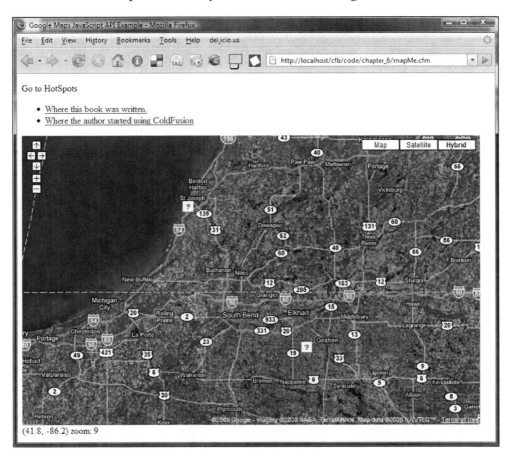

Let us look at the calling code page called `mapMe.cfm` in the 'chapter' directory. (Do remember to get your own Google code to make this work. `http://www.google.com/apis/maps/`.) You will just need the Google code to run the calling code correctly. Refer to the following code:

```
<!DOCTYPE html PUBLIC "-//W3C//DTD XHTML 1.0 Strict//EN"
  "http://www.w3.org/TR/xhtml1/DTD/xhtml1-strict.dtd">
<html xmlns="http://www.w3.org/1999/xhtml">
  <head>
    <meta http-equiv="content-type" content="text/html;
                                                charset=utf-8"/>
    <title>Google Maps JavaScript API Example</title>
    <script type="text/javascript" src="jquery.js"></script>
   <cf_geoMap
        googleKey="--replace this with your Google API key--"
        mapContainer="gmaps_container"
        mapInfo="gmaps_info"
           latitude="41.8"
           longitude="-86.2"
           zoom="9">
     <cf_geoLocation
        bubbleText="3.5 versions since I started and two companies
later the ColdFusion world is just getting better. Adobe has invested
more than a vision into the language. It's time for another book to
help people get a rounded view of ColdFusion fast and full!"
           popLink=""
           latitude="42.043423"
           longitude="-86.51531"
             zoom="9"
             icon="images/writeBook.gif">
     <cf_geoLocation
        bubbleText="I began working with ColdFusion at version 4.5
during the Allaire days."
           popLink="nestMe.cfm"
           latitude="41.54700"
           longitude="-85.9438"
             zoom="9"
             icon="images/writeBook.gif">
    </cf_geoMap>
  </head>
  <body onload="">
   <p>Go to HotSpots
   <ul>
      <li><a href="#" class="gmaps_container" tabIndex="1">Where this
book was written.</a></li>
      <li><a href="#" class="gmaps_container" tabIndex="2">Where the
author started using ColdFusion</a></li>
```

```
        </ul>
        </p>
          <div id="gmaps_container" style="width: 800px; height: 500px">
          </div>
          <div id="gmaps_info"></div>
        </body>
    </html>
```

What we see in our code is a standard page of ColdFusion code. We are creating a map that is targeted at a `div`-based container later on the page. There is also an infomation `div`. If you look at the browser view, you will see the longitude and latitude along with the current zoom. We then use our nested tag technology in ColdFusion that shows the locations present on the map. If you look at the map, you will see that these locations are marked with a box and a blue question mark.

If you want to go to any of these locations, you have two choices. You can either click directly on the location, or you can click on the link that is available above the map. The included library is based on the `tabIndex` attribute. At the end, we just need to wade through all the Google map APIs once, and then remember how to do it the next time we want to use it. Here, we have a library with all the functionality shared by the Google interface with a `jQuery` plug-in library. We have taken it even further along the way and wrapped that library functionality into custom tags.

Here is the `geoMap` custom tag:

```
    <cfswitch expression="#thisTag.ExecutionMode#">
      <cfcase value="start">
          <cfparam name="attributes.bubbleText" default="">
          <cfparam name="attributes.popLink" default="">
          <cfparam name="attributes.relPath" default="">
          <cfset location = arrayNew(1)>
      </cfcase>
      <cfcase value="end"><cfoutput>
      <script
    src="http://maps.google.com/maps?file=api&amp;v=2&amp;key="#attributes
    .googleKey#" type="text/javascript"></script>
      <script type="text/javascript" src="jq_gmaps.js"></script>
        <script type="text/javascript">
        var locations_data = { locations: [<cfloop from="1" to="#arrayLen(
    location)#" index="iLoc">
      {
          simpleContent: "#location[iLoc].bubbleText#",
          maximizedContent: "#location[iLoc].popLink#",
          latitude: #location[iLoc].latitude#,
          longitude:      #location[iLoc].longitude#,
```

```
          zoom:   #location[iLoc].zoom#,
          icon:  "#location[iLoc].icon#"
    },</cfloop>
    ]};
    $(document).ready(function(){
    $("###attributes.mapContainer#").gmaps({
          data: locations_data,
          infopanel: $("###attributes.mapInfo#").get(0),
          center: [#attributes.latitude#, #attributes.longitude#],
            zoom: #attributes.zoom#,
            relativepath: "#attributes.relPath#"
    });
    });
     </script></cfoutput>
          <cfset thisTag.GeneratedContent = "">
    </cfcase>
</cfswitch>
```

Here is the nested geoLocation custom tag:

```
<cfswitch expression="#thisTag.ExecutionMode#">
   <cfcase value="start">
          <cfparam name="attributes.bubbleText" default="">
          <cfparam name="attributes.popLink" default="">
   <cfscript>
          baseTagData = getBaseTagData("cf_geoMap");
          arrayAppend(baseTagData.location,attributes);
   </cfscript>
   </cfcase>
   <cfcase value="end">
     <cfset thisTag.GeneratedContent = "">
   </cfcase>
</cfswitch>
```

From the above code, it is evident that the nested tag is quite simple. Here we can see the start tag call of the geoMap tag. Then, the geoLocator tag can be called as many times as it gets called. It adds a structure as a new array element to the location variable in the parent tag. This is done with the getBaseTagData() function. We then add all the attributes of the nested geoLocation tag to the parent variable, and then we can call the end tag of the geoMap tag.

Let us look at some of the calling code in more detail and the new view in the browser. First, we will have a look at the link **Where the author started using ColdFusion**.

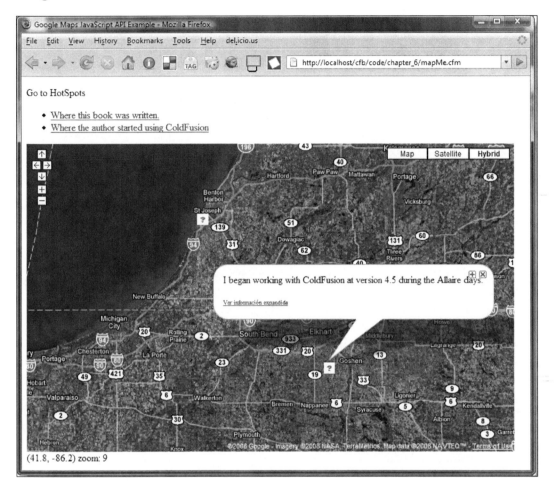

Not only did our link move to the center of the map, but we also got a pop-up box with the contents of our geoLink attributes. Here is that segment of the code for your review.

```
<cf_geoMap
    googleKey"--replace this with your Google API key--"
    mapContainer="gmaps_container"
    mapInfo="gmaps_info"
        latitude="41.8"
        longitude="-86.2"
            zoom="9">
```

```
    <cf_geoLocation
        bubbleText="3.5 versions since I started and two companies
later the ColdFusion world is just getting better. Adobe has invested
more than a vision into the language. It's time for another book to
help people get a rounded view of ColdFusion fast and full!"
            popLink=""
            latitude="42.043423"
            longitude="-86.51531"
              zoom="9"
              icon="images/writeBook.gif">
    <cf_geoLocation
        bubbleText="I began working with ColdFusion at version 4.5
during the Allaire days."
            popLink="nestMe.cfm"
            latitude="41.54700"
            longitude="-85.9438"
              zoom="9"
              icon="images/writeBook.gif">
    </cf_geoMap>
```

It was the second link and all the attributes are the settings for the second location. If we have locations that are off the map, it will still link to them from the external links. If we click on the link in the view message box, or click on the 'plus' sign at the top of the message box, we will see that it loads the HTML of simple text into the page. This could have been about any HTML page. We could even call up AJAX pages on these links and interact with them. Imagine we built a sales application that ran from a sales individual's remote tablet PC on the road. Each time he or she made a sale of house signing, he or she could do things like take a picture of the house and use the form inside the map in order to upload the photo from his or her digital camera directly to the home office. He or she could fill out the form of details and by using his tablet PC, he or she could even get the customer signature, perhaps, right inside this window. Imagine how much fun the customer had in just signing the sales contract.

You will also find that changing the zoom has the map redrawn in its current Google version. Now, we can look at the other location. We would just click on **Where this book was written**.

Here is another view of the map when we click on the link at the top of the map for **Where this book was written**. This moves the selected item and relocates the center of the map. There are many useful functions and simple integrations possible when we write custom tags to put things together.

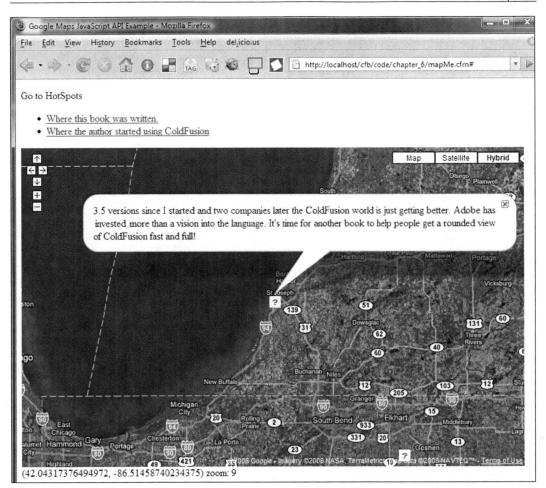

This is just an idea of how you could take this type of functionality and use it within an application. Wrapping this inside a custom tag makes things much simpler.

ColdFusion JavaScript

Chris Jordan created the inverse of what you would think of when combining technologies with ColdFusion. He has a plug-in library that allows you to code JavaScript in the same way you code ColdFusion. You can go to his website at `http://cjordan.us/jquery/plugins/?page=CFJSdemo` and you will find examples of how he does JavaScript in the CF way.

You might wonder why you would do that. Well, it makes things simpler. His work is a good example of an approach to development. One thing it adds to JavaScript is the natural ability to handle 'lists' in JavaScript in the same way as in ColdFusion. How about doing time formatting in the same way in both the locations? It is something handy for making life simpler. The library can be obtained at http://jquery.com/plugins/project/CFJS.

Multiple State Form Items

Now that we can use ColdFusion functions in JavaScript, we are going to look at another custom tag to show the power of ColdFusion along with an external set of libraries. This custom tag saves repetition of ColdFusion code with sets of CFLoops and CFIF conditional statements. It also saves us from toggling between the browser and the server.

```
<cfscript>
myData = queryNew("display,value");
queryAddRow(myData);
querySetCell(myData,"display","Apples");
querySetCell(myData,"value","ignore");
queryAddRow(myData);
querySetCell(myData,"display","Oranges");
querySetCell(myData,"value","ignore");
queryAddRow(myData);
querySetCell(myData,"display","Peaches");
querySetCell(myData,"value","ignore");
</cfscript>
<html>
<head>
    <title>Fancy List</title>
    <script src="jquery.js"></script>
    <script src="jquery.cfjs.js"></script>
</head>
<body>
<h3>This is the fancy list example.</h3>
<form method="post">
   <cf_multiState
     name="myFruit"
     states="bid,sell,ignore"
     default="ignore"
     data="#myData#" />
   <input name="submit" type="submit" value="submit">
</form>
<cfdump var="#form#" label="Form Submit Values">
</body>
</html>
```

We are just building a prototype for this component. We would add even more features to it if it was a real-life custom tag. In our example, we will take a farmers' market into consideration. This is a 'chalkboard' page that helps us to see which fruit the boss wants to buy and sell. Here is how the resulting page appears in the browser:

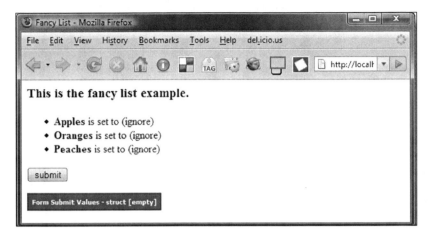

This is how the page appears before the form is submitted. If we click on **submit**, it will put the form values on the page. This page is intended to look like a chalkboard. Perhaps, the results will go out as email. The boss has not yet made his decision yet. He just wants a proof of concept where he can have 'buy', 'sell', and 'ignore' as options. We could do this with three radio buttons each. Yet, if we had done that, the page would have grown very large in size because the actual list of products at the market is around seventy items that are normally bought and sold. In this scenario, the custom tag that we have written by using the custom library will be a better choice. Now, the boss comes in and we click on **Apples**. The action turns to **bid**. Then, we click on the **Peaches** item twice. It turns to **bid** and then to **sell**.

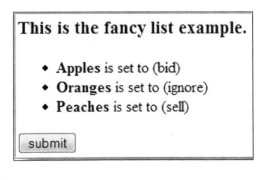

Now, we **submit** the text and it shows us the results and also resets all the items to the default value. Again, we did not build any round-trip persistence into this application as it is only a prototype.

Here we observe that the page returns the items as required. We can add more features, or use this custom tag repeatedly.

Inside the Fancy Form Tag

Le us take a peek inside the tag to see the working of some of the browser-side ColdFusion such as JavaScript.

```
<cfswitch expression="#thisTag.executionMode#">
   <cfcase value="start">
         <cfparam name="attributes.states" default="Yes,No,ignore">
         <cfparam name="attributes.default" default="ignore">
         <cfset data = attributes.data>
   </cfcase>
   <cfcase value="end">
   <cfoutput>
     <ul><cfloop query="data">
```

```
            <li id="#attributes.name#_#data.currentRow#">
                <strong>#data.display#</strong> is set to (<span
id="#attributes.name#_#data.currentRow#_value">#attributes.default#</
span>)
                <input type="hidden"
                id="#attributes.name#_#data.currentRow#_display"
                 name="#attributes.name#_#data.currentRow#_display"
                 value="#data.display#">
                <input type="hidden"
                id="#attributes.name#_#data.currentRow#_action"
                name="#attributes.name#_#data.currentRow#_action"
                value="#data.value#">
            </li>
        </cfloop></ul>
        <script>
            #attributes.name#_list = '#attributes.states#';
            #attributes.name#_list_len = #listLen(attributes.states)#;

            jQuery('li').bind('click', function() {
                var myId = jQuery(this).attr('id');
                var myValue = jQuery('##'+myId+'_value').text();
                var myListPos =
                jQuery.ListFindNoCase(#attributes.name#_list,myValue);
                if(myListPos == #attributes.name#_list_len) {
                    myListPos=1;
        } else  {
                    myListPos++;
        }
                var newValue =
                jQuery.ListGetAt(#attributes.name#_list,myListPos);
                jQuery('##'+myId+'_action').val(newValue);
                jQuery('##'+myId+'_value').text(newValue);
        });
        </script>
        </cfoutput>
        </cfcase>
</cfswitch>
```

You can see that there are default values for some of the variables. We loop through
the dataset passed into the tag and create code to go back to the browser. This is
normal ColdFusion code. But it is observed that some of the code is being generated
to go back to the browser. Here is a section of the code that we get inside the browser
generated from the ColdFusion code on the server:

```
<script>
myFruit_list = 'bid,sell,ignore';
myFruit_list_len = 3;
```

```
jQuery('li').bind('click', function() {
        var myId = jQuery(this).attr('id');
        var myValue = jQuery('#'+myId+'_value').text();
        var myListPos = jQuery.ListFindNoCase(myFruit_list,myValue);
    if(myListPos == myFruit_list_len) {
        myListPos=1;
    } else  {
        myListPos++;
    }
        var newValue = jQuery.ListGetAt(myFruit_list,myListPos);
        jQuery('#'+myId+'_action').val(newValue);
        jQuery('#'+myId+'_value').text(newValue);
});
</script>
```

Now, if we look at the generated browser code, we will find a command called `jQuery.ListGetAt(...)` in the code. This is an interesting situation because there are no list functions such as these native to JavaScript. This library adds some of the ColdFusion power to JavaScript.

Summary

There is tremendous power inside and outside ColdFusion. We will continue to learn and grow in knowledge with this language. We looked at `jQuery` for our examples, and we have observed that there is much more than just this library. Explore a little bit, and you will find it very interesting.

In this chapter, we have learned the following things:

- Wrapping the ThickBox library in ColdFusion custom tags
- Using ColdFusion custom tags to integrate Google maps on our pages
- Creating a multi-state element that has more states than radio buttons and wrapping it up inside a ColdFusion custom tag so that we can re-use it in our applications.

7
Authentication and Permissions

In this chapter, we will be looking into the native solutions that are packed into ColdFusion. Also, we will be looking at the built-in features for doing authentication and permission management. We will also look at some of the custom alternatives that give us more control with code of about the same ease-of-use as the built-in features.

How ColdFusion Recognizes Users

Browsers have unique IDs that mark the session that is being used. Browsers can also have cookies. If the browser is allowing cookies, then things will be easier. Without cookies, we will have to pass the user identification in every communication that comes back to the server from the browser. The following table shows the key permission functions that we will be using in this chapter. These are the most commonly used functions, but if needed, you can look at some more functions, or consider rolling your own solution. Now, we will look at some built-in common solutions that prove beneficial:

Key permissions functions	Description
cfLogin	This is a wrapper tag used in login code. The inner contents of the tag runs only if the session does not show that someone is logged in.
cfLoginUser	This tag is run inside the `<cfLogin>` tag body. This tag declares the user's unique ID, password, and permission roles.
cfLogout	This tag simply logs the current user out of the session if he or she is logged in.

Key permissions functions	Description
cfFunction	This tag has an optional attribute called "roles" that will manage access to the tag based on the current user having one of the roles in the list.
isUserInRole	This function allows you to check against the current session user roles declared in the cfLoginUser tag. If the current user has all the roles, it returns true.
isUserInAnyRole	This function allows you to check against the current session user roles declared in the cfLoginUser tag. If the current user has any of the roles, it returns true. If none of the roles match, then it returns false.
getAuthUser	This tag returns the ID of the currently logged in user. If there is no user logged in, it will check the cgi.remote_user variable.

Looking at the tags, we can see that there are two basic groups of functions here. We have a group of functions that achieve setting the current user for a session or deleting a user. The other set of functions manage permissions validation actions.

ColdFusion actually recognizes browsers, and not users. Each time you start a standard browser, it creates a unique identification. Using this ID and cookies, ColdFusion allows us to create an authenticated user identity. We will also have a page to check the user status. Let us look at the code.

```
<cfset objCFC = createObject("component","checkUser")>
<cfoutput>The current user is: (#getAuthUser()#).<br />
        Based on the role test the user checks for being in the role
test returns: (#isUserInRole('test')#)<br />
        Based on the role test the user checks for being in the role
test and test2 returns: (#isUserInRole('test,test2')#)<br />
 <cftry>Based on the CFC hasTestPermission() method: (#objCFC.
hasTestPermission()#)<br />
        Based on the CFC hasOneOfRoles() method: (#objCFC.
hasOneOfRoles()#)<br />
 <cfcatch>
  <cfdump var="#cfcatch.message#" expand="false" label="CFC
Test">)<br>
 </cfcatch>
 </cftry>
</cfoutput>
<a href="login_form.cfm">Login Form</a> 
<a href="logout.cfm">Logout</a>
```

When we first run the page, the results are very predictable. There will be no user, unless you are on a system where your server logs you into the web server. You can also expect `false` from both the permissions. This is because we are not logged in, and we will have no permission roles at this time. Here are the browser results for the first pass made:

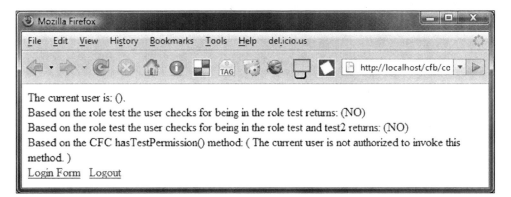

We have another file running along with this file that will be needed to make it work. That file is called the `Application.cfc` file. This file is used to create an active application and session, without which your login will not work. Let us move to our login page and enter some key login information. We are going to put the information on this page as it is an online demonstration application. Here is the login page in the browser and the code:

```
<cfparam name="form.user" default="">
<cfparam name="form.password" default="">
<cfoutput>
 <form action="login_check.cfm" method="post"> User:<br />
  <input name="user" type="text" value="#form.user#"><br />
       Password:<br />
  <input name="password" type="password" value="#form.password#">
<br /><br />
  <input type="submit" value="Login">
 </form>
</cfoutput>
```

The beauty of good software is that the complexity is wrapped up for simpler interfaces. When you enter the username, you will be able to read the text. When you enter the password, it obscures each letter to hide the text. In other words, the password is encrypted. A quick and functional way to secure assets is to use the built-in functionality. Enter `first` for the username and `demo` for the password. Refer to the following code:

```
<cfparam name="form.user" default="">
<cfparam name="form.password" default="">
<cflogin>
 <cfif form.password EQ "demo">
  <cfset roles = "">
  <cfswitch expression="#form.user#">
   <cfcase value = "first">
    <cfset roles = "test">
   </cfcase>
   <cfcase value="admin">
    <cfset roles = "test,test2,test3">
   </cfcase>
  </cfswitch>
  <cfloginuser name="#form.user#" password="#form.password#"
               roles="roles"><a href="checkUser.cfm">Back to
checkUser.cfm page.</a>
  <!--- don't use with built in login <cflocation url="checkUser.cfm"
                                      addtoken="false"> --->
  <script>location.href="checkUser.cfm";</script>
 <cfelse> Sorry but your user name and password are not correct.
 <br />
  <cfinclude template="login_form.cfm">
 </cfif>
</cflogin>
```

Here, we check the login information only if there is no one logged into the built-in authentication system for ColdFusion. If you hit this page and someone has already logged into the system, it will appear as a blank page. In this simplified system, it just checks for the password `demo` and logs in using the username that has been passed. In a real system we would check a step further.

The current user is: (demo).
Based on the role test the user checks for being in the role test returns: (NO)
Based on the role test the user checks for being in the role test and test2 returns: (NO)
Based on the CFC hasTestPermission() method: (The current user is not authorized to invoke this method.)
Login Form Logout

Now when we visit our `checkUser.cfm` page, we will get some interesting results. In `UserInRole()`, we pass the same comma-delimited list as used in the CFC methods. We get yes for `test` and it passes in the `roles` attribute inside the CFC method. When we use two or more `roles` in a comma delimited list, then we get different results.

In the previous code, you will notice that we have commented out the CFLocation. This is because the login did not work correctly when that code was used. There are a number of solutions to this issue. The end of the matter is the way in which the CFLocation tag does not work in combination with the `<CFLogin>` tag. It is better to either keep the user on the same page with a message that they are correctly logged in, or use JavaScript for changing the location. We can use a combination of these two, if we want to make it convenient for those who have their JavaScript turned off.

We also see that by using the permission feature of the CFC methods, we can block access to the methods based on the current user's permissions. We wrapped this with a try and catch method to prevent the page from failing. It might be a better practice to build a custom permissions check function rather than hard-coding the permissions as your site gets bigger and more featured. We will have a look at it in the custom section that follows.

Another thing to note is that the actual login made by using the built-in `<CFLogin>` tag may not show the current user until the next time that the page is requested. This can be a problem if it is assumed to be available immediately upon the same request as the login. So one needs to be careful with this one. There are ways around this, but when it is combined with the need to write extra code to get around it, we have the option of writing some custom code that does even more than the built-in features. Perhaps this type of need would be best filled with custom authentication.

Custom Authentication (Additional Power)

In this section, we will look at a customized way to handle authentication that gives us all the core features that we need along with some additional enhancements. We are going to create a CFC for the user and nest the logic for authentication inside the user object. We will instantiate the user class as a session-based object. We will also take this logic and wrap it up into the Application.cfc so that it becomes portable and easier to implement in our programs. In the end, we will have more function and flexibility than the native authentication permission handling system. Here is the code for the session start of the Application.cfc:

```
<cffunction name="onSessionStart" output="false">
 <cfscript>
// create default session stat structure and pre-request values
   session._stat.started = now();
   session._stat.thisHit = now();
   session._stat.hits = 0;
// at start of each session update count for application stat
   application._stat.sessions += 1;
// create an instance of the user class
   session._user = createObject("component","user").init();
 </cfscript>
</cffunction>
```

Here, we see that the user object is created and it will persist for the entire session. This will allow us to re-use the object during any request to the server as long as the session has not ended. We can also put some common login code into the user object, which will keep us from cluttering up the code that uses these functions. The common interface will allow us to change some of the internals of the user functionality without having to change the pages that use them. This means the same page requests could actually be logging in the user on an LDAP server-based authentication, a database, or even a system that uses some other methods.

Authentication Data Model

This is a basic representation of how the authentication or permission model is set up in our more advanced example of the site. There are three separate tables with 'many-to-many' relational join tables. Here, we will illustrate the power of having logic packaged up into CFCs. This is because we will not be looking at the database or the code inside those objects. We do not need to know how they work internally. Of course, anyone who would like to get more details can search and see how they can be modified.

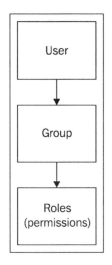

The user can belong to one or more groups. The group has one or more role-based permissions. We would do this in an indirect manner because it adds another layer of complexity that we have handled previously as the code for it is complete.

Normally, each time you add permissions to or remove permissions from a site, you have to go and manually do it for every user it affects. It doesn't take a genius to figure out that the more the things and users that are being managed, the more difficult it becomes. The normal response is to dumb-down the permissions model on a site to make it manageable. This scenario will help us assign users to groups just as a company does to an organizational chart. In fact, this type of construct would allow a company to remake an organizational chart in order to map out these permissions and then hand them over to the systems administrator with each of the users' groups defined.

The end benefit lies when we choose to add some special edit permissions to the edit group on a site, and then we have a super editor that has other permissions. We can assign people and give permissions to those groups without having to manage it on such a small scope inside our sites.

There are a couple of data objects that we use to connect to the permissions model but the main one will be used all over our application. This is the **User** object. We will store that data object in the session scope as we listed earlier. There are a few other classes present inside the administration interface. Here is a screenshot of the main site administration at this time. (Remember we are prototyping this interface. So we are not going to get distracted with design perfection now.)

Here, we see a general interface that will allow an administrator to edit the users, groups, and roles. Let us take a look at the users list view. We are using the CF8 AJAX technology to manage the users on this site. It will make things simpler. We have more information in the database than we have exposed for this prototype but it is a part of the actual process. We do not need to make a functional model. But with CF8, it can be done faster than before.

In our prototype, we can choose to list and then click on a user to edit his or her record, or we can just choose to create a new record. There is some logic that is required on CF8 AJAX pages hidden in this code if we desire to have a solid function. Review the code to see how the application works. The issue arose when we were prototyping the page and when if the form was submitted more than once. CFLocation did not change our issues. So we created a location based on the AJAX page function. Since we were using the AJAX UI for layout, this was a logical solution.

Remember that the grid we see for the user list can sort the data as well. You must also notice that in our site we include a default user for guests. It is just the style of this prototype. We should design the model so as to fit the needs of the site and the business that the site is designed to service. You may also see more modifications to the code if we mess with the prototype more along the way. Its basic function will remain the same but do not get confused if the code that you have downloaded is not an accurate match, or if we add some additional function to the code before you get to grab it.

Here, we see that each user is able to belong to one or more groups. Each group has its own permissions. Both the users and the groups can have an associated relationship with other data. This is the reason why we see the checkbox associations in these edit/add pages, but not in the roles page. We have re-used the logic so that the same page serves several functions. It will search in order to check if the data has been submitted. If it has submitted by using the class objects, the data will be stored in the database for any new records or changes. There are several tips for forms processing. Moreover, there is a special way in which the CF AJAX forms work. So, we should certainly use it as a reference.

How to Use Advanced Authentication

The authentication that comes with ColdFusion is good, but there are some things that can be added to the features that are being offered out of the box. We can see that there is administration that can be taken and used in their sites by anyone who wishes to do that.

Let us look at the following code. We now have a rich authentication system that will help us see how we can simplify and enhance our authentication on this prototype site. Remember this is not intended to be a perfect practice that will work for all situations. We are looking at it in order to learn to do site authentication. Each site should consider its special security needs. Here, we will look at the default template in a site:

```
<cflayout name="loPage" type="border" style="hight:100%;width:100%;">
 <cflayoutarea name="loHeader" position="top">
  <h1 style="margin:0px;text-align:center;">Building Site
    Administration</h1>
 </cflayoutarea>
 <cflayoutarea name="loSidebar" position="left"
   style="padding:4px;width:160px;">
  <cfoutput>
   <cfif NOT session._user.isUser()>
    <a href="#request._api.app.path#index.cfm?action=login">Login
    </a>
   <cfelse>
    <a href="#request._api.app.path#index.cfm?action=logout">Logout
    </a>
   </cfif>
   <h3>Site</h3>
   <ul>
    <li>Home</li>
    <li><a href="#application._api.site.path#/admin">Admin</a></li>
   </ul>
```

```
   </cfoutput>
  </cflayoutarea>
  <cflayoutarea name="loMain" position="center" style="padding:4px;">
   <cfinclude template="#request._api.app.path##request.attributes.
action#.cfm">
  </cflayoutarea>
  <cflayoutarea name="loFooter" position="bottom" style="text-align:
center;">
   <em>This is the site home page.</em>
  </cflayoutarea>
 </cflayout>
```

This template is based on the CFAJAX UI. We use the following line to pull in the page in the same directory in order to fill the loMain center section of the layout:

```
<cfinclude template="#request.attributes.action#.cfm">
```

The default page is based on the request.attributes.action, which has a default of main. Refer to the following screenshot.

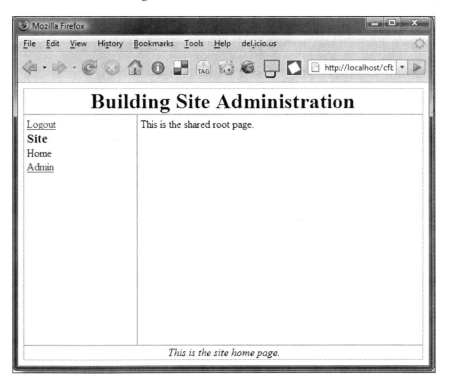

Anyone can click on the **Admin** link but we can see that this page is already secure. It is not appropriate page content unless someone has admin role permissions. We will modify the code block with a method in our custom authentication. This could have been done with the standard built-in authentication if we had built a site with that model. Here is a modification of the previous page:

```
<h3>Site</h3>
<ul>
 <li>Home</li>
 <cfif session._user.isAuthorized("admin")>
  <li><a href="index.cfm">Admin</a></li></cfif>
</ul>
```

Here we see that the **Admin** menu item in the sidebar has been wrapped with logic to check if the current user has the **Admin** role permission. If there is not an administrator logged into the site, then the screen will appear as follows:

With a simple change, we can choose to selectively display content only if the permissions are set for the current user. This is very nice. Let us have a look at the code that will be used to block unauthorized users in sections of the site. **Admin** is stored in a common directory. We have a settings file in that directory that checks if the current user has permission to access that directory. Here is the file:

```
<cfscript>
// check to see if current user has administrative permissions.
```

```
session._user.isAuthorized("admin","#application._api.site.path#index.
cfm");
</cfscript>
```

Here, we are using a combination of an API that we have modified for the code example and our package for reuse through the user object. We are using the same command that we used to determine if the content on the main page should show the **admin** sidebar link. Now, we have added another item to the page. This second argument in our object method is a URL link. If the user is not authorized, it sends him or her to that URL. In this case, it would send the user to the homepage of the site. If we want we can tag on a little more content, and it would send them to a message page for the site and tell them why they ended up at that location.

```
<cfscript>
// check to see if current user has administrative permissions.
session._user.isAuthorized("admin","#application._api.site.path#index.
cfm?action=message&_msg=You don't have permission to access that
page.");
</cfscript>
```

This is a great way to make managing the site even better than the authentication power that comes as a standard with ColdFusion. Yet, there is one more thing that we should cover about the power of this authentication. This is the power of 'AND' and 'OR' authentication. Here is a code sample to check multiple authentications with someone logged into a site on the basis of standard authentication. Let us say you want to allow people who are administrators or people having both staff and edit role permissions to view the site.

```
<cfif isUserInRole("admin") OR isUserInRole("staff,editor")>
 <!--- Permission Section of Code --->
</cfif>
```

The above aim can be achieved by adopting the following (feel free to use and modify this code as you wish, it is and has been open-source under the Apache library for years.):

```
<cfif session._user.isAuthorized("admin|staff,editor")>
 <!--- Permission Section of Code --->
</cfif>
```

The comma in both the authentication modes represents logic that all the items connected by commas have to be there for the function to evaluate as 'true'. The custom method allows us to pass multiple checks into evaluation just to see if any of them is 'true'. It also allows permissions that are required to be stored in a variable allowing a very flexible solution.

Extra Notes

Our code has lots of extra features in our example application for us to build on, if we choose. It is based on the CF8 AJAX UI. There are some features in `scriptCFC.cfc` that work better with the UI than the `<cflocation>` tag. Our system has the following built-in features:

- LOGIN
- LOGOUT
- Registration
- Get Password
- Administration

  ◦ User Management
  ◦ Group Management
  ◦ Roles (permissions) Management

We should remember that the needs of the client and an integration with the current systems may dictate these requirements.

Summary

We have looked at the basic concepts of authentication. In this chapter, we have seen how to use the authentication that comes standard with CF and we have also seen an example of extended and more powerful authentication built as a CF8 UI-based prototype site. In this chapter, we have covered the following:

- Core ColdFusion authentication tools
- Custom authentication
- Extended granular user permissions model
- Controlling site content based on current user permissions
- Redirecting the user to another page and protecting content based on permissions
- Extended 'AND' and 'OR' permissions for both the standard and the enhanced models
- The features built into the CF8 AJAX UI prototype

CF AJAX User Interface

8

AJAX is a term that changed the face of the Web. The topics in this chapter are enough to drive the upgrade or purchase of ColdFusion repeatedly. The power of the functions helps developers and site owners in a number of ways that prove worthy of this version holding the AJAX label.

In this chapter, we will find out what makes AJAX different from HTML and regular server-oriented web pages. We will also look at how ColdFusion interacts with AJAX in order to assist us with layout, menus, toolbars, and form features. This helps us conclude that ColdFusion has made our applications easier. In this chapter, we will cover the following:

- Comparing HTML, server, and browser technology sites
- ColdFusion AJAX layout features
- ColdFusion widgets (dynamic divs, menus, panels, tool tips, windows)

Over time, we have had different technologies that come and go. Some technologies actually mature or morph into a new form. It seems the newer technology assimilates the former concepts and standards into a newer and more functional solution. Here are some of the technologies that have been available over the years.

HTML-Based Websites

These websites were present at the beginning of the Web. There were two dominant features that were added to the Web during this time. We had page layouts and links. With the layout, we were able to organize page content so that the users had headers and side bars. Finally, we had links that helped us jump dynamically from one location to another just by clicking on a linked item.

Server-Side Languages

The next integration was done by server-side languages. ColdFusion, Perl, and PHP were among the ones that provided some more power in these areas. The pages included sections that were dynamically written to HTML after the page was requested by the end user. This allowed us to start building applications that also took into consideration how many people had visited the web page. These applications grew into systems that provided major shopping sites, auction sites, search engines, and complete business systems for companies.

Browser-Side Applications

The idea of placing a part of the program power on the client (inside the browser to start the internet concepts) predates the Web. There were different types of applications and tools to accomplish client-side applications. These included Java applets, JavaScript code inside the browser, and Flash. Over time, the only two that have survived with any dominance are Flash and JavaScript. There are some other tools that also work with the client machine, that is, they work through the browser, like media players.

Flash

Flash provided presentation improvement to the Web. There were many tools that were available at that time. Flash is a tool with unique power. Its power was so exhilarating that it motivated Adobe to buy out Macromedia and build a future around this technology. Flash includes much more than fancy animations and video feeds. It is actually an application platform. It works to provide regular business applications on the browser as Flex applications and AIR applications on the desktop. There is an interface that allows Flex and AIR applications to work with AJAX. Flex is another topic altogether, but realize it is a popular way to do AJAX now.

JavaScript

The ability of JavaScript and the power of browsers to interact with it became an integral part of AJAX. In one generation, we had static web pages. In the next generation, we had pages that were dynamically generated after they were requested. The newer AJAX allowed the page available inside the browser to communicate with the server without a page reload. This made the user experience much better.

Now, there were applications being written that were not considered previously. Excellent examples of those applications were the online mapping applications. You could get directions from one location to another and the map would update without having to load another page. Other examples include live galleries of photos where the new selections appear in the current page. The user experience has greatly matured. In fact, users are no longer annoyed as they do not have to wait for the next page to load. This is the power of an AJAX application.

ColdFusion AJAX

Web servers were designed to work with AJAX. This proved to be one of the most remarkable features in this version of ColdFusion. The features of integration are focused in two areas. This includes the data and development features along with the user interface.

Layout

There are four layout containers in ColdFusion 8. These include the div, layout, pod, and window containers. They give us great power and flexibility.

By default, this will generate div tags and this can work for any container type. We are going to create a page that allows us to pass the name and date of a form to another page. The difference is that the page will not reload. It will be passed through an AJAX request. Let us look at how we can do this in ColdFusion.

```
<html>
<head>
   <title>CFDiv Example</title>
</head>
<body>
<h2>Ticket Example</h2>
<cfform>
     <cfinput name="purchaser" type="text"> Name<br />
     <cfinput name="forDay" type="datefield"> Date<br />
</cfform>
<cfdiv
```

```
        bind="url:ticket_reply.cfm?purchaser={purchaser}&forDay={forDay}"
                  id="dynaDiv" style="background-color:##DDDDDD;">
    </body>
    </html>
```

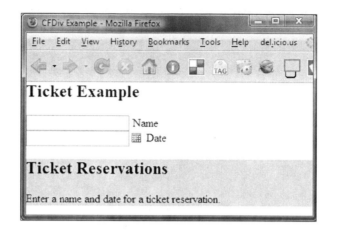

Here we have a simple form implemented in CF. You might notice that there is no submit button attached to the form. You may also notice the div section. In this style, it will submit content whenever any field is updated. We handle the logic of dealing with it on the second page. First, we will look at the use of the CFDiv tag. Note that inside the bind attribute, we have { } brackets. They are the CFAjax equal of the ## marks used in normal CF output. It allows JavaScript to know that, inside the client browser, they will be dynamically updated through the entries in the form. Here is the response page code:

```
<h2>Ticket Reservations</h2>
<cfif url.purchaser NEQ "" and url.forDay NEQ "">
    <cfoutput>
        We have a ticket reserved for #url.purchaser# for the date of
#url.forDay#.
    </cfoutput>
<cfelse>
        Enter a name and date for a ticket reservation.
</cfif>
```

We can see that the page is quite simple, and works in a simple manner. The only difference is that the page is being requested via AJAX. This is how the page looks when you fill in both the form fields:

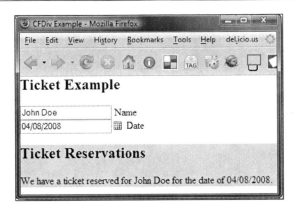

In our example, we can see that the contents typed into our input form fields is pushed to the `<cfdiv>` without even refreshing the page. It is a simple AJAX example as this content is actually passed through the `Ticket_reply.cfm` file with the new CF8 features.

`<cflayout />`

There are two types of layouts, horizontal layouts and vertical layouts. This tag helps us control the elements within those orientations. This tag creates a tabbed region or a set of bordered regions that can include top, bottom, left, right, and center regions. This is done with a nested tag called `cflayoutarea`. Each block of content inside the layout is stored inside a `cflayoutarea` tag. The layout container can either be a border, hbox, tab, or vbox container.

Border Example

```
<html>
<head>
    <title>CFDiv Example</title>
</head>
<body>
<h2>Ticket Example</h2>
<cflayout
    type="border"
    name="myLayout">
    <cflayoutarea name="region1"
        position="top" align="center">
    <strong>Header Section</strong>
    </cflayoutarea>
    <cflayoutarea name="region2"
        position="left">
    <h3>Region 2</h3>
        <p>This is a content section.</p>
```

```
    </cflayoutarea>
    <cflayoutarea name="region3"
        position="center">
    <h3>Region 3</h3>
        <p>This is a content section.</p>
    </cflayoutarea>
    <cflayoutarea name="region4"
        position="right">
    <h3>Region 4</h3>
        <p>This is a content section.</p>
    </cflayoutarea>
    <cflayoutarea name="region5"
        position="bottom">
        Footer Section
    </cflayoutarea>
</cflayout>
</body>
</html>
```

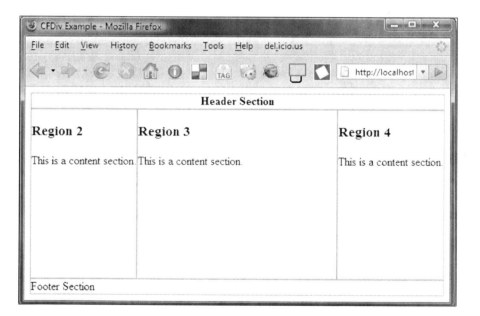

This proves to be a faster way of putting things together. It is also a great way to prototype sites. You will note that some of the regions like the center region will not support all the attributes. Just remove those attributes, if you are getting an error and add them back again to solve the issue. You must notice that you can control the alignment of the individual regions.

There are additional features to the border-type layout areas. You can set align, closable, collapsible, initCollapsed, initHide, maxSize, minSize, name, onBindError, overflow, size, source, splitter, style, and title attributes. You must remember that some of the attributes may not work on every position. If you get an odd error, try to remove the elements from that section.

HBox/VBox Example

Layouts do not need to be full page; they can be nested. You may find that the hBox and the vBox layouts are good for the layout of the inner content. In this example, there are no essential attributes for the layout area. The optional attributes are name, onBindError, overflow, size, source, and style. Here, we are just going to look at the base functionality. We will be using the layout shown in the previous figure, but we need to remove the left and right center sections. By using the center section, we will nest the layout inside it. We will also color the background of each section so that the layout sections are easily visible.

```
<html>
<head>
    <title>CFDiv Example</title>
</head>
<body>
<cflayout
    type="border"
    name="myLayout">
<cflayoutarea name="region1"
    position="top" align="center">
    <strong>Header Section</strong>
</cflayoutarea>
<cflayoutarea name="region3"
    position="center">
<cflayout name="myHBox" type="hbox">
    <cflayoutarea style="background-color:##FFDDDD;">
        <p>Box Region 1</p>
    </cflayoutarea>
    <cflayoutarea style="background-color:##DDFFDD;">
        <p>Box Region 2</p>
    </cflayoutarea>
    <cflayoutarea style="background-color:##DDDDFF;">
        <p>Box Region 3</p>
    </cflayoutarea>
</cflayout>
</cflayoutarea>
<cflayoutarea name="region5"
    position="bottom">
```

```
        Footer Section
    </cflayoutarea>
</cflayout>
</body>
</html>
```

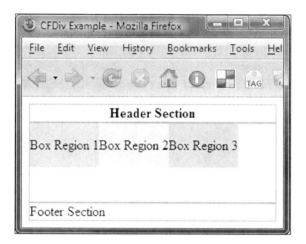

This is how the screen apperas when we change the inner hBox layout to `style="width:33%"`. (We actually set the middle one to 34% to make sure that it adds up to 100%.)

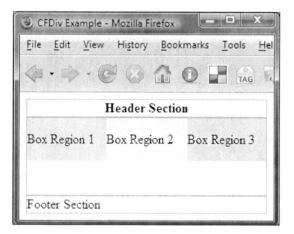

Now, we will make a minor change to the `type` attribute of the inner layout tag. We will change it to vBox. You can see these are some concepts that have been used in Flash forms and Flex for a long time now. It is good to see this functionality being packaged up for simpler use in CF. This means that good design will be possible without expecting the developers to master, or pretend to master the markup.

Tab Example

Here, we are going to create a layout with a left sidebar, header, and footer and then nest our tabs inside the center section of the outer layout container. The current CF documents do not mention that you must include a `title` attribute for the tab text. We also set our overflow to hidden. Like any other layout, you may have to change these a little so that it works with your scenario. Here is the code and the screen as it appears. You should set your width with the `style` attribute if you are going to set a label and make it interactive.

```
<html>
<head>
    <title>CFDiv Example</title>
</head>
<body>
<cflayout
     type="border"
     name="myLayout">
     <cflayoutarea name="region1"
       position="top" align="center">
       <strong>Header Section</strong>
   </cflayoutarea>
   <cflayoutarea name="region2"
       position="left" style="width:120px"
       title="Sidebar Section" collapsible="true">
   <ul>
       <li>One</li>
       <li>Two</li>
```

```
            <li>Three</li>
        </ul>
    </cflayoutarea>
    <cflayoutarea name="region3"
          position="center" overflow="hidden">
    <cflayout name="myTabs" type="tab">
    <cflayoutarea
          title="Tab 1">
          <p>Box Region 1</p>
    </cflayoutarea>
    <cflayoutarea
          title="Tab 2">
          <p>Box Region 2</p>
    </cflayoutarea>
    <cflayoutarea
          title="Tab 3">
          <p>Box Region 3</p>
    </cflayoutarea>
    </cflayout>
    </cflayoutarea>
    <cflayoutarea name="region5"
           position="bottom">
           Footer Section
    </cflayoutarea>
</cflayout>
</body>
</html>
```

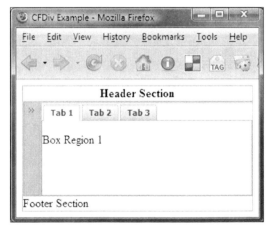

Pods are good for doing things such as sidebar content. At the time when the chapter was written, the pod could not be set to 100% for width; it had to be set to a fixed width. Usually, sidebars have fixed width, so this should not be a big issue. Here is the code that will be used. Again, we will modify the outer layout by adding this to the inner content nested within the sidebar section.

```
<html>
<head>
   <title>CFDiv Example</title>
</head>
<body>
<cflayout
    type="border"
    name="myLayout">
  <cflayoutarea name="region1"
    position="top" align="center">
      <strong>Header Section</strong>
  </cflayoutarea>
  <cflayoutarea name="region2"
    position="left" size="120">
      <strong>Sidebar Section</strong>
  <ul>
      <li>One</li>
      <li>Two</li>
      <li>Three</li>
  </ul>
        <cfpod name="myPod" title="Pod 1"
          width="118" height="40">
          This is pod content.
        </cfpod>
        <cfpod name="myPod2" title="Pod 2"
          width="118" height="60">
          This is more pod content.
        </cfpod>
  </cflayoutarea>
  <cflayoutarea name="region3"
    position="center" overflow="hidden">
    Main Content Region
  </cflayoutarea>
  <cflayoutarea name="region5"
    position="bottom">
    Footer Section
```

```
    </cflayoutarea>
  </cflayout>
  </body>
  </html>
```

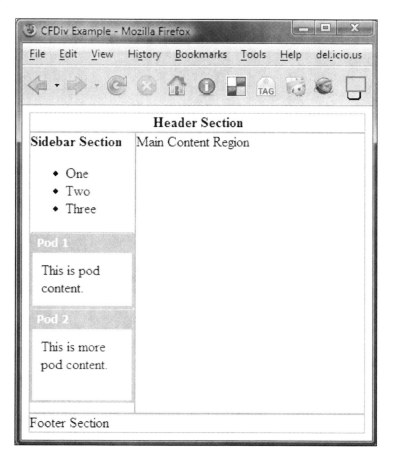

This is another element that will be used and will be enjoyed frequently. Many companies block the actual pop-up windows because of all the abuse on the Internet. There is a way to create a pop-up window that is actually not another window. The window is a pseudo-window inside the same browser window or tab. This window can be hidden and revealed on demand with JavaScript access to the DOM. One of the best things about ColdFusion is how easy it is do all this.

What characterizes a CF pop-up window? They have title bars and float over the other content. They can be modal to prevent interaction with the page around the pop-up window while they are active. The window can be dragged, closed, and resized. If you want, it is also possible to have more than one window on the screen. Let us look at the code.

```
<html>
<head>
    <title>CFDiv Example</title>
    <script>
    // Configuration for second window
    var config =
    {x:100,y:100,width:300,modal:false,closable:false,
     dragable:true,resizeable:true,initShow:false,minheight:150,minwidt
h:150}
    </script>
</head>
<body>
<cflayout
        type="border"
        name="myLayout">
    <cflayoutarea name="region1"
        position="top" align="center">
        <strong>Header Section</strong>
    </cflayoutarea>
    <cflayoutarea name="region2"
        position="left" size="140">
        <strong>Sidebar Section</strong>
    <ul>
        <li>One</li>
        <li>Two</li>
        <li>Three</li>
    </ul>
    <cfpod name="myPod" title="Control 1"
        width="138" height="60">
     <form>
        <input
          type="button" value="Show Window"
          onClick="ColdFusion.Window.show('window1')">
        <input
          type="button" value="Hide Window"
          onClick="ColdFusion.Window.hide('window1')">
     </form>
    </cfpod>
```

```
        <cfpod name="myPod2" title="Control 2"
            width="138" height="85">
        <form>
            <input
              type="button" value="Make Window"
              onClick="ColdFusion.Window.create('window2', 'Created In
Browser Window', 'popWindowContent.cfm', config)">
            <input
              type="button" value="Show Window"
              onClick="ColdFusion.Window.show('window2')">
            <input
              type="button" value="Hide Window"
              onClick="ColdFusion.Window.hide('window2')">
        </form>
        </cfpod>
        </cflayoutarea>
        <cflayoutarea name="region3"
            position="center" overflow="hidden">
            Main Content Region
        </cflayoutarea>
        <cflayoutarea name="region5"
            position="bottom">
            Footer Section
        </cflayoutarea>
    </cflayout>

    <cfwindow name="window1" title="Popup Window"
        draggable="false" resizable="false"
        height="300" width="300" x="50" y="50">
    This is a stubborn window that has limited features.
    </cfwindow>
    </body>
    </html>
```

We will make a solution that has the following features for this example. It will have two pop-up windows. The first pop-up window will be created by using the custom tag <cfwindow/> and the other one will be created using a JavaScript call. We will put the attributes for the features of the window that we have created on the fly in the header section inside a set of script tags. The other pop-up window will be placed in the code at the very end of the body tag section.

You will notice that we are using browser dom element events to trigger our window creation, hide, and show functions. This gives a preview of our new program integration of ColdFusion browser side. Remember that JavaScript is case sensitive. You must get the ID of the items that are being referenced, correctly. You must also get all the functions and structures case perfect. Most of the time, things are written with all the letters of the word as lowercase after the first letter of the word. The first letter of the word in the first word is typically in lowercase, and each of the joining words start with uppercase. These are not rules but they are generally considered good practice. If you make this a habit, you will find that you have less bugs while working with JavaScript code or creating it. Note that ColdFusion is spelled just as the proper name is spelled.

Again, you will see that the window shown in the following screenshot is nested inside the layout with which we have been working so far. The buttons are also inside our pods, so we can show some of the combined advantages of using ColdFusion layout features. Like any layout, you are expected to do some adjustments in order to get it just right. Yet, for most developers, this is easier than trying to manage the HTML design. This is a great way to do the prototypes without taking a designer's time for a proof of concept.

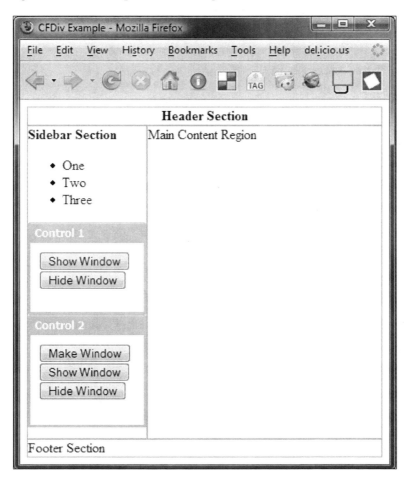

The following figure shows a pop-up window that has a close button but does not allow itself to be dragged or resized. The front window that is overlapping shows the window that loads its content from another URL that is requested. This window does not have a close button, but it does have the drag and resize abilities. It is fairly obvious that you can create, hide, and show windows from JavaScript based on the buttons available on the sidebar inside the pods. These windows are hidden by default. But, there is also an attribute called initShow that allows the window to be shown by default.

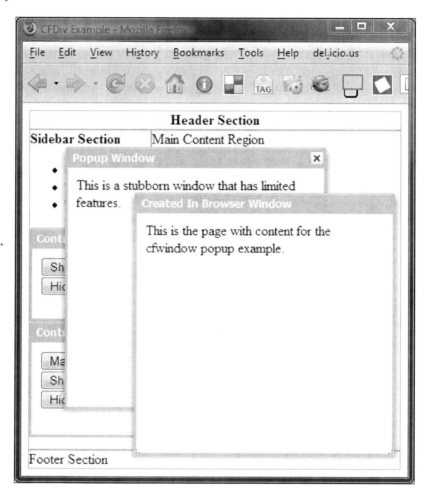

There are some other features of this window, which may be of interest to you. We can have a specific section of the code based on events. This means that when we show or hide the window, it can have an event target that is called when that event occurs. If we put a form in a window and need to verify whether it was filled out, then things like these can be very valuable. There may be other uses as well.

Menus and Tool Tips

When people build websites, most of the navigation is presented in a see and click format. Menus are more common with desktop style applications than websites. This is not because menus are a bad idea, but because there is no standard HTML menu function. It should also be noted that just because ColdFusion allows us to add menus to our sites, it does not mean that it is always the best use-case scenario. We also have no standard tooltip element in HTML. This adds a standard solution for people building ColdFusion-based websites.

We now have the power and flexibility to create menus. These can be set as either horizontal or vertical. The default menu, if not set, is vertical. You can even nest menus inside menus for levels. Only the top menu can be a horizontal menu. All menu items except dividers must have a display attribute. Horizontal menus have dividers, and divider items are therefore not needed.

Menus are considered to be active if they perform an action. This could be a web link or a JavaScript function. Let us build a simple page with a vertical menu in the sidebar to explore this concept.

```
<html>
<head>
   <title>CFMenu Example</title>
   <script>
   </script>
</head>
<body>
<cflayout
    type="border"
    name="myLayout">
<cflayoutarea name="region1"
      position="top" align="center">
<strong>Header Section</strong>
 </cflayoutarea>
<cflayoutarea name="region2"
      position="left" size="140">
  <cfmenu name="sbMenu" type="vertical">
  <cfmenuitem display="Home" href="javascript:alert('Home')" />
  <cfmenuitem display="Shop" />
  <cfmenuitem display="About Us" href="javascript:alert
                                      ('About Us')" />
  </cfmenu>
 </cflayoutarea>
<cflayoutarea name="region3"
     position="center" overflow="hidden">
```

```
     Main Content Region
       <p id="status"></p>
  </cflayoutarea>
  <cflayoutarea name="region5"
      position="bottom">
      Footer Section
  </cflayoutarea>
</cflayout>
</body>
</html>
```

The following screenshot shows the results of this code. In fact, you can see that the status bar shows the contents of the **About Us** hyperlink. It is a JavaScript call to the alert function that is displayed as expected. With this type of function, you may rethink how you can do some of your website organization. You could have your site link from **About Us** to a pop-up window rather than a whole separate page. This would give visitors the desired information and keep them on track as to what generated the interest in the **About Us** details.

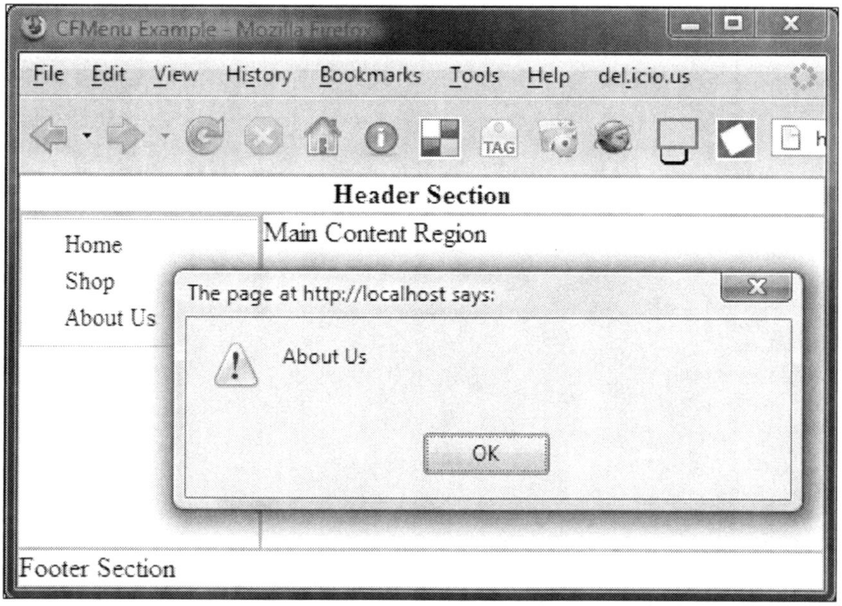

Another important aspect of the AJAX standard features of ColdFusion is that we do not need to include the JavaScript AJAX libraries at the top of our page. ColdFusion takes care of it for us. Now let us put some nested menus under the **Shop** menu in our page. Let us add a **Specials** link, a **Search** link, and a **Policies** link. Now, we will add three submenu items to our page under the **Shop** menu. We will also put a divider in the midst of them to show the functionality.

We choose to show the horizontal version of the menu in the center section for this demonstration for three reasons. The first reason is that inside the nested section of the page, our menu pushes off to the side. This issue may be temporary. So do not count it out, just because it didn't work at this moment. The second reason is that we wanted to make sure to cover that option as well. The third reason is that historically, menus failed to cover the select boxes properly.

```html
<html>
<head>
   <title>CFMenu Example</title>
   <script>
   </script>
</head>
<body>
<cflayout
         type="border"
         name="myLayout">
   <cflayoutarea name="region1"
         position="top" align="center">
    <strong>Header Section</strong>
   </cflayoutarea>
   <cflayoutarea name="region3"
         position="center" overflow="hidden">
    <cfmenu name="sbMenu" type="horizontal">
    <cfmenuitem display="Home" href="javascript:alert('Home')" />
    <cfmenuitem display="Shop">
    <cfmenuitem display="Catalog" />
    <cfmenuitem display="Specials" />
    <cfmenuitem divider="true" />
    <cfmenuitem display="Order History" />
    </cfmenuitem>
    <cfmenuitem display="About Us" href="javascript:alert('About
                                      Us')" />
      </cfmenu>
    <br />
      <form style="padding-left:80px">
          <select>
           <option>Menu Checker</option>
          </select>
      </form>
   </cflayoutarea>
   <cflayoutarea name="region5"
         position="bottom">
          Footer Section
   </cflayoutarea>
</cflayout>
</body>
</html>
```

Remember that since we can have the nested menus inside the `cfmenuitem` tags, we will need to close all the `cfmenuitem` tags either with an end tag or with a slash in the same tag. The following screenshot illustrates the new look that the menu gives when the shop menu is selected. We can see that it covers the select box nicely, and as we would expect.

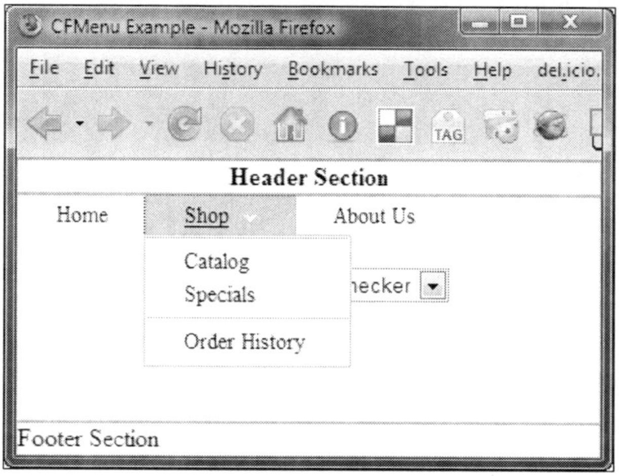

`<cftooltip />`

Tooltips are a great way to show more content. We can show definitions of words or clues about why things are on the page, or on the forms. There are lots of special attributes to control 'enter' and 'exit' types of delays. The tag also allows us to call the content from the nested pages and place it in the page. We are going to highlight the word 'tooltip' and show it as a tip that is pulled by loading a different page. We will also set a tooltip for the select box on the page. Note that we have placed HTML tags on both the tips, and they work just fine.

```
<html>
<head>
    <title>Tool Tips Example</title>
    <script>
    </script>
</head>
<body>
<cflayout
        type="border"
        name="myLayout">
    <cflayoutarea name="region1"
        position="top" align="center">
    <strong>Header Section</strong>
    </cflayoutarea>
```

```
    <cflayoutarea name="region3"
        position="center" overflow="hidden">
    <p>
This is an example of a <cftooltip sourcefortooltip="myTip.
cfm">tooltip</cftooltip> where the tip is actually pulled from another
web page. If you wanted this could even be dynaic content. Mouse over
the word tooltip in the fist sentence to see the tip.
    </p>
    <br />
        <form style="margin-left: 160px;">
    <cftooltip tooltip="This is our <strong>static</strong> tip.">
        <select>
            <option>Tip Checker</option>
        </select>
    </cftooltip>
      </form>
    </cflayoutarea>
    <cflayoutarea name="region5"
        position="bottom">
        Footer Section
    </cflayoutarea>
</cflayout>
</body>
</html>
```

This is what we get when we place our pointer over the tooltip text that calls the contents of the tip from another webpage.

You will also notice that the tooltip covers the select box with expected perfection. Here, **tooltop** is the tip source.

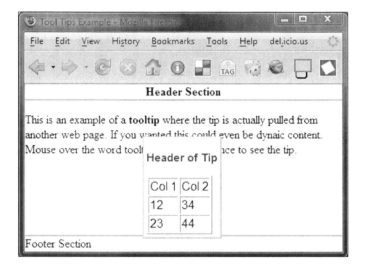

Styling Notes

Each of the UI elements has a default generic style. We can create our own styles to manage these UI elements and give them some more personalized essence. Do not forget to look at the actual styles that are generated to manage these elements. Changing something may have cascading effects that we do not desire. Make one change at a time and test it under cross-browser situations. Just use the examples and you will find it easier than heading out on your own. This will make things possible for you.

Tips

If you use AJAX forms in dynamic divs or windows, then you will have to include some kind of features on the outermost container page. This could include creating a dummy CFC that is called with CFAjaxProxy. You do not need to do anything else to get it done. Yet without it, you may think AJAX is not working right. The issue is that the libraries must be on the outer container page. If you have a `cfform` on the outer page, then ColdFusion will know how to include the proper JavaScript libraries with the page. Without that, you will just need to include some CFC via the CFAjaxproxy tag.

Summary

There is much more you can do with AJAX. There are developers who have been programming with ColdFusion since its very early versions. They did not have all these pre-packaged helpers. As we learn and use other libraries and different methods of adding to these, we must also add our own UI custom tags to enhance what we are learning as the native features of ColdFusion. Here is a summary of what was covered in this chapter:

- The difference between AJAX and Flash RIA (Rich Internet Interface) technologies.

- The <cfdiv /> tag—This is a region of HTML that can be dynamically populated by a bind expression. This also works directly with ColdFusion forms.

- The <cflayout /> tag—A horizontal or vertical layout container.

- The <cfmenu /> tag—A menu bar or the root of a drop-down menu.

- The <cfpod /> tag—An area of the browser with an optional title bar and a body that contains display elements.

- The <cftooltip /> tag—This allows you to add dynamic tooltips to your form AJAX element items.

- The <cfwindow /> tag—This allows you to create an on-page pop-up window that will neither be blocked, nor be failed by the browser pop-up blockers. This is because even though it looks like a different window, it is actually a part of the same HTML page.

9
CF AJAX Forms

Each of us has different needs. These needs dictate what we call the 'best AJAX features' in ColdFusion. These AJAX features refer to its form features, which will be very popular among those who consider them to be the best features. The main reason for CF's popularity is that it has lots of power and speed in building new AJAX forms with CF8.

In this chapter, we will have a look at the following form features:

- CFGrid for table-based data
- CFInput with features like Autosuggest
- CFSelect
- CFTextArea with its new rich text editing
- CFTree

Forms

One of the most common problems with forms is when you have to go back to the server in an HTML-based site. This means it not only takes the time for the data to come back but it also takes extra time since the graphics and page layout details are checked and reloaded. You might think that it is always cached. Yet, sometimes with different browsers, form information can be cached during a session. This means that the developer may need to turn caching for that particular page off. In this case, the whole page will get reloaded each time the server gets a request. Very often, this results in slower pages on forms. Here, you may routinely need dynamic information.

We will look at the grid example first, and then we will have a look at autosuggest. You may have been using some of the features on the Web without having much knowledge about them. Good design is harder to notice than bad design. In fact, one of the things you will notice about a well-designed application is how much you don't notice. It just has a powerful workflow.

The grid tag in CF8 replaces a former Java-based tag with AJAX technology. This tag allows us to build interactive tables of data for the users. With the grid tag, we get paging and sorting built in with no extra work. Let's build a general grid and add the features in. The first thing we have to do is to set the cfgrid format attribute to html.

```
<cfscript>
    oProduct = createObject("component","product").init('cfb');
    rsProducts = oProduct.getRecordset();
</cfscript>
<html>
<head>
    <title>Grid Example</title>
</head>
<body>
<h2>Grid Example</h2>
<cfform>
    <cfgrid name="products" query="rsProducts"
        format="html" striperows="yes">
    </cfgrid>
</cfform>
</body>
</html>
```

This gives us a simple grid. Now, let us see the data stored in the table. We will see that without adding the cfgridcolumn tag, it will show all the columns in the recordset. You will also notice that we have added the striperows attribute. This is a quick way to help the user get a more modern-looking grid for to use. At this point, sorting is available, and is standard. We can arrange any column in either ascending order or descending order. The row in which we are currently is highlighted. If the end user desires, they can change the size of the columns as it has an in-built column sizing feature. If that is not enough, they can re-order the columns by dragging them around.

Design is outside the scope of this book. Yet, we have the ability for all of the ColdFusion AJAX controls to go in and manage the CSS being called for the look and feel of the AJAX components. This is far more than what we get from a flat table using CFLoop. It also takes far less code for live development. Here is the view we get with this initial code.

Grid Paging

In the next example, we will remove the request for a new page and place a bind variable right inside the tag. This means that we will remove the query attribute from the grid. ColdFusion will create all the AJAX code needed for this to work on the browser, and send it without any manual assistance by the developer. We will also add in a `pagesize` attribute. When there is more than one page of data, the appropriate navigation controls will be added to the grid. We need to remember that the grid column tags must be included when we move into the AJAX mode. This isn't a big issue and is a good practice to follow.

```
<html>
<head>
   <title>Grid Example</title>
</head>
<body>
<h2>Grid Example</h2>
<cfform>
   <cfgrid name="products"
        format="html" striperows="yes"
        pageSize="3"
        bind="cfc:product.getGridRecordSet(
          {cfgridpage},{cfgridpagesize},
          {cfgridsortcolumn},{cfgridsortdirection})">
```

```
        <cfgridcolumn name="name" header="Product" width="120"/>
        <cfgridcolumn name="description" header="Description"
width="300"/>
        <cfgridcolumn name="price" header="Price" width="120"/>
    </cfgrid>
</cfform>
</body>
</html>
```

Now we need to create a custom method that extends our former simple data object. We could do this as a query but we would rather write the code once, and re-use it over and over again. After all, that is the peculiarity of the AJAX grid tag. Let's look at the function we need to add to our base class in the `product.cfc` file to make it work.

```
<cffunction name="getGridRecordSet" access="remote"
returntype="struct">
        <cfargument name="page" type="numeric" required="yes">
        <cfargument name="pageSize" type="numeric" required="yes">
        <cfargument name="gridSortColumn" type="string" required="no"
default="">
        <cfargument name="gridSortDirection" type="string" required="no"
default="">
        <cfscript>
        var products = "";
        var sort="#arguments.gridSortColumn# #arguments.
gridSortDirection#";
        products = getRecordSet(order:trim(sort));
        return QueryConvertForGrid(products,
                arguments.page, arguments.pageSize);
        </cfscript>
</cffunction>
```

This will be created in layers because we need to maximize our code reuse. AJAX offers a more elegant way to code. We create base object classes in order to make programming more elegant. We have added the above method to the base class. Now, we will be able to do simpler implementation and re-use the base method. This may also be the first time when many users will see the use of the super method type, which is a standard feature of CFCs in ColdFusion. Here is the code for the class we will use to create an object through the binding attribute of the grid tag. Note that for security purposes, we need to set the DSN manually in the code as we are invoking a method, and not creating a persistent CFC object. This provides minimal code to interact with a very elegant AJAX grid. We are only taking the arguments and passing them directly to the base class method.

```
<cffunction name="getGridRecordSet" access="remote"
returntype="struct">
        <cfargument name="page" type="numeric" required="yes">
```

```
    <cfargument name="pageSize" type="numeric" required="yes">
    <cfargument name="gridSortColumn" type="string" required="no"
default="">
    <cfargument name="gridSortDirection" type="string" required="no"
default="">

    <cfscript>
    init('cfb');

    return super.getGridRecordSet(
        page:arguments.page,
        pageSize:arguments.pageSize,
        gridSortColumn:arguments.gridSortColumn,
        gridSortDirection:arguments.gridSortDirection
      );
    </cfscript>

</cffunction>
```

We can now go through our grid records without reloading the whole page. Of course in our example, there is little difference. But in a real-life application, it would be very profound. This shows the power of AJAX and the beauty of an integrated server-side implementation.

Grid Updates and Deletes

Now we will be making a few minor changes that will allow us to update and delete rows in the grid. We will need to have a front end and back end to manage this transaction. The highlighted code given here is no big challenge to change in this grid tag. The following changes are to be made:

1. We set an attribute tag for `edit` mode.

2. We set two attributes for adding in the `delete` functionality. We set `delete` to `'true'` and pass text in for the visible link on the grid.

3. We set the `onChange` attribute to `cfc` and then the method will take the update requests. It will require all the variables to be passed back to the CFC. Apart from this, we have the following case:

```
<html>
<head>
<title>Grid Example</title>
</head>
<body>
<h2>Grid Example</h2>
<cfform name="bob">
    <cfgrid name="products"
            format="html" striperows="yes"
            pageSize="3"
        selectMode="edit"
        delete="true" deletebutton="X"
        onChange="cfc:product.updateRow({cfgridaction},
        {cfgridrow},{cfgridchanged})"
        bind="cfc:product.getGridRecordSet(
            {cfgridpage},{cfgridpagesize},
            {cfgridsortcolumn},{cfgridsortdirection})">
    <cfgridcolumn name="name" header="Product" width="120"/>
    <cfgridcolumn name="description" header="Description"
                  width="300"/>
    <cfgridcolumn name="price" header="Price" width="120"/>
    </cfgrid>
</cfform>
</body>
</html>
```

This takes care of the modifications in the AJAX grid. Now we need to update the CFC with a function to handle the request made by the grid. The data being passed back and forward between the browser and the server is a JSON data structure. JSON is a data package technology that is popular for text-based data transfers. This works in a manner as similar to the update request. Here is an example of JSON data structure:

```
function: saveGridRow
arguments:
{
"action":"U",
"row":
{
"ID":2,
"NAME":"Watermelon Plant",
"DESCRIPTION":"This is likely the largest and sweetest of the cucumber
family.",
"PRICE":"3.25"
},
"changed":{"PRICE":"3.23"}
}
```

You can see that there are three base `arguments` that will be passed to our CFC. These are `'action'`, `'row'`, and `'changed'`. The `action` will either have `'U'` or `'D'` in our code. `'U'` stands for updates and `'D'` stands for deletes. The row argument contains a structure that has an `ID`. It also contains the field names and field values of each of the data rows being modified. Lastly, we have a variable with the data field being updated and its new value. Let's have a look at how we can handle this new request from our CFC.

The common logic of pulling in the argument data and the basics is just the same. For those new to CFCs that inherit functions, the following is an example. We have some basic variables in the pseudo-constructor method `init()`, which is called here. This scenario requires us to either pass the DSN here, or have it stored in the `init`. This is because when we use CFCs for Web Services or for AMF (Flash Remoting), they are not persistent objects. We branch either to update or delete specific database rows.

The update logic in our example is more flexible than required as only one field is updated at a time. Each time the user edits a field and moves away from it, the data to be updated is immediately sent back to the server. This is a bit different from some other databases where you need to move off a line before the update is made. People can choose either of these methods. The important thing is to know how it works. Now we use the variables of the objects in order to retrieve some of the basic fields so as to process the data. The object knows its own table name because it is set in the `init` function. It knows the primary key field, and it uses this in the query. The fields and values come from the arguments.

This makes this code so that it never has to be updated for it to move from one grid implementation to the next. Yes, more code reuse! Let's look at what a grid with an edit cell looks like.

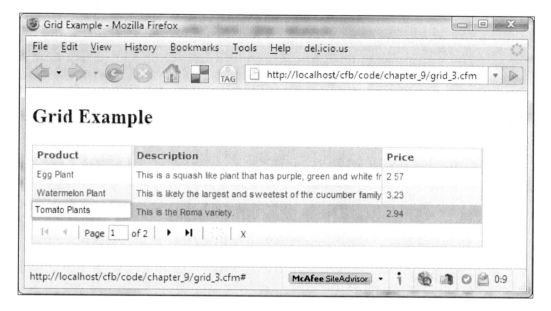

Next, we see a more compact JSON data package. There are some pointers for understanding the JSON data packaging technologies that are included under version 8 of ColdFusion.

```
arguments:{"action":"D","row":{"ID":5,"NAME":"Carrots","DESCRIPTION":"
Beta vitamins in store.","PRICE":1.24},"changed":{}}
```

Here is an example of a delete request. This is simpler than an update request. We take the same information that we already have and extract the data from both the objects that are stored in the `init()` method. The rest of the information can be extracted from the grid AJAX request as well.

```
<cffunction name="updateRow" access="remote" output="false">
<cfargument name="action" type="string" required="yes">
<cfargument name="row" type="struct" required="yes">
<cfargument name="changed" type="struct" required="yes">
<cfscript>
 var fields = "";
      var field = "";
      var value = "";
      init('cfb');
      </cfscript>
      <cfswitch expression="#arguments.action#">
         <!--- Process updates --->
```

```
            <cfcase value="U">
                <!--- Get column field and value --->
                <cfset fields=StructKeyList(arguments.changed)>
                <cfset field=ListFirst(fields)>
                <cfset value=arguments.changed[field]>
                <!--- Perform actual update --->
                <cfquery datasource="#variables.dsn#">
                UPDATE #variables.table#
                SET #field# = <cfqueryparam value="#value#">
                WHERE #variables.pKeyField# = #arguments.row[variables.
pKeyField]#
                </cfquery>
            </cfcase>
            <!--- Process deletes --->
            <cfcase value="D">
                <!--- Perform actual delete --->
                <cfquery datasource="#variables.dsn#">
                DELETE FROM #variables.table#
                where #variables.pKeyField# = #arguments.row[variables.
pKeyField]#
                </cfquery>
            </cfcase>
        </cfswitch>
    </cffunction>
```

Linked Grids

So far, we have had good data management capabilities. Another type of grid function that may be useful would be a grid designed with hyperlinks. Mixing hyperlinks and an edit grid should be avoided now. You can do several things with the linked grid. You could create links so that it reloads the same page for another detailed page to drill down in another grid for reporting purposes. If you use "Row" instead of "Single" as the value for selectMode, then we will observe that it passes the entire row of data as a delimited string. Now, we will proceed with the value "Single".

```
<html>
<head>
<title>Grid Example</title>
</head>
<body>
<h2>Grid Example</h2>
<cfform name="bob">
        <cfgrid name="products"
        format="html" striperows="yes"
        pageSize="3"
        selectOnLoad="yes" preservepageonsort="yes"
        selectMode="Single"
        delete="true" deletebutton="X"
```

```
                onChange="cfc:product.updateRow({cfgridaction},
                                     {cfgridrow},{cfgridchanged})"
                bind="cfc:product.getGridRecordSet(
                        {cfgridpage},{cfgridpagesize},
                        cfgridsortcolumn},{cfgridsortdirection})">
                <cfgridcolumn name="ID" display="false"/>
                <cfgridcolumn name="name" header="Product" width="120"
                 href="grid_4.cfm" hrefkey="ID" target="_blank"/>
                 <cfgridcolumn name="description" header="Description"
                                     width="300"/>
        </cfgrid>
        </cfform>
        </body>
        </html>
```

We made the following changes to the grid. First we changed the `cfgrid`
`selectMode` attribute to `Single`. This returns a single value with the hyperlink on
the link cell. The next thing was to add a hidden `ID` field. The value returned with
the hyperlink has to be the name of a column data field. If there is no column, then
the field will not be available to the hyperlink. Lastly, we add the `href` attribute to
the page with the target URL in the link. The required values will be automatically
appended to the end of the URL when it is selected from the web page. The value
passed is designated in the `hrefkey` attribute field. If you wish to get it loaded in a
specific frame rather than in the same window or tab, then you can use the `target`
attribute in a manner similar to any other `href` tag.

That was a good introduction to using the CFGrid AJAX tag in ColdFusion 8. We can
do a few other things that will prove to be helpful in understanding the concept well.

This is one of the most versatile packages in the language. Just as in HTML, the input can represent buttons, check boxes, date fields, file selectors (these are not supported at this time for AJAX submissions), hidden, image, password, radio buttons, reset buttons, submit buttons, and text entry boxes. We will look at several features to get us started in using these power tags in ColdFusion. You may also note that if the type attribute isn't defined it defaults to text. In this chapter, we will take into consideration the AJAX versions of these tags.

Binding Page Elements

Now, we will have a look at the binding power of the new ColdFusion AJAX. We will be binding the attributes of elements to other objects. In the following code, we can see that we have three cfinput tags nested in a cfform. The third input has a bind attribute with the name of the first cfinput element. This means that, at any time, we can change the value in the first cfinput and leave the field for the third one to update.

```
<html>
<head>
<title>CFInput Example</title>
</head>
<body>
<h2>CFInput Example</h2>
<cfform name="bob">
        <cfinput name="boxOne" /><br/>
        <cfinput name="boxTwo" /><br/>
        <cfinput name="boxThree" bind="{boxOne}" />
</cfform>
</body>
</html>
```

In the previous example, we can see that there are no values entered in the bottom window. In the top window, the text entered in the first box has immediately appeared in the third box upon leaving the first box. Thus, the binding technology makes it easier to build a natural intuitive functionality into our pages.

Binding Immediately upon Load

There are times when we want the values to be set as the form loads. This is done by using the `bindOnLoad` attribute. We will modify the previous example and look at the results.

```
<html>
<head>
<title>CFInput Example</title>
</head>
<body>
<h2>CFInput Example</h2>
<cfform name="bob">
    <cfinput name="boxOne" value="Pre-Set Value" /><br/>
    <cfinput name="boxTwo" /><br/>
    <cfinput name="boxThree" bind="{boxOne}" bindonload="true" />
</cfform>
</body>
</html>
```

Note that the first box and the third box have the same content. This is not because both values were set at the server, but because as the form gets loaded, the value of the first box is immediately set to match the third box. This is how the `bind` attribute naturally works in ColdFusion 8.

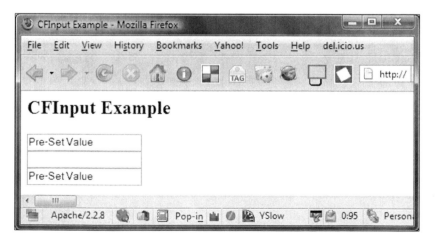

Now, we will have a look at one the techniques of masking our text fields. This is something that is often used when we work more with forms. This example has been tested with and without masking the first text field, and it is observed that the `bind` feature pulls an exact copy of what is in the field to which it is bound at that time. As a result, we need to be sure that we put a `mask` attribute on both the fields. Refer to the following code.

```
<html>
<head>
<title>CFInput Example</title>
</head>
<body>
<h2>CFInput Example</h2>
<cfform name="bob">
        <cfinput name="boxOne" value="1234567890"
                                mask="999-999-9999" /><br/>
        <cfinput name="boxTwo" /><br/>
        <cfinput name="boxThree" bind="{boxOne}"
                bindonload="true" mask="999-999-9999" />
</cfform>
</body>
</html>
```

The following screenshot shows the results.

Now, we can see that both the text boxes have a phone number format once the page form is loaded. There are several masking options that are present in the ColdFusion documentation.

The Date Requestor

The date requestor is a great addition to the form tools in ColdFusion 8. The AJAX date requestors were not available for the standard HTML functionality in ColdFusion forms. We have a very simple piece of code that helps us understand this new feature. There are many other features as well, but for now, we will take up this particular tag.

```
<html>
<head>
<title>CFInput Example</title>
</head>
<body>
<h2>CFInput Example</h2>
<cfform name="bob">
        <cfinput name="boxOne" type="datefield" /><br/><br/>
        <cfinput name="boxTwo" /><br/><br/>
        <cfinput name="boxThree" />
</cfform>
</body>
</html>
```

It would be good if the date requestor appeared at the top of all the other content. This will be of great help as the different types of form elements such as select boxes can be an issue with this type of technology. The user also has the option of clicking the close button without entering a date. Check the ColdFusion documents on how to format the data as per the clients' needs. In the following example, we have used the default settings.

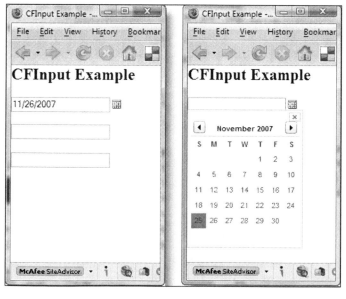

If you choose, you can also pass a list in a `dayNames` attribute for the name of the days. There is a `monthNames` attribute that works the same way as `dayNames`. Some cultures and businesses look at the calendar in different ways. Another function that can assist you is the `firstDayOfWeek` attribute. You use a 0 (zero) to a 6 for the day you would like your week to start on.

The Autosuggest Box

The autosuggest box is a product of the AJAX era. This is not a native DOM element that is a part of HTML. Yet it works with it in an efficient manner. We will have a look at the hard-coded suggest list. All you need is to pass a list into the tag. This can also be done with a variable via ColdFusion variables.

```
<html>
<head>
<title>CFInput Example</title>
</head>
<body>
<h2>CFInput Example</h2>
<cfform name="bob">
    <cfinput name="boxOne" type="text"
    autosuggest="Albert,Amos,Andy,Ann,Betty,Bob,Charlie,Dan,Doug,
                Ernest,Frank,Fred,Sam,Samantha,Stan" />
<br/>
</cfform>
</body>
</html>
```

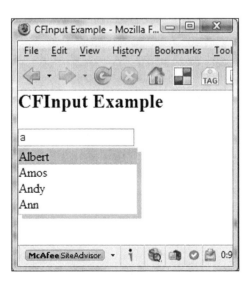

This list functionality starts with a default of 10 items in the list. We can also change that if we want with the `maxResultsDisplayed` attribute. We can also set the box so it does not start giving results until enough characters have been typed in. This will make our auto-request lists more efficient when we are using CFCs for searching data. The field that sets the minimum length is `autosuggestMinLength`. Another method is to set a delay in order to make ensure not many requests are sent back to back. The default value is half a second. This is done with the `autosuggestBindDelay` attribute.

There are two attributes left. These are very AJAXed attributes. The first attribute is the `showAutosuggestLoadingIcon`. When the user is wondering if data is coming from the server, this attribute asks them to wait as the data gets loaded. Another attribute is the `typeAhead` attribute. This attribute works with the previous one in order to make things easier. When it is set to true, it fills in the first close match, so data entry can be done much faster. Let's look at the last two in the following code sample, which demonstrates the bind pulling data from a CFC.

```
<html>
<head>
<title>CFInput Example</title>
</head>
<body>
<h2>CFInput Example</h2>
        <cfform name="bob">
        <cfinput name="boxOne" type="text"
            autosuggest="cfc:names.getUsers({cfautosuggestvalue})" />
<br/>
</cfform>
</body>
</html>
```

The code for `autosuggest` is very simple. We need to make sure we pass in the variable name `cfautosuggestvalue` as our binding value, for it to work. We see that we have moved our data into the CFC, and we are parsing it with a proper loop and a conditional logic check. In real life, this is more likely to be a query request. Just loop through the query request and append the values to an array in order to pass it back to our `autosuggest` element.

```
<cfcomponent output="false">
<cffunction name="getUsers" access="remote" output="false">
        <cfargument name="suggestValue" required="true">
        <cfset var retNames = ArrayNew(1)>
        <cfset var myNames = "Albert,Amos,Andy,Ann,Betty,Bob,
            Charlie,Dan,Doug,Ernest,Frank,Fred,Sam,Samantha,Stan">
        <cfset var iName = "">
```

```
        <cfloop list="#myNames#" index="iName">
            <cfif findNoCase(arguments.suggestValue,iName)>
            <cfset arrayAppend(retNames,iName)>
            </cfif>
        </cfloop>
    <cfreturn retNames>
</cffunction>
</cfcomponent>
```

This time we will look up with our 'b' character and see that AJAX is connected to our CFC, and the CFInput autosuggest type is working well. Not only that but if we look closely, we can see that the autosuggest starts at the start of the word. We should set our code when using queries to use a "LIKE '#variable#%'" to match functionality.

The select box is a very useful form element. It is one of the most popular AJAX items. The technique that we will be discussing will work for two or more select boxes. We are also going to create a CFC that feeds off one of the standard data sources in ColdFusion installations. We will have more data to work with this way. Let's look at the CFC in which we will extract the code. Now, we will call our CFC HR.cfc for human resources.

```
<cfcomponent output="false">
<cfset this.dsn="cfdocexamples">
<cffunction name="getDepts" access="remote" returnType="array">
    <cfset var rsData="">
    <cfset var myReturn=ArrayNew(2)>
    <cfset var i=0>
```

```
            <cfquery name="rsData" datasource="#this.dsn#">
                SELECT dept_id, dept_name
                FROM app.departmt
                ORDER BY dept_name
    </cfquery>
            <cfloop query="rsData">
                <cfset myReturn[rsData.currentRow][1]=rsData.dept_id>
                <cfset myReturn[rsData.currentRow][2]=rsData.dept_name>
            </cfloop>
        <cfreturn myReturn>
        </cffunction>

<cffunction name="getEmployees" access="remote" returnType="array">
<cfargument name="dept_id" type="numeric" required="true">
        <cfset var rsData="">
        <cfset var myReturn=ArrayNew(2)>
        <cfset var i=0>
<cfquery name="rsData" datasource="#this.dsn#">
        SELECT emp_id, lastname, firstname
        FROM app.employee
        WHERE dept_id = #arguments.dept_id#
        ORDER BY lastname, firstname
</cfquery>
<cfloop query="rsData">
        <cfset myReturn[rsData.currentRow][1]=rsData.emp_id>
        <cfset myReturn[rsData.currentRow][2]=rsData.firstname & ' '
& rsData.lastname>
</cfloop>
<cfreturn myReturn>
</cffunction>
</cfcomponent>
```

Here we have two standard queries. The `getDepts()` method does not require any arguments because it pulls its data directly. The `getEmployees()` method gets a department ID passed, so it will only pull back the employees with a matching ID for the department selected in the first select box. In both the cases, we loop though the returned result, and create a two-dimensional array for returning the data to AJAX running on the browser. Once again, all the data packaging and handling has been provided under the covers by ColdFusion. Now let's look at the following code. This code should be sent to the browser to do the related `select` function with the `cfselect` tags.

```
<html>
<head>
<title>CFSelect Example</title>
```

```
    </head>
    <body>
    <h2>CFSelect Example</h2>
    <cfform name="bob">
       Departments:<br/>
        <cfselect name="dept_id"
          bind="cfc:hr.getDepts()"
          bindonload="true" />
     <br/>
     <br/>
          Employees:<br/>
          <cfselect name="emp_id"
          bind="cfc:hr.getEmployees({dept_id})" />
    </cfform>
    </body>
    </html>
```

From the above, we can see the compact AJAX code, which we can use with ColdFusion custom tags along with the new AJAX libraries. This is what we would see if we selected **HR** in the first select box, and then selected the second select box.

There are times when a text box is just not enough. Then we have to turn to a textArea HTML element. This can be better since it allows us to have more than one line and also to scroll through large content. Yet, it has many other limitations. For example, we could not embed a picture in the content, create tables, or justify the text in each line. This is where a rich text editor comes into the picture. ColdFusion has one built into AJAX forms. Here is a simple page that allows us to create content, and send it back to the same page. If the content is there, then it will display it above the editor, once the page is reloaded.

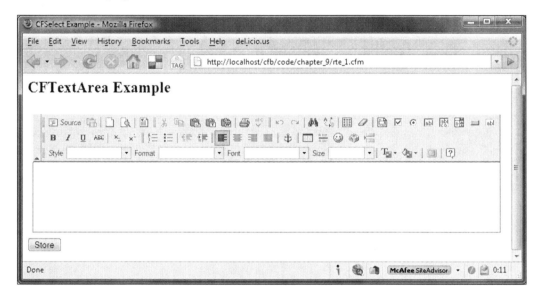

```
<html>
<head>
<title>CFSelect Example</title>
</head>
<body>
<cfif structKeyExists(form,"rtext")>
<h2>Submitted Rich Text</h2>
<cfoutput>#form.rtext#</cfoutput>
</cfif>
<h2>CFTextArea Example</h2>
<cfform name="bob">
   <cftextarea richText="true" name="rtext" />
    <cfinput name="submit" type="submit" value="Store">
</cfform>
</body>
</html>
```

This is quite simple. Yet, most of the time, this would be way too much information on the page. Let's see if we can simplify the toolbars, a little bit in the following code, and see the results of this change.

```html
<html>
<head>
<title>CFSelect Example</title>
</head>
<body>
<cfif structKeyExists(form,"rtext")>
<h2>Submitted Rich Text</h2>
<cfoutput>#form.rtext#</cfoutput>
</cfif>
<h2>CFTextArea Example</h2>
<cfform name="bob">
    <cftextarea richText="true" name="rtext"
                        toolbar="Basic" />
    <cfinput name="submit" type="submit" value="Store">
</cfform>
</body>
</html>
```

The following results are obtained:

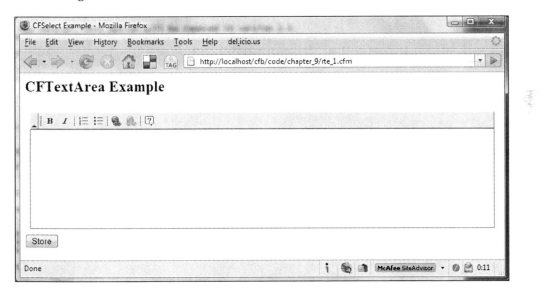

There are two default toolbars that are standard in ColdFusion. It is possible on a server where developers have access to modify the file that contains the toolbars, and thus create additional sets. This is located in the CFIDE folder in the following subdirectory file:

`/scripts/ajax/FCKeditor/fckconfig.js`

We can read the instructions about creating toolbars in the ColdFusion Developers' Guide. The following screenshot shows the HTML that came out of the editor when submitted back to the page. This can be stored in a file or in a database. The content could be part of a page, or this could even be used to create an entire CMS (Content Management System).

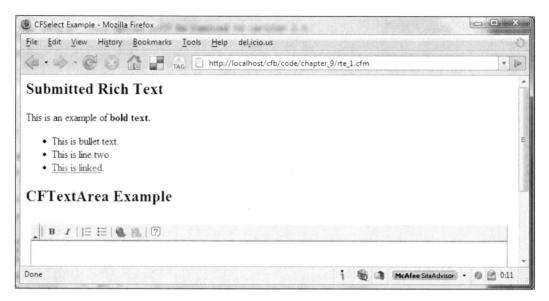

The tree tag has some excellent features that allows us to expand and collapse branches with nested content. When we bind the tag to the source, it only loads the data it needs. This makes things more efficient and gets them displayed faster. It is possible to use this tag without the AJAX binding, but we will concentrate only on the AJAX usage. While doing it this way, we only use one `cftreeitem` tag. The following example explains how the tree and the data provider for the tree work together.

```
<cfcomponent output="false">
<cffunction name="getNodes" returntype="array" output="false"
access="remote">
    <cfargument name="nodeitemid" required="true">
    <cfargument name="nodeitempath" required="true">
  <cfscript>
   var myReturn = arrayNew(1);
 var myElement = structNew();
    if(arguments.nodeitemid == ""){
```

```
            arguments.nodeitemid = 0;
    }

            myElement.value = arguments.nodeitemid + 1;
            myElement.display = "Node #nodeitemid#";
            myReturn[1] = myElement;
    return myReturn;
    </cfscript>
    </cffunction>
    </cfcomponent>
```

This is the data provider at this point of time. We will add all of our methods to this CFC as we proceed. The following example adds one level to the level that had been requested. It then returns an array back to the browser for the AJAX logic to handle insertion into the tree. Here is the code we will write to make the actual page work.

```
<html>
<head>
<title>CFTree Example</title>
</head>
<body>
<h2>CFTree Example</h2>
<cfform name="bob">
<cftree name="dirTree" format="html">
        <cftreeitem bind="cfc:objTree.getNodes({cftreeitemvalue},
                                    {cftreeitempath})">
</cftree>
</cfform>
</body>
</html>
```

This is as simple as a tree can be. The variables like the rest of the AJAX tags are the values of the variables that are created by the tag. You must use the binding variables listed for the purpose of interaction with the CFC for it to function correctly. The data sent to ColdFusion under the hood to add the fifth node to the tree was a nodeitemid of 6 and a nodeitempath of "2\\3\\4\\5". You might have noticed that the root node is not listed in the path details. When we call the tree data, it must return a single layer of data. It may not contain more than one layer.

If you would like to see the data that goes between your server and the browser, you might consider using the tool "Service Capture". This will give you all kinds of details about what is going on between the browser and the server.

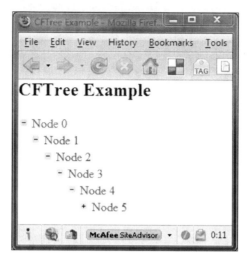

The Directory Tree

We will create a tree from the `examples` directory. In trees, we have "leaf nodes". The leaf nodes don't have any leaves or items after them. They are placed at the end of the path. In this case, the files will be our leaf items. Let's look at the markup page code. Here the tag sends the same information to the CFC. This time, we will use a different method that we have added to the CFC. The CFC on each request gets the information, and sends it back as a one-dimensional array.

```
<html>
<head>
<title>CFTree Example</title>
</head>
<body>
<h2>CFTree Example</h2>
<cfform name="bob">
<cftree name="dirTree" format="html">
  <cftreeitem bind="cfc:objTree.getDir({cftreeitempath},
                                {cftreeitemvalue})">
</cftree>
</cfform>
</body>
</html>
```

Now, we will have a look at the new method that we have added to our CFC so as to supply our tree view. The main method uses a private method in our CFC. This method is how we return the actual directory listing. Managing your code inside your CFCs in a similar manner makes cleaner code possible. This tag was one of the reasons why we would not have written our getDir() method completely in CFScript. Since this acts as a separate step in logic that can be encapsulated, it makes sense to factor and simplify the code.

```
<cffunction name="getPathDirectory" output="false" access="private">
<cfargument name="path" required="true">
<cfset var myReturn = "">
<cfdirectory action="list" directory="#arguments.path#"
name="myReturn" sort="asc">
<cfquery dbtype="query" name="myReturn">
        SELECT *
        FROM myReturn
        ORDER BY type
</cfquery>
<cfreturn myReturn>
</cffunction>
```

The above code describes the getPathDirectory() method. We receive the path and value arguments from the AJAX page that has been called. Remember to make sure that the order of your arguments matches with the order of the calling code. Then, for good practice we var all the variables we will be using in our method. This is not required. We are doing it because you never know when you might have to re-use code, and this is just a good habit to make sure all code remains thread safe. The value item is the key for this block of code. If the nodeitemvalue is empty, then the value returned is simple. When we click on the items that are directories, they contain the current path in the value variable. This means that we can continue to append the path to nested directories and achieve the effect of a file requestor.

Now, there are a couple of other features in this method. We are adding file and folder pictures. This is done by including the img attribute in the element structure. We use the leafnode attribute on file types to prevent the plus expansion tree indicator from showing up in the browser window. The last thing we will do is pass just a generic alert hyperlink when someone clicks on a file, rather than a folder. This can be modified as per the needs of any project that we are currently working on.

```
<cffunction name="getDir" returntype="array" output="false"
access="remote">
    <cfargument name="nodeitempath" required="true">
    <cfargument name="nodeitemvalue" required="true">
<cfscript>
    var myReturn = arrayNew(1);
```

```
        var myElement = structNew();
        var myPath = getDirectoryFromPath(GetCurrentTemplatePath());
        var mySlash = right(myPath,1);
        var myDir = "";
        var myValue = "";
        var i = 0;
          if(arguments.nodeitemvalue NEQ ""){
        myValue = "#mySlash##arguments.nodeitemvalue#";
        myValue = replace(myValue,"#mySlash##mySlash#","#mySlash#",
                                                          "ALL");
        myPath = "#myPath##arguments.nodeitemvalue#";
    }
arguments.nodeitemvalue = replace(arguments.nodeitemvalue,"#mySlash##m
ySlash#","#mySlash#","ALL");
        myDir = getPathDirectory("#myPath#");
        for(i=0;i <= myDir.recordCount; i++){
        if(len(myDir.type[i])){
            myElement = structNew();
        if(myDir.type[i] == "file"){
        myElement.leafnode = true;
        myElement.img = "document";
        myElement.href = "javascript:alert('This would select the
                                        file (#myDir.name[i]#)')";
        myElement.value = "#myDir.name[i]#";
    } else {
        myElement.leafnode = false;
        myElement.img = "folder";
        myElement.value = "#myValue##mySlash##myDir.name[i]#";
    }
        myElement.display = "#myDir.name[i]#";
        arrayAppend(myReturn,myElement);
    }
    }
    return myReturn;
    </cfscript>
    </cffunction>
```

The following are views of the tree showing the results of our new code. We can see that it does an incredible amount of processing with very little coding by the programmer. Now that we have this programming snippet of code, it has become easier for us. We can take this method in the CFC and re-use it any number of times.

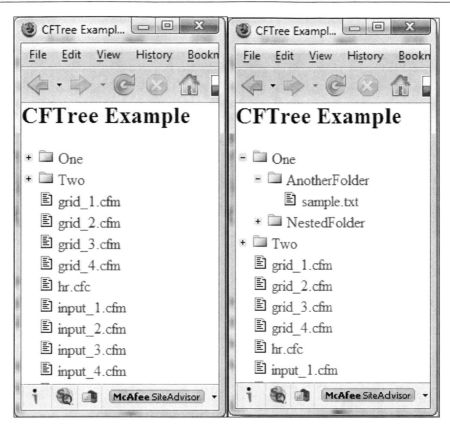

Summary

In this chapter, we have seen the benefit received from the combined power of tag-based encapsulation with AJAX functionality. Further, we have also discussed the following:

- `<cfgrid/>` tag—A dynamic, editable, sortable data grid. This can also be used for hyperlinked grids.

- `<cfinput/>` tag—An input control that could be a normal input or date field input with a popup calendar. There is also the ability to create an autosuggest box.

- `<cfselect/>` tag

- `<cftextarea/>` tag—This is a tag that allows you to insert a rich text WSYWIG HTML editor right onto your HTML page.

- `<cftree/>` tag

- How to use the bind attribute with tags.

10
CF AJAX Programming

This chapter deals with AJAX programming in ColdFusion. ColdFusion acts a great platform not just because of its code features, but because of its characteristics as to how the code interacts with other features. ColdFusion is a language with depth and power. Yet, as we developers know, it seems real power always requires a bit of custom code. In this chapter, we will have a look at the following topics:

- Binding
- Proxy connections
- JSON features
- Spry data integration
- Debugging

Binding

When it comes to programming, the two most commonly used features are CFAJAXProxy and binding. The binding feature allows us to bind or tie things together by using a simpler technique than we would otherwise have needed to create. Binding acts as a double-ended connector in some scenarios. You can set the bind to pull data from another ColdFusion tag on the form. These must be AJAX tags with binding abilities.

There are four forms of bindings, on page, CFC, JavaScript, and URL. Let's work through each style so that we will understand them well. We will start with on page binding. Remember that the tag has to support the binding. This is not a general ColdFusion feature, but we can use it wherever we desire.

On Page Binding

We are going to bind 'cfdiv' to pull its content to show on page binding. We will set the value of a text input to the `div`. Refer to the following code. ColdFusion AJAX elements work in a manner different from how AJAX is written traditionally. It is more customary to name our browser-side HTML elements with `id` attributes. This is not the case with the binding features. As we can see in our code example, we have used the `name` attribute. We should remember to be case sensitive, since this is managed by JavaScript. When we run the code, we will notice that we must leave the input field before the browser registers that there has been a change in the value of the field. This is how the event model for the browser DOM works.

```
<cfform id="myForm" format="html">
    This is my edit box.<br />
    <cfinput type="text" name="myText">
</cfform>
<hr />
And this is the bound div container.<br />
<cfdiv bind="{myText}"></cfdiv>
```

Notice how we use curly brackets to bind the value of the 'myText' input box. This inserts the contents into 'div' when the text box loses focus.

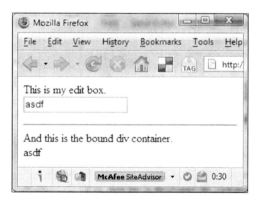

This is an example of binding to in-page elements. If the binding we use is tied to a hidden window or tab, then the contents may not be updated.

CFC Binding

Now, we are going to bind our `div` to a CFC method. We will take the data that was being posted directly to the object, and then we will pass it out to the CFC. The CFC is going to repackage it, and send it back to the browser. The binding will enable the modified version of the content to be sent to the `div`. Refer to the following CFC code:

```
<cfcomponent output="false">
    <cffunction name="getDivContent" returntype="string"
access="remote">
            <cfargument name="edit">
            <cfreturn "This is the content returned from the CFC for
the div, the calling page variable is '<strong>#arguments.edit#</
strong>'.">
    </cffunction>
</cfcomponent>
```

From the previous code, we can see that the CFC only accepts the argument and passes it back. This could have even returned an image HTML segment with something like a user picture. The following code shows the new page code modifications.

```
<cfform id="myForm" format="html">
    This is my edit box.<br />
    <cfinput type="text" name="myText">
</cfform>
<hr />
And this is the bound div container.<br />
<cfdiv bind="cfc:bindsource.getDivContent({myText})"></cfdiv>
```

The only change lies in how we bind the `cfdiv` element tag. Here, you can see that it starts with CFC. Next, it calls `bindsource`, which is the name of a local CFC. This tells ColdFusion to wire up the browser page, so it will connect to the CFC and things will work as we want. You can observe that inside the method, we are passing the bound variable to the method. When the input field changes by losing focus, the browser sends a new request to the CFC and updates the `div`. We need to have the same number of parameters going to the CFC as the number of arguments in our CFC method. We should also make sure that the method has its access method set to remote. Here we can see an example results page.

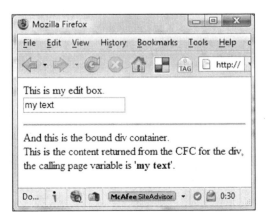

It is valid to pass the name of the CFC method argument with the data value. This can prevent exceptions caused by not pairing the data in the same order as the method arguments. The last line of the previous code can be modified as follows:

```
<cfdiv bind="cfc:bindsource.getDivContent(edit:{myText})"></cfdiv>
```

JavaScript Binding

Now, we will see how simple power can be managed on the browser. We will create a standard JavaScript function and pass the same bound data field through the function. Whenever we update the text box and it looses focus, the contents of the `div` will be updated from the function on the page. It is suggested that we include all JavaScript rather than put it directly on the page. Refer to the following code:

```
<cfform id="myForm" format="html">
    This is my edit box.<br />
    <cfinput type="text" name="myText">
</cfform>
<hr />
And this is the bound div container.<br />
<cfdiv bind="javascript:updateDiv({myText})"></cfdiv>
<script>
updateDiv = function(myEdit){
    return 'This is the result that came from the JavaScript function
with the edit box sending "<strong>'+myEdit+'</strong>"';
}
</script>
```

Here is the result of placing the same text into our JavaScript example.

URL Binding

We can achieve the same results by calling a web address. We can actually call a static HTML page. Now, we will call a `.cfm` page to see the results of changing the text box reflected back, as for CFC and JavaScript. Here is the code for our main page with the URL binding.

```
<cfform id="myForm" format="html">
    This is my edit box.<br />
    <cfinput type="text" name="myText">
</cfform>
<hr />
And this is the bound div container.<br />
<cfdiv bind="url:bindsource.cfm?myEdit={myText}"></cfdiv>
```

In the above code, we can see that the binding type is set to URL. Earlier, we used the CFC method bound to a file named `bindsource.cfc`. Now, we will bind through the URL to a `.cfm` file. The bound **myText** data will work in a manner similar to the other cases. It will be sent to the target; in this case, it is a regular server-side page. We require only one line. In this example, our variables are URL variables. Here is the handler page code:

```
<cfoutput>
    'This is the result that came from the server page with the edit
box sending "<strong>#url.myEdit#</strong>"'
</cfoutput>
```

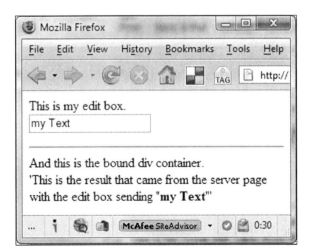

This tells us that if there is no prefix to the browse request on the bind attribute of the `<cfdiv>` tag, then it will only work with on-page elements. If we prefix it, then we can pass the data through a CFC, a URL, or through a JavaScript function present on the same page. If we bind to a variable present on the same page, then whenever the bound element updates, the binding will be executed.

Bind with Event

One of the features of binding that we might overlook its binding based on an event. In the previous examples, we mentioned that the normal event trigger for binding took place when the bound field lost its focus. The following example shows a bind that occurs when the key is released.

```
<cfform id="myForm" format="html">
    This is my edit box.<br />
    <cfinput type="text" name="myText">
</cfform>
<hr />
And this is the bound div container.<br />
<cfdiv bind="{myText@keyup}"></cfdiv>
```

This is similar to our first example, with the only difference being that the contents of the `div` are updated as each key is pressed. This works in a manner similar to CFC, JavaScript, and URL bindings. We might also consider binding other elements on a click event, such as a radio button. The following example shows another feature. We can pass any DOM attribute by putting that as an item after the element `id`. It must be placed before the @ symbol, if you are using a particular event. In this code, we change the input in order to have a class in which we can pass the value of the class attribute and change the binding attribute of the `cfdiv` element.

```
<cfform id="myForm" format="html">
    This is my edit box.<br />
    <cfinput type="text" name="myText" class="test">
</cfform>
<hr />
And this is the bound div container.<br />
<cfdiv bind="{myText.class@keyup}.{myText}"></cfdiv>
```

Here is a list of the events that we can bind.

- @click
- @keyup

- @mousedown
- @none

The @none event is used for grids and trees, so that changes don't trigger bind events.

Extra Binding Notes

If you have an ID on your CFForm element, then you can refer to the form element based on the container form. The following example helps us to understand this better.

```
Bind = "url:bindsource.cfm?myEdit={myForm:myText}"
```

The ColdFusion 8 documents give the following guides in order to specify the binding expressions.

1. cfc: componentPath.functionName (parameters)

 The component path cannot use a mapping. The componentPath value must be a dot-delimited path from the web root or the directory that contains the page.

2. javascript: functionName (parameters)
3. url: URL?parameters
4. ULR?parameters
5. A string containing one or more instances of {bind parmeter}, such as {firstname}.{lastname}@{domain}

The following table represents the supported formats based on attributes and tags:

Attribute	Tags	Supported Formats
Autosuggest	cfinput type="text"	1,2,3
Bind	cfdiv, cfinput, cftextarea	1,2,3,5
Bind	cfajaxproxy, cfgrid, cfselect cfsprydataset, cftreeitem	1,2,3
onChange	cfgrid	1,2,3
Source	cflayoutarea, cfpod, cfwindow	4

Multiple Radio Buttons or Check Boxes and Multiple Select

We can also do binding of multiple radio buttons or check boxes. This is done by giving the same name attribute to the radio button collection or to the check box. We can use unique IDs to allow the use of the HTML `<label></label>` tags for extending the selection to the contents of `for` tags, based on the usage of the matching ID of the check boxes or radio buttons. In HTML, the use of a `for` tag would appear like the following, thus making the user interface better.

```
<label for='firstRadio'>
    <input id='firstRadio' value='1' type='radio'>
</label>
```

When we have check boxes or multiple select, the results of the bind are treated like a list. If more than one item is selected, they are stored by separating them with commas similar to any other returning form data.

Spry Binding

Spry is an independent AJAX library that works with the browser DOM. Spry uses the same curly bracket type of parameters for binding. There are some differences in implementation though. Another thing that you can bind to your forms is the Spry data in what is called a Spry dataset. You would do that as shown in this example:

```
{spryDataset.dataField}
```

If we wish to bind deeper into a Spry dataset in more detail, we can use standard Spry dataset notation to refer to the data.

 To include a literal brace character in a bind expression, excape the character with a backslash.

CFAJAXProxy

This is another very popular AJAX programming feature. This tag allows us to bind AJAX component changes to CFCs, JavaScript, and URLs without the requirement of an AJAX component to pass through it. It also allows us to interact with CFCs directly from JavaScript without binding to any other AJAX component. The JavaScript interface is created for us, and we can reuse the CFC as if it was present locally inside the browser JavaScript. It is very simple and acts as a good solution. Let's take a look at how it works.

CFAJAX Proxy Binding

We are going to build two text boxes that do arithmetic. The application only adds or subtracts. The first line of our code binds to the radio button set with the name `calcType`. We will bind to the click event. When either of the buttons is clicked, the call is made to the JavaScript function `doCalc()` passing the value of the radio button selected. Then the JavaScript function extracts the values of the two boxes and makes sure that they are floating-point numbers. If we didn't convert them, it would see them as text, and append the first text item to the second text item, or we would get some sort of error in subtraction. Then the results are stored and displayed with the alert function.

```
<cfajaxproxy bind="javascript:doCalc({calcType@click})">
<cfform id="myForm" format="html">
    Enter Two Numbers.<br />
    <cfinput type="text" name="number1" id="number1"><br />
    <cfinput type="text" name="number2" id="number2"><br />
    <label for="calcAdd">
       <cfinput type="radio" value="add"
           name="calcType" id="calcAdd">
     Add</label><br />
   <label for="calcSubtract">
     <cfinput type="radio" value="subtract"
           name="calcType" id="calcSubtract">
     Subtract</label><br />
</cfform>
<script>
doCalc = function(thisCalc){
    var myResult = 0;
    var number1 = parseFloat(document.getElementById('number1').
value);
    var number2 = parseFloat(document.getElementById('number2').
value);
    switch(thisCalc){
    case 'add':
        myResult = number1 + number2;
        break;
    case 'subtract':
        myResult = number1 - number2;
        break;
    }
alert(myResult);
}
</script>
```

This is what we would see if we entered '23' and '11' and had selected the subtract radio button:

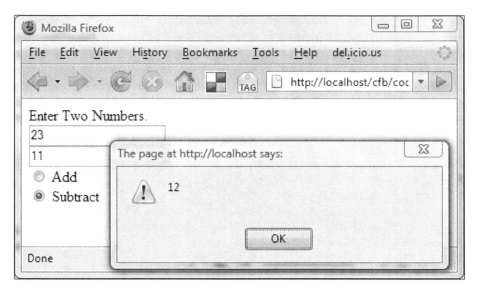

We could have sent the results to either a CFC or URL as we did earlier. We do not need to have visible results in this example either, but it was just to show what was going on. We can see that one of the uses of CFAJAXProxy is to bind.

CFC Proxy Class Objects

Another use of CFAJAXProxy is to extend the remote methods of a CFC into the currently loaded AJAX page on the browser. This function is not binding, but rather an actual proxy. This means that we will extend the functionality of the remote methods right into the web page without writing extensive code. We will be converting our math webpage to support multiplication and division. We could do this easily in the browser. But we want to show the power of extending CFCs, so we will add these two functions in our CFC and work with them from there.

```
<cfajaxproxy bind="javascript:doCalc({calcType@click})">
<cfajaxproxy cfc="serverMath" jsclassname="remoteMath">

<cfform id="myForm" format="html">
    Enter Two Numbers.<br />
    <cfinput type="text" name="number1" id="number1"><br />
    <cfinput type="text" name="number2" id="number2"><br />
    <label for="calcAdd">
    <cfinput type="radio" value="add"
     name="calcType" id="calcAdd">
```

```
      Add</label><br />
      <label for="calcSubtract">
        <cfinput type="radio" value="subtract"
       name="calcType" id="calcSubtract">
      Subtract</label><br />
      <label for="calcMultiply">
        <cfinput type="radio" value="multiply"
       name="calcType" id="calcMultiply">
      Multiply</label><br />
      <label for="calcDivide">
        <cfinput type="radio" value="divide"
       name="calcType" id="calcDivide">
      Divide</label><br />

</cfform>

<script>
jsMath = new remoteMath();

doCalc = function(thisCalc){
    var myResult = 0;
    var number1 = parseFloat(document.getElementById('number1').
value);
    var number2 = parseFloat(document.getElementById('number2').
value);
    switch(thisCalc){
        case 'add':
           myResult = number1 + number2;
           break;
        case 'subtract':
           myResult = number1 - number2;
           break;
        case 'multiply':
           myResult = jsMath.doMultiply(number1,number2);
           break;
        case 'divide':
           myResult = jsMath.doDivide(number1,number2);
           break;
}
alert(myResult);
}
</script>
```

The first modification to our code is to use the CFAJAXProxy tag in order to generate a proxy connection to the remote CFC component. We use an alias name of remoteMath for this component. This becomes a JavaScript class that helps in creating a local object that proxies between this page and our CFC. We then add two more radio buttons so that we have an interface for doing the multiplication function and the division function in our example. The next new line is where we create an object called jsMath in this example. This is not actually JavaScript math, but a JavaScript object that uses the remoteMath class to build an object for communicating with the CFC. Lastly, we check the value of the selected radio button. Then we use our jsMath object, and communicate with the remote server. The name of the remote method is the same as we use on our object and then we pass the argument parameters to the server. The return value is put in our myResult variable just as we did from JavaScript in add and subtract. If we use the same numbers and click **Divide**, the following result will be obtained. Here is the screenshot of the page in action and the CFC code.

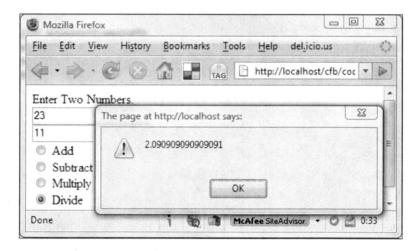

```
<cfcomponent output="false">
    <cffunction name="doDivide" access="remote">
        <cfargument name="number1">
        <cfargument name="number2">
        <cfreturn arguments.number1 / arguments.number2>
    </cffunction>
    <cffunction name="doMultiply" access="remote">
        <cfargument name="number1">
        <cfargument name="number2">
        <cfreturn arguments.number1 * arguments.number2>
    </cffunction>
</cfcomponent>
```

Now in a real-world application, we might be looking for some data or updating a database if we were doing this type of proxy function interaction. The point is that all the coupling and AJAXing is done with little code. It is truly a remarkable work as the Adobe engineers have worked hard for this connectivity. This is how ColdFusion has become better than ever before!

One thing that we have not yet dealt with is the callback functions. There are two standard types of callback object methods in remote CFC proxy classes, the setCallbackHandler() method and the setErrorHandler() method. We are going to modify our code so that the results are automatically sent to these handlers with our CFC interaction. Here is the final code for our examples.

```
<cfajaxproxy bind="javascript:doCalc({calcType@click})">
<cfajaxproxy cfc="serverMath" jsclassname="remoteMath">
<cfform id="myForm" format="html">
    Enter Two Numbers.<br />
    <cfinput type="text" name="number1" id="number1"><br />
    <cfinput type="text" name="number2" id="number2"><br />
    <label for="calcAdd">
    <cfinput type="radio" value="add"
      name="calcType" id="calcAdd">
     Add</label><br />
    <label for="calcSubtract">
    <cfinput type="radio" value="subtract"
        name="calcType" id="calcSubtract">
     Subtract</label><br />
    <label for="calcMultiply">
    <cfinput type="radio" value="multiply"
        name="calcType" id="calcMultiply">
     Multiply</label><br />
    <label for="calcDivide">
    <cfinput type="radio" value="divide"
        name="calcType" id="calcDivide">
     Divide</label><br />
</cfform>
<script>
jsMath = new remoteMath();
doCalc = function(thisCalc){
  var number1 = parseFloat(document.getElementById('number1').value);
  var number2 = parseFloat(document.getElementById('number2').value);
    jsMath.setCallbackHandler(showResult);
    jsMath.setErrorHandler(showError);

switch(thisCalc){
```

```
        case 'add':
            showResult(number1 + number2);
    break;
        case 'subtract':
            showResult(number1 - number2);
    break;
        case 'multiply':
         jsMath.doMultiply(number1,number2);
    break;
        case 'divide':
         jsMath.doDivide(number1,number2);
     break;
    }
    }
    showResult = function(result){
        alert(result);
    }
    showError = function(statusCode,statusMsg){
        alert("status: "+statusCode+"\n"+statusMsg);
    }
</script>
```

We set the callback handers inside our `doCalc()` function for the `jsMath` object. These methods are default names in the ColdFusion AJAX plumbing. It should be noted that we do not want to create remote methods with these names in our CFCs. We removed the variable that we were using and have now created another function called `showResult()` for handling the addition and subtraction. Now, let us look at the multiply case statement block and the divide case statement block for our code. There is no evidence as to how the output from these calls is being handled. This is why we have declared the `setCallbackHandler()` and `setErrorHandler()` methods. In those methods, we put the name of the callback handler functions without their parents. This is a standard way to handle the referencing of a callback handler in JavaScript. We can see that the standard parameters are passed to the error handler. Run the modified code and pass in a zero for the bottom number, and this is what you will see. We could produce much more elaborate code for handling the error. We could pass structured code back to the success method, and do much more there also. We kept this example as simple as possible to help us understand the power and features of how ColdFusion AJAX programming works for both binding and proxy functions.

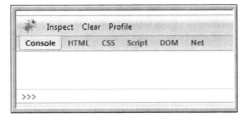

This handles all the data type conversions between ColdFusion and browser JavaScript variables and structure.

This makes ColdFusion the easiest and fastest application for doing AJAX. Also, this platform provides a high level of power and ease to developers.

Client Debugging

There are a number of tools that can make AJAX programming more effective. We will look at Firebug and the built-in debugger that is a part of ColdFusion.

Firebug

One of the best tools available for AJAX development is Firebug. This tool is a plug-in for Firefox with many abilities. The one we will look at specifically here is the ability to drill down into the DOM structure of a browser page. We are going to look at how this tool works. First, we will have a look at the previous example and take the radio button for our divide selection. Here is a screenshot of the page in which we run firebug. Refer to `http://www.getfirebug.com/` for the features of this plug-in.

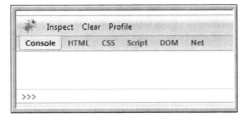

We see the **Inspect** menu item at the top. If we click on it, then we will be able to click on the radio button besides the **Divide** text. This in turn will give us the following in our console view.

If we then go to the right pane of firebug and click on the **DOM** item, we will get the structure details of the object. There are several types of objects that are explained in detail in ColdFusion and this gets loaded with AJAX pages. These can be entered by clicking on the **Console** tab present in the left panel. Then as you can see, you have an entry line at the bottom where you can enter any DOM object name or any JavaScript function, and it will allow us to see what is available with that item. If you're going to dive deeper into AJAX, these are the tools to make the journey much simpler. If you don't have a library loaded that supports it, you can still use the common DOM element shortcut. This means that for the radio button above with the id **calcDivide,** we could use the full **DOM** of **document.getElementById (calcDivide)** or we can use the shortcut version **$ ('calcDivide')**, and press Enter.

Now, we don't see the item within the context of the HTML page. We just see the item we have requested. If we were calling an existing JavaScript structure or a simple value, we would see that too. With a similar item, we can click on it, and then have a look at the DOM model for that particular item as we did earlier. The additional items that the ColdFusion AJAX includes are listed here. We would just enter them in the prompt line as we did for the radio button ID.

- `ColdFusion.Layout.getBorderLayout` (name)
- `ColdFusion.Grid.getGridObject` (name)

- `ColdFusion.Layout.getTabLayout` (name)
- `ColdFusion.Tree.getTreeObject` (name)
- `ColdFusion.Window.getWindowObject` (name)

To get more information about these topics, you can look at the ColdFusion documents that consist of **EXT** and **YUI** library files. The name of course is the same as you assigned while creating the item. Also, we need to remember that JavaScript is case sensitive.

Built-In Debugging

This is a very useful feature. All you have to do is to change the URL in the address bar to get this working. Now, if you are running ColdFusion on a live site, this feature should be shut off in the ColdFusion Administrator. Here is the URL with and without debugging. The only difference is we have added an extra variable to the URL. Just add it to the last variable after the question mark in the URL.

`http://localhost/cfb/code/chapter_10/bind_7.cfm`

`http://localhost/cfb/code/chapter_10/bind_7.cfm?cfdebug`

Here is the screenshot of the debugging window.

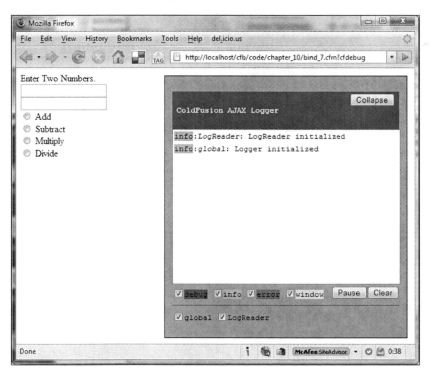

We can see that there are a number of features to this debugging window. We can **Collapse** the window to get it out of the way. It can also be dragged around the screen to move it out of the way, if collapsing is not enough. It is dragged by holding the mouse button down over the dark grey area where the title is. We can toggle to obtain information on the type of debugging. This will also toggle the information that is already present. When we have more information, it will create a scroll bar so as to move through the log. The pause and clear buttons are great features.

Logging Features

Not only is debugging built in, but the system is designed to allow us to send logging to the window so that it becomes easier. Let's open our Firebug console and log the element we were looking at earlier. There are a number of logging features, and it is a better way for managing our build or debugging interaction with the logger.

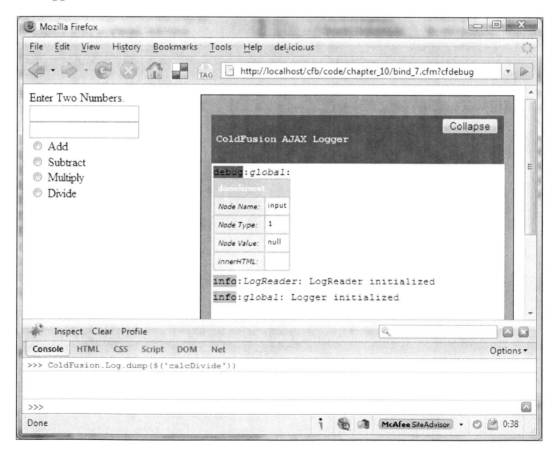

Here, we observe that we do not get as many details as we used to get in the DOM panel of the Firebug console. Remember that the $() shortcut is a part of Firebug. Normally, you either need to have that in another AJAX library, or you have to use the old method that we mentioned earlier. Here are the types of log functions that are included with the debugger.

- `ColdFusion.Log.dump`
- `ColdFusion.Log.debug`
- `ColdFusion.Log.error`
- `ColdFusion.Log.info`

The `ColdFusion.Log.dump` has a special function whereas the remaining three only change the tag that is before the log item. One thing that can be done is to design custom tags and CFCs, so that they have a 'test' mode that can be run. This would allow them to interact with the debugging tools and make a more sustainable product. This would mean there would be more quality assurance for all our software.

Customization

When it comes to coding, there are many things that can be done. This is a two-fold scenario. The primary way to customize is more on design than on coding. If we are inclined, we can actually go as far as replacing all the code of core AJAX functions. Generally, before going that far, it might be a better idea to look at individual libraries and see if there is something present already that can help us achieve our goals.

We are going to look at another tag in ColdFusion 8 known as `<CFAjaxImport/>`. Most of the look-and-feel of the AJAX tags is controlled by CSS files. Using this tag, we can substitute custom styles for these tags. This will be coded as in the given example. The `cssSrc` attribute specifies the URL, relative to the web root of the directory that contains the CSS files used by ColdFusion AJAX features, with the exception of the rich text editor. This directory must have the same directory structure, and contain the same CSS files, and image files required by the CSS files, as the `web_root/CFIDE/scripts/ajax/resources` directory.

```
<cfAjaxImport cssSrc="/mySite/myCSS/">
```

We can also change the `scriptSrc` attribute. Similar to CSS styles, you need to include structure of the same scripts as found in the `/cfide/scripts/` directory. This is where hackers can extend the core power that ships in ColdFusion. If you use this attribute, you will not be able to use it more than once in a request.

Another important thing about this tag is the ability to declare the AJAX tags that need modification. As developers, we often forget, as we think about code, the challenge of designing a site to the owner's satisfaction. We are often negligent in this aspect. The following table shows the tags that can be put in the tag attribute list to set what is modified by the cfAjaxImport tag.

Tag Attribute Value	Used For
cfdiv	cfdiv tags
cfform	Forms that are in cfpod, cfwindow, or cflayoutarea tag bodies
cfgrid	AJAX format cfgrid tags
cfinput-autosuggest	cfinput tags that use the autosuggest attribute
cfinput-datefield	HTML format cfinput tags that use the datefield attribute
cflayout-border	cflayout tags with a type attribute value of border
cflayout-tab	cflayout tags with a type attribute value of tab
cfmenu	cfmenu tags
cfpod	cfpod tags
cfsprydataset-JSON	cfsprydataset tags that generate Spry JSON data sets
cfsprydataset-XML	cfsprydataset tags that generate Spry XML data sets
cftextarea	HTML format cftextarea tags
cftooltip	cftooltip tags
cftree	HTML format cftree tags
cfwindow	cfwindow tags

Automatically Wired AJAX Links

This function allows you to connect the links inside a cfdiv, cflayoutarea, cfpod, or cfwindow control to the containing control. This code would load the local file as the content of the container. It will not load a file from a remote site to protect it from cross-site script attacks.

```
<cfdiv height="600" width="600" name="ajaxDiv">
    <cfoutput>
        <a href="#AjaxLink('LinkOne.cfm')#">Link One</a>
        <br />
        <a href="#AjaxLink('LinkTwo.cfm')#">Link Two</a>
    </cfoutput>
</cfdiv>
```

Execute JavaScript after Loading Content

There are two times when content is loaded. First, when the page is loaded and then when the content within a section such as a `cfdiv`, `cflayoutarea`, `cfpod`, or `cfwindow` is loaded. You want the browser DOM to be created before any JavaScript is called. This function helps in ensuring that the code isn't run prematurely. Here is an example of how to run the command when the whole page is loaded.

```
<html>
<head>
<title>Enter Mail Login Details</title>
<script>
init = function() {
ColdFusion.Window.show('loginwindow');
}
</script>
</head>
<body>
    <cfwindow name="loginwindow" title="Enter Login Details"
        draggable="false" closable="false" resizable="false"
        width="450" height="200">
    <cfoutput>
    <form action="#cgi.script_name#" method="post" name="loginform">
    <table width="400" class="loginTable" cellpadding="5">
      <tr>
      <td>username:</td>
      <td><input type="text" name="username"></td>
      </tr>
      <tr>
      <td>password:</td>
      <td><input type="password" name="password"></td>
      </tr>
      <tr>
      <td> </td>
      <td><input type="submit" name="login" value="Login"></td>
      </tr>
    </table>
    </form>
    </cfoutput>
    </cfwindow>
    <cfoutput>
    <form action="#cgi.script_name#" method="post" name="changePasswor
dForm">
    <table width="400">
      <tr>
```

```
      <td>old password:</td>
      <td><input type="password" name="password"></td>
      </tr>
      <tr>
      <td>new password:</td>
      <td><input type="password" name="password"></td>
      </tr>
      <tr>
      <td> </td>
      <td><input type="submit" name="login" value="Login"></td>
      </tr>
    </table>
    </form>
    </cfoutput>
    <cfset AjaxOnLoad("init")>
</body>
</html>
```

This example is a little longer than our previous examples. But it makes sure that the user is logged in before he or she attempts to change a password. It's not a complete example but is intended to explain in a real-world application how to use the tag for illustration purposes. There are missing pieces. So DO NOT use it as it is!

Other Cool Commands

There are three JSON functions built into ColdFusion. Most of the time, you will find this is used in CF8 AJAX, where it is handled automatically. Yet, if you are working with Yahoo data or sending something to jQuery, then you might require the ability to work with JSON data along with built-in functions. You can dump the results with CFDump on the server side, and with the debugging dump function.

- JSONencrypt() converts to JavaScript object notation
- JSONdecrypt() converts from JavaScript object notation
- isJSON() checks to see if a variable's content is in a valid JSON format

Spry is an AJAX library created by ADOBE. It does many amazing things. The first time I came across the curly bracket data alias style of coding that we use in ColdFusion AJAX was in Spry. Shortly thereafter, I also found similar practice in ActionScript coding. This may not have been the first time it came to my attention. If we are going to work with Spry AJAX pages, then we need to convert data to Spry-based data for in-browser usage. The ins and outs of Spry could end up being as much text as we have on CFAJAX, if not more.

- CFSpryDataset()

Post for CFAJAX Calls

We will complete this chapter with a tip on how to send data to the browser via Post, instead of sending it via standard URL variables. We can send more data through a Post than we can though URL style variables.

```
<html>
<head>
<script type="text/javascript">
function cfcViaPost()
{
    Var pickyObject = new pickyCFC();
    pickyObject.setHTTPMethod("POST");
    pickyObject.doSomething();
}
</script>

</head>

<body>
    <cfajaxproxy cfc="pickyCFC">
    <cfinput type="button" name="test" onclick="cfcViaPost();">
</body>
</html>
```

Summary

It seems to me like there were so many subjects it was hard to tell where to stop. With that said you should think there is still plenty of content that isn't contained in this chapter. We have covered the following:

- Binding between object data and container objects
- Binding between CFCs and container objects
- Binding between URLs and container objects
- Binding between JavaScript and container objects
- How to make binding objects event sensitive
- Binding on multi-item objects like radio buttons, check boxes or multi-select boxes
- CFAJAXproxy for binding objects to JavaScript functions
- CFAJAXproxy to extend connectivity of CFCs to JavaScript class objects
- Success and Exception Handling on CFC proxy class objects execution

- Client Debugging with Firefox and Firebug
- Client Debugging with CFDebug in the browser
- Logging to the Client debugger
- Customization for AJAX component CFCs and Scripting
- Auto-wired AJAX Links
- OnLoad JavaScript function triggering
- Overview of JSON features
- Sending CFC targeted data via form Post versus URL type data

11
Working with PDF

PDF is a well-known technology. Not only is adding this feature better for the end users, but everyone who has a product wants to add PDF to the feature list. This tells us that if we can add PDF abilities to our web applications, it should increase the popularity and acceptance of our creations too. With the first version of ColdFusion by Adobe, the owner of PDF technologies, has included many PDF features into this version.

In this chapter, we will be looking at how to create a PDF document from common web pages. The output of the page will go to PDF, rather than HTML. We will see how to deliver the PDF to the browser, or to a file. We will also look at how to create and use PDF forms to collect and retrieve end-user data. Then, we will look at how to take the content of PDF pages and send them to printers available on the server where ColdFusion is running. In this chapter, we will also have a look at the different ways in which we can reorganize pages of PDF documents into a new PDF file from one or more separate PDF source documents.

Generating PDF Pages

Now, we all know that the end user can buy Adobe Acrobat and print the content of a page to a PDF file. Yet, what if someone could come to the website we build, and the reports and content could come to the browser as live PDF generated on demand, without them having to purchase additional software?

Our First PDF Page Conversion

Let's look at the code for a simple page, and then look at the same code converted into PDF content. We are going to take a combined page where we have data being put out into a standard HTML list. Then, we will place the data in a CFDump below the list. We could set many more fancy features for the page by using CSS and HTML. Most of the CSS features are supported, and this is a very powerful tool for page creation.

Here is the code we will using so that we have a bulk of content to place on the page. We will create an array of structures for our sample page data.

```
<cfscript>
myData = arrayNew(1);

for(i=1;i<20;i++){
    newStruct = structNew();
    newStruct.id = i;
    newStruct.value = "This is item #i# of the data.";
    arrayAppend(myData,newStruct);
}

</cfscript>
```

Now, we will include this data on a page and wrap the content with the ColdFusion <cfdocument /> tag. We could add many attributes to change the features of the document, but there is an essential attribute. This is the format attribute. Before ColdFusion was an Adobe product, it had the ability to create either Flash Paper or PDF. With the ownership of Adobe, there is little need to mention Flash Paper for much more than legacy support in this chapter.

```
<cfinclude template="data.cfm">
<cfdocument format="PDF">
    <cfoutput>
      <ul><cfloop
          from="1" to="#arrayLen(myData)#"
          index="iItem">
      <li>#myData[iItem].value#</li></cfloop>
      </ul>
    </cfoutput>
    <cfdump var="#myData#">
</cfdocument>
```

Now if you run this code, you will see two pages. The first page will be the bullet list we expect but the second page sort of gets clipped as it goes across the margin. It would be the same with anything that goes across the margin of a page. This is something we will have to be aware of when we are working with this technology. But most of these issues are easy to overcome.

Splitting into Sections

Here, we will create sections. We will put the list into one section and the dump content in another section. There are additional attributes for customizing the look of each session beyond the defaults we set for the pages. The defaults are set in the `<CFdocument/>` tag for the document. The sections will inherit all document attributes that are not explicitly declared.

```
<cfinclude template="data.cfm">
<cfdocument format="PDF">
  <cfdocumentsection>
    <cfoutput>
      <ul><cfloop
          from="1" to="#arrayLen(myData)#"
          index="iItem">
        <li>#myData[iItem].value#</li></cfloop>
        </ul>
    </cfoutput>
  </cfdocumentsection>

  <cfdocumentsection>
      <cfdump var="#myData#">
  </cfdocumentsection>
</cfdocument>
```

Adding Headers and Footers and Variables

Now we have multiple sections of content, and it would be good if we could set the headers and footers for the pages. We could actually set the headers and footers down to the level of each section if we so desired. We will be using `<CFdocumentitem/>` to add these features to our pages.

```
<cfinclude template="data.cfm">
<cfdocument format="PDF">

  <cfdocumentitem type="header">
  <h1>Example Header</h1>
  </cfdocumentitem>

  <cfdocumentitem type="footer">
  <h3>Example Footer</h3>
  </cfdocumentitem>

  <cfdocumentsection>
    <cfoutput>
      <ul><cfloop
          from="1" to="#arrayLen(myData)#"
          index="iItem">
        <li>#myData[iItem].value#</li></cfloop>
        </ul>
    </cfoutput>
  </cfdocumentsection>
```

```
    <cfdocumentsection>
        <cfdump var="#myData#">
    </cfdocumentsection>
</cfdocument>
```

We can run the previous code and see that it is absolutely easy to put headers and footers on our pages. You may refer to the main ColdFusion documents for additional features on these topics. One important thing we should know is that if things don't look right in our header, we may work with changing the margins in order to get it right.

Adding Page Breaks and Variables

The <CFdocumentitem/> element will be used again to add page breaks. Let's look at our code. Here, we see that there are a number of variables that we have added to our footer item. The following list shows the currently available dynamic cfdocument-scoped variables.

- currentPageNumber
- totalPageCount
- totalSectionNumber
- currentSectionNumber

```
<cfinclude template="data.cfm">
<cfdocument format="PDF">

    <cfdocumentitem type="header">
    <h1>Example Header</h1>
</cfdocumentitem>

<cfdocumentitem type="footer">
    <h3>Example Footer <cfoutput>(Page #cfdocument.
        currentPageNumber# of #cfdocument.totalPageCount#
</cfoutput>
    </h3>
</cfdocumentitem>

<cfdocumentsection>
    <cfoutput>
    <h5>First Set</h5>
        <ul><cfloop
            from="1" to="#arrayLen(myData)#"
            index="iItem">
        <li>#myData[iItem].value#</li></cfloop>
        </ul>
<cfdocumentitem type="pagebreak" />
    <h5>Second Set</h5>
```

```
            <ul><cfloop
                from="1" to="#arrayLen(myData)#"
                index="iItem">
            <li>#myData[iItem].value#</li></cfloop>
            </ul>
        </cfoutput>
    </cfdocumentsection>
    <cfdocumentsection>
        <cfdump var="#myData#">
    </cfdocumentsection>
    </cfdocument>
```

In the previous code, we can see that some `<h5>` HTML head tags are added so that
we could identify the segments and see where the page breaks are present. The
`<CFdocument type="pagebreak" />` is needed to move to a new page after the first
segment. Now, we can run the code and see it live on our browsers.

Adding Bookmarks

There are many things we can do with the robust technology built into ColdFusion
for building PDFs on the fly. We will look at one last feature before we move on.

```
<cfinclude template="data.cfm">
<cfdocument format="PDF"
            bookmark="yes">
<cfdocumentitem type="header">
    <h1>Example Header</h1>
</cfdocumentitem>
<cfdocumentitem type="footer">
    <h3>Example Footer</h3>
</cfdocumentitem>
<cfdocumentsection name="bullet list">
<cfoutput>
        <ul><cfloop
            from="1" to="#arrayLen(myData)#"
            index="iItem">
        <li>#myData[iItem].value#</li></cfloop>
        </ul>
</cfoutput>
</cfdocumentsection>
<cfdocumentsection name="data dump">
        <cfdump var="#myData#">
</cfdocumentsection>
</cfdocument>
```

Now, you may need to click on the bookmark option for your PDF viewer to see the
results. It was amazingly simple to put the bookmarks into our PDF document.

Saving PDF Documents

There is only one change needed to shift from sending the document to the browser to storing it in the file system. We just need to add the attribute `filename` to our `<CFdocument/>` tag. We will store it in the same directory as the file where it is running.

```
<cfinclude template="data.cfm">
<cfdocument format="PDF"
          bookmark="yes"
fileName="#getDirectoryFromPath(getCurrentTemplatePath())
                                        #document_6.pdf">

<cfdocumentitem type="header">
    <h1>File Store Example</h1>
</cfdocumentitem>

<cfdocumentitem type="footer">
    <h3>Example Footer</h3>
</cfdocumentitem>

<cfdocumentsection name="bullet list">
<cfoutput>
    <ul><cfloop
        from="1" to="#arrayLen(myData)#"
        index="iItem">
    <li>#myData[iItem].value#</li></cfloop>
    </ul>
</cfoutput>
</cfdocumentsection>

<cfdocumentsection name="data dump">
    <cfdump var="#myData#">
</cfdocumentsection>

</cfdocument>
```

Printing from the Server

When we look at printing our PDF documents from the server, we must approach the concept of printing in a different manner. It is also worth noting that while writing this book, we must declare the exact name of the printer because there isn't a default printer function. Perhaps this is best, since we are using a server and not a personal computer to do the printing. Printing from a network server may have several implications.

Let's start by modifying one of our documents and making the content print to a server. We are going to use OKI C3200n as it is the printer present in our network. But, we must remember that the name of the printer is case-sensitive. If needed, we can find these names in the server, in the ColdFusion Administrator Console.

```
<cfinclude template="data.cfm">
<cfdocument format="PDF" name="toPrint">

<cfdocumentitem type="header">
    <h1>Example Header</h1>
</cfdocumentitem>

<cfdocumentitem type="footer">
    <h3>Example Footer <cfoutput>(Page #cfdocument.currentPageNumber#
of #cfdocument.totalPageCount#)</cfoutput></h3>
</cfdocumentitem>

<cfdocumentsection>
<cfoutput>
    <h5>First Set</h5>
        <ul><cfloop
            from="1" to="#arrayLen(myData)#"
            index="iItem">
        <li>#myData[iItem].value#</li></cfloop>
        </ul>
<cfdocumentitem type="pagebreak" />
    <h5>Second Set</h5>
        <ul><cfloop
            from="1" to="#arrayLen(myData)#"
            index="iItem">
        <li>#myData[iItem].value#</li></cfloop>
        </ul>
</cfoutput>
</cfdocumentsection>

</cfdocument>
<cfprint type="pdf"
    source="toPrint"
    pages="2"
    printer="OKI C3200n" />
Your document has been sent to the printer.
```

We have simply added the `<cfprint/>` tag to our document and have used the variable "toPrint". This variable did not exist in our original example. We modified the `<cfdocument/>` tag to include a name attribute that tells ColdFusion what variable to store the PDF document in. We then set the printer just to print page 2 to our network printer. Substitute this with your own printer name on your system. This is it!

We have this same document stored as a file, and it would have been easy to pull it from the same directory. Here is the code that would accomplish the task of printing directly from a file. We included some text at the end of both these examples to let the user know that something has happened. A blank page certainly would not be the proper way to handle this practice.

```
<cfprint type="pdf"
    source="document_4.pdf"
    pages="2"
    printer="OKI C3200n"/>
Your document has been sent to the printer.
```

There are many attributes and options. We should explore this tag with thought about what we can do with it until we feel we have mastered the attributes. It might be good to go into the details, now and then, to get familiar with all the features.

Working with PDF Forms

When we build web forms, they do not appear like the paper forms that we have used for years in business. Sometimes, this gives us more flexibility than we could have on paper. Other times it just doesn't present as well. The Web is nice and is very flexible but we have perfected the art of doing business on paper long before the Web was even a consideration. PDF forms are a combination of the flexibility of web forms and the perfection of paper-based business processes. Let's look at how ColdFusion can use PDF technology to bring these two concepts together.

There are two major PDF integration functions that are made possible through ColdFusion. The first function is to populate the PDF form. This form can either be stored or sent to the browser, depending on whether the destination attribute is set or not. The second function is to read the contents of a PDF document's data and store it in a variable structure. Now they are brought down to simple integration functions by the power of ColdFusion. In both these cases, we will need to create our forms outside ColdFusion. This is very simple with the Adobe Acrobat software. We have included in the book files the PDF Forms needed to do all the exercises without using Acrobat. Of course, we can acquire a demonstration version to try this out from Adobe.com, if we so desire.

Populating PDF Forms with Data

While working with inserting data into PDF Forms, the data format used is an XML document. The picture here is a filled-out PDF Form being sent back to the data department. We can add logic to the required fields, and do something similar to what we do on web forms by using PDF forms. We put one required field, which is employee ID, on our testing form. It will prevent submission and display a generic warning if this field is left empty. We will leave it empty in our sample data for better understanding. We actually used the read function of this tag to get the XML structure so that the form can be filled. There is no need to create this manually, when it is so easy to just use the built-in features of ColdFusion.

```
<cfpdfform
    action="populate"
    source="timesheet.pdf"
    XMLdata="timesheet_data.xml"/>
```

This is all it takes to pull the `timesheet.pdf` file, and fill in the data with the contents of the file named `timesheet_data.xml`. Here are the results being sent back via email:

This opens the door to many other possibilities. We could have the employee timesheets stored as PDF files rather than HTML forms. These forms could be made available in a list for open weeks that have not gone into payroll processing at this time. The additional rules beyond that would be a part of any standard site. The management would decide how it was done, and we would just add the logic to our pages.

The `populate` function can also be used to create a stored version of the populated document. We would just need to add a destination attribute to the tag. What is the possibility of integrating the systems of different companies? We are going to create a data merge into a PDF form, and submit it to show how more specialized systems could be integrated using PDF forms. This would be practical if companies are working together and one of the companies had a standard timesheet. The other company already has a different time system. Using these techniques, the timesheet submissions could be automated based on the data entered in another system. So this code pulls the data from a web page, and places it in our timesheet ready to store. There should be security and other features added, but this should give you an idea on how to use this type of feature.

```
<cfpdfform
    action="populate"
    source="timesheet.pdf"
    XMLdata="http://localhost/cfb/code/chapter_11/employeeTime.cfm"/>
```

Now we have got the data from a local file, from a web server, and this will show us how to populate the data with unique variables. We need to use the subform tag for any nested levels. When we look at the results of reading the data in the next section, the result data variable dumped to the page will show us the nested structure to make this process simple to achieve. Here is the code for the form in our book example. We see that the data is nested in a subform called `form1` and then we use the names of the form fields and populate them with the appropriate data. This will make things easier for our users as they do not have to fill in details that can be assumed. They will also have the ability to change these fields if they choose to do so. If there are fields with the same name, then we need to add the index field to the `param` tag.

```
<cfpdfform
    action="populate"
    source="timesheet.pdf">
  <cfpdfsubform name="form1">
      <cfpdfformparam name="EmployeeName" value="Mary Jane" />
      <cfpdfformparam name="Date" value="#dateFormat(now())#" />
      <cfpdfformparam name="Required" value="32" />
  </cfpdfsubform>
</cfpdfform>
```

We see that the data from PDF forms can be moved back into the server with a submission button, or it can be emailed. If the users choose to email the data, it will come as an attachment in XML format. This could be sent to a unique email address, and we could use ColdFusion to parse the email folder and process the data. If the form is submitted via the Web, we can put the site target page address into the button of our PDF document. The next section covers how we read data from PDF forms.

We might also want to consider using some of this technology to create old-fashioned hard copies of documents where we take existing PDF documents and merge the data for just-in-time print integration.

```
<cfinclude template="data.cfm">
<cfdocument format="PDF">

<cfdocumentsection>
<cfoutput>
    <ul><cfloop
        from="1" to="#arrayLen(myData)#"
        index="iItem">
    <li>#myData[iItem].value#</li></cfloop>
    </ul>
</cfoutput>
</cfdocumentsection>

<cfpdfform
    action="populate"
    source="timesheet.pdf"
    XMLdata="timesheet_data.xml" />

</cfdocument>
```

In this example, we have used the code from the second CFDocument example. If we look at the example, we will see that the orientations of the two examples do not need to match. The main document is portrait, and the form we created is landscape in orientation. Yet they merge well together. Using this multiple form of merging, we can create some very personalized forms on the fly.

Reading Data from PDF Forms

Firstly, we will look at how we can read a blank form. If administration creates a form and sends it to us, or to the design department, then we can use the following technique to get the fields present in the form.

```
<cfpdfform action="read"
    source="timesheet.pdf"
    XMLdata="dataXML"
    result="dataResult" />

<cfdump var="#dataResult#" />
<cfdump var="#dataXML#" />
```

This will show us a structure view and a text representation of the XML string in the document. In some ways, this is so much easier than working with HTML forms. There are still many aspects that are not as dynamic as common HTML forms are, on a server such as ColdFusion. Yet, if that is a business requirement, then we should do some research about integrating our systems into LiveCycle by Adobe. There is a free version available under some business conditions.

If we take the form that we have populated earlier, change the data, and submit it back to the server via the Web, we will see the results of the page on the screen. Here is the code we are using to catch the contents of the PDF being sent back to the server.

```
<cfdump var="#form#">
```

It is quite simple to get the results of the PDF back from the server. The best thing about it is that it can come back as a standard form.

Manipulating PDF Documents

There are many ways in which we can change PDF documents. Here is a list of things we can do to manipulate PDF documents with ColdFusion. This is not a complete list, but it should give us a great idea of the power that we have in this new version of ColdFusion.

- We can take individual pages out of documents.
- We can merge documents together into another new document.
- We can add watermarks to or remove watermarks from documents.
- We can delete pages from documents.
- We can use DDX instructions to manipulate documents.
- We can set passwords and encrypt documents.
- We can read or set information about a document.
- We can generate thumbnails of our documents.

Merging Documents

Here is a simple code example to merge the documents. This is just an example to show how flexible the merge process can be.

```
<cfpdf action="merge"
    destination="#employee#_packet.pdf"
    overwrite="yes">
     <cfpdfparam source="contract.pdf" password="#employeePassword#" />
```

```
      <cfpdfparam source="benefits.pdf" />
      <cfpdfparam source="timeSheet.pdf" />
      <cfpdfparam source="ethics.pdf" />
      <cfpdfparam source="#position#.pdf" />
</cfpdf>
```

This shows us that we can merge both memory variable copies of documents such as the contract document and set a password on that individual part of the document. We can use dynamic variables to include things on the fly such as the position document describing the duties and information about the position that a particular person has accepted with the company. The information could also be packaged and sent immediately to the employee via email, or as hard copies if needed.

Deleting Pages

Here is a sample code to delete pages from a document. This example is pretty good because the footers of the pages in the resulting document say 1 of 4 and 2 of 4 in the final document when there are only 2 pages left. This is because similar to paper documents, PDF documents are what they were when they were generated. This makes a great way to verify that things are actually working as we expected. One big thing to watch out for here is that if you don't declare what the new document will be called, then the old document will get overwritten.

```
<cfpdf action="deletepages"
    pages="3-4"
    source="document_4.pdf"
    destination="newDoc_4.pdf">
```

Encrypting PDF Documents

There are times when a password is not considered to be secure enough for a PDF document. On these occasions, the solution is the power of encrypting the document. Here is a code sample to achieve this.

```
<cfpdf action="protect"
    source="generatedPDF"
    destination="secure.pdf"
    encrypt="AES_128"
    newOwnerPassword="thePassword"
    permissions="none"
    overwrite="yes" />
```

This code allows a person who has the permissions to open the file, but they can't print it or modify it. There are many permissions and they are listed at the end of the chapter. The point here is that we have lots of power to control our documents even after they "leave the building" as we put it.

Generating Thumbnails

Thumbnails of our PDFs can be created in either PNG, JPEG, or TIFF formats. Here is an example of code that will generate thumbnails of our timesheet PDF document. The tag stores the files in a nested thumbnails directory as it was left unnamed. This tag will create a thumbnail for every page in the document. We put a border around the image tag in HTML to make sure the outer edges of the thumbnail were distinct.

```
<cfpdf action="thumbnail"
    source="timesheet.pdf"
    format="png"
    imagePrefix="timesheet"
    overwrite="yes" />

<cfpdf action="thumbnail"
    source="document_4.pdf"
    format="png"
    imagePrefix="pdfThumb"
    overwrite="yes" />

Document_4.pdf pages<br />
<img src="thumbnails/pdfThumb_page_1.png" border="1">
 
<img src="thumbnails/pdfThumb_page_2.png" border="1">
 
<img src="thumbnails/pdfThumb_page_3.png" border="1">
 
<img src="thumbnails/pdfThumb_page_4.png" border="1">
<br />
Timesheet.pdf<br />
<img src="thumbnails/timesheet_page_1.png" border="1">
```

Here is a screenshot of the result after running this code. There isn't actually any control built in to control the size of these documents in a single stage. It is possible to use the CFImage tag to manipulate graphics with some of the amazing simplicity and power we have become accustomed to in ColdFusion.

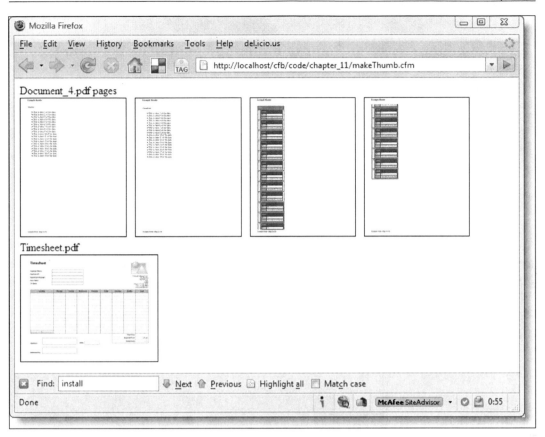

Adding Watermarks

Watermarks are a touch of class and a personalization that has been popular for many years. This is simple to achieve using ColdFusion and PDFs as well. Here is a sample code page that will achieve the goal. We have two types of watermarks here. The first is from a JPEG file. The png watermark didn't work as well as the jpg file. The second one includes a PDF as a watermark. This one has been rotated to make it look just a bit fancier.

```
<cfpdf action="addwatermark"
    pages="2-3"
    foreground="yes"
    image="logo.jpg"
    opacity="2"
    source="document_4.pdf"
    destination="watermark_1.pdf"
    overwrite="yes">
```

```
<cfpdf action="addwatermark"
    pages="2-3"
    foreground="yes"
    copyFrom="timesheet.pdf"
    rotation="-35"
    opacity="2"
    source="document_4.pdf"
    destination="watermark_2.pdf"
    overwrite="yes">
```

Final Thoughts

There are also permissions that can be set for documents to determine what someone is allowed to do with the PDF document in their possession. Here is a list of features we can restrict with the permissions attribute. We can use one or more in a comma-delimited list.

- All
- AllowAssembly
- AllowDegradedPrinting
- AllowCopy
- AllowFillIn
- AllowModifyAnnotations
- AllowModifyContents
- AllowPrinting
- AllowScreenReaders
- AllowSecure
- None

There is a whole level of power available using the DDX instructions, but that is definitely outside an introduction to using PDF with ColdFusion chapter. It is something that you should Google for and get more information on, if this is an area of interest in your ColdFusion development. Don't forget that there are many PDF files in the samples directories of the book files.

Summary

In this chapter, we can actually create content that can reach outside the browser through stored PDF documents and later have those files submit data back to the server. Here is a summary of what we have covered in this chapter.

- Generating PDF vis-a-vis HTML
- Page Headers and Footers, and Page Breaks
- Document Sections
- Output Variables
- Creating Bookmarks
- Printing from the Server
- Merging PDF Documents
- Deleting Pages from PDF Documents
- Encrypting PDF Documents
- Generating Thumbnails from PDFs
- Adding or Removing Watermarks in PDF Documents

12

Building Search Abilities

How much of our life is spent on looking for things? Knowing where something isn't can be almost as valuable as knowing where something is. If it isn't there, then the time and resources aren't wasted looking in the wrong place. If it is there, then locating it is the goal, and not the quest to locate it. The time we save in this quest can be put to better use somewhere else.

We will cover the following subjects just to make sure that we have a broad base of methods to manage our future search capabilities. We will look at searching with a database in the simple form of a dynamic FAQ system. We will look at the power of Verity that is included in ColdFusion. We will also learn how to integrate a third-party search solution.

Database Searching

When it comes to customized searches, this is a popular choice. If a person is familiar with SQL data, then he or she can use this technique repeatedly. This will be a very good solution for shopping carts and more where the searched information is part of the local site data. This can be a standalone feature for the site, or it can also be extended to integrate with some search engine tools. Searching a data table is one of the standard skills that we have learned in SQL. In this chapter, we will cover the integrated aspects of Coldfusion.

Verity Search Solutions

There are three main processes to build search abilities. They are as follows:

1. Create the collection
2. Index the collection
3. Build a search interface

Built-In Search Engine

Verity comes in package with ColdFusion. One of the reasons why people pay for ColdFusion is the incredible power that comes with this tool. It should be noted that one of the most powerful standalone commercial search engines is this tool. Some of the biggest companies in the world have expanded internal services with the help of the Verity tool that we will learn about.

We can see that in order to start, we must create collections. The building of search abilities is a three-step process. There is a standard ColdFusion tag to help us with each of these functions.

1. Create collections
2. Index the collections
3. Search the collections

These collections can contain information about web pages, binary documents, and can even work as a powerful way to search cached query result information. There are many document formats supported. In the real business world, the latest bleeding-edge solutions will still store a previous version. Archived and shared documents should be stored in appropriate formats and versions that can be searched. The ColdFusion manual has a big list of formats that are supported in this tool.

Creating a Collection

Now let us get started. The first thing is to make our collection. We will start by going to the ColdFusion Administrator under **Data & Services**.

Here, we will be able to add collections and edit existing collections. There is one default collection included in ColdFusion installations. This is the **bookclub** demonstration application data. We will be creating a collection of PDF documents for this lesson. We have placed a collection of ColdFusion, Flex, and some of the Fusion Authority Quarterly periodicals in a directory for indexing. Here is the information screen for adding the collection through the administrator.

Add New Verity Collections	
Name	devDocs
Path	C:\ColdFusion8\verity\collections\documents Browse Server
Language	English (Basic)
Enable Category Support	☑
Create Collection	

We choose to select the **Enable Category Support** option. Also, there are libraries available for multiple languages if that is appropriate in a collection. We now see that there is a new collection for our **devdocs**. There are four icons to work with this collection. They are, from right to left, index, optimize, purge, and remove actions. The **Name** link takes us to the index action. The collection gives us the number of actual documents present, and the **size** of the index file on the server. The screen will show the details of the index as to when it was last modified, and the language in which it is stored. It lists the categories, and also shows the actual path where the index is stored.

Verity Collections

Actions	Name	Documents	Size (Kb)
🔲🔲🔲🔲	bookclub	0	28
🔲🔲🔲🔲	devdocs	0	0

Here is a code version of creating a collection that would achieve the same thing. This means that it is possible to create an entire administrative interface to manage collections. It is also possible to move from tags to objects, and wrap up all the functions in that style.

```
<cfcollection
   action="create"
   collection="devdocs"
   path="c:\ColdFusion8\verity\collections\documents" />
```

If we have categories in our collection, and we want to get a list of the categories, then the following code must be used:

```
<cfcollection
    action="categoryList"
    collection="bookClub"
    name="myCats" />

<cfdump var="#myCats#">
```

We should find that while learning about and working with any new ColdFusion structure, we should observe the results on the screen.

Indexing a Collection

We can do this through the administration interface. But here, we will do it as shown in the the following screenshot. This is a limited directory that we have used as an example for searching.

This is the result of the **devdocs** submitted above.

This gave a result of 12 documents with a search collection of the size, 4,611 Kb. Now, we will look at how to do the same search using code and build the index outside the administrator interface. This will require the collection to be built before we try to index files into it. The creation of the collection can also be done inside the administration interface or in code. It should also be noted that ColdFusion includes a security called Sandbox Security. These three core tags for Verity searching among many others can be blocked if you find it better for your environment. Just consider what is actually getting indexed and what needs to be searched. Hopefully, documents will be secured correctly and it will not be an issue.

When we are making an index, we have to make sure that we can either choose to use a recursive search or not. A recursive search means that all the subdirectories in a document or web page search will be included in our search. It should also be noted that the service will not work for indexing other websites. It is for indexing this server only.

```
<cfindex name="myCats" action="refresh"
    collection="bookClub" recurse="true"
    type="path" extensions=".html .htm .cfm .cfml"
    key="c:\inetpub\wwwroot\documents\"
    urlpath="http://localhost/documents/" />
```

Your collection has been indexed.

It is important to note that there is no output from this tag. So we need to put some text on the screen to make sure the person using the site can know that the task has been completed. If we want to index a single file rather than a whole directory path, we can do it with this code:

```
<cfindex action="refresh"
    collection="bookClub" recurse="true"
    type="file" extensions=".pdf"
    key=" c:\inetpub\wwwroot\documents\ColdFusion\cf8_devguide.pdf"
    urlpath="http://localhost/documents/ColdFusion" />
```

Your collection has been indexed.

Searching a Collection

Now we have created collections and indexed the contents of those items. It is time to start knowing that something which we are looking for is not present in that collection. Not only will we learn how to find things but will also learn how to narrow our results in order to get more of what we want and less of what we do not require. The results will only be the links to the documents that contain the results for which we were looking.

The Search Form

We are going to build a search form that is simple, which will again reinforce the value of code reuse in ColdFusion. The techniques that we will use will involve including this page on another page, and using variables that can be set on either page. It should also be noted that this page can also be run independently. The scenario of running it independently will only allow for a singe default search result page. Here is the code.

```
<cfparam name="form.params" default="">
<cfparam name="target" default="searchVerity">
<cfoutput>
<form method="post" action="#target#.cfm">
   <p>
     Enter your search term(s) using AND, OR, NOT and parens.
     Surround an exact phrase with quotes.
   </p>
   <input type="text" name="params" size="75" value="#form.params#">
   <br />
   <input type="submit" value="Search">
</form>
</cfoutput>
```

We can see here that we have a variable called `params` that is passed through the `form` scope. We do this setting of `form` scope by setting our `form method` attribute to `post`. If we did not do that, the variables would return as URL variables. There is also an on-page variable called `target`. Its default value is set to `searchVerity` which is used in the `action` attribute of the form. The `action` attribute will direct the data of the form to the specified page. This page, as you will see, is included onto the search pages. So the `params` we set will be displayed in that form again when the actual search results are presented.

The Results Page

Our results code is opposite. The top items are the same default parameters as present on the form code. If we look at the bottom of the page, we will see that the form page is included, and it will be displayed above the search results. In this first example, there will be no change.

The next item we see is the actual search function. The `name` attribute is where the results of the search will be stored. The `collection` is the name of the Verity collection, where the information has been indexed. The `criteria` are the search parameters that were entered on the form. Then, we can choose how many context passages can be retrieved from a single document. Lastly, it sets how much context to pull for reference, and the maximum number of rows of results if found to pull.

The results are returned in a record set, which ColdFusion refers to as queries. Since this is stored in a record set, it can be treated the same way as other queries, and we will use a `cfoutput` to loop through the records for display. We will show the number of records returned before the loop for the user. Then, we will show the URL link to the results since this result set happens to contain web-accessible results.

```
<cfparam name="form.params" default="">
<cfparam name="target" default="searchVerity">
<cfsearch
    name="foundResults"
    collection="devDocs"
    criteria="#form.params#"
    contextPassages = "1"
    contextBytes = "300"
    maxrows = "100">
<cfinclude template="searchVerityForm.cfm">
<hr />
<h3>Search Results</h3>
This search returned a total of <cfoutput>#foundResults.recordCount#</
cfoutput> results.
<cfoutput query="foundResults">
<hr />
<p>
    File: <a href="#foundResults.URL#" target="_blank">#foundResults.
title#</a> (score=#foundResults.score#)<br />
    Highlighted Summary: #foundResults.context#
</p>
</cfoutput>
```

This is the type of content that we would get from searching for `cfajaxproxy` in our current data set where the examples were created.

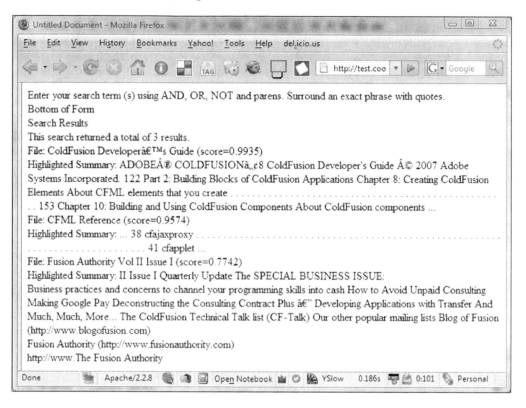

We can see that we get a reference link, a score on the chances of the returned results matching the searched query, then, we get a summary with the highlighted summary results. We can set the highlighting, but we have retained the default settings here. As the second result shows, the occurrences in our summary text are bolded. There are two ways to see the common fields in the query record set returned by the search tag. The first would be to go through the documents, but often, it would be helpful to see the actual results by using the `CFDump` tag.

Search Techniques

One consideration for using this search engine is that it runs a little differently from say Google. Now do not think that only this search engine is the right way to do things. The point to be noted is that we must consider the user habits and the training needed to achieve the best results by using this technique. As programmers, we are more familiar with the logical use of AND, OR, and NOT in phrases. Not to be outdone, we will also find that lawyers and other professions are actually as good as we are in this practice. The other general tip that may be of use is to add an * before or after a word to allow mixing of partial finds. This means that 'fish*' would find fish and fishing. The wild card modifier can be added before or after a search word. It should also be noted that a comma is translated as an OR in searches.

When we get ready to graduate to some more advanced searching, the ColdFusion documents also contain additional wild cards. The "?" represents a single character. The [ ] square brackets will find any one of the characters within them. Using the curly brackets { }, we can place a comma-delimited list of items to search for in our collection. The ^ symbol is the same as the NOT keyword, but it will allow us to find things like occurrences of words that do not have a character in them. The dash can be used within brackets to declare a range of characters. The last thing to note here is that if we want to look for a character such as "?", then we must place this \ slash in front of it within the search parameters. There are actually many other tips for finding things in collections. What we end up discovering is that the base tool set of Google has been created to make things simple. Yet, because it is the most common search tool, it is likely to be a standard based on which things are graded. As most of the terms are common here, it is fine.

To exclude a term from a search, place a "–" in front of the item. If we wish to include an item, then we lead the item with a + character. Phrases can be declared by placing double quotes around the phrase. If we have a query stored, we should be able to find something by declaring the field with a colon and then the item being searched for in that request. Lower case will find all results normally. We can code the criteria attribute to pass only lower case using the `lcase()` ColdFusion function if that can help.

There are a number of operators that need to be researched as the search engine power matures on a site. There are five basic types of operators (concept, relational, evidence, proximity, and score) and each of these types is of a magnitude that needs to be explored. With practice, we can attain mastery over this. One such master has built a business called Knowledge Watch in Michigan, USA (`http:www.knowledgewatch.com`). He has a business that runs based on ColdFusion search abilities, and vending result sets to the customers. He is a living proof that the information age is a good business to serve with ColdFusion.

If we find a client who has a need to search ColdFusion, Verity should be considered a very viable solution. There is much more information than could be covered in a chapter. Someone can run an entire seminar track just on ColdFusion's capabilities. It is not likely that we will push Google or Yahoo out of the market. But it is quite likely that we will be able to complete all the core needs of our clients.

PDF Linking to Searches

This is a great tip for working PDF searches into the mix. We just spoke about the differences in searches and this is one place where it comes into view. We can actually pass the search terms through to Acrobat. The search engine in Acrobat is different. Some detailed searches do not work in a similar manner. We will look at an example of how it works. While we will find that most of the searches work well, the ones that do not can be adjusted after the document loads.

In our example, we will say we have technical documents and we are looking for `ECMAScript edition 3`. Verity finds the Programming Actionscript 3 document for us. We want to be able to pass the search through, so when the document loads, we get search results. We will show a simple working concept here, and save the perfecting of the techniques for another book. Here is what we would pass through the URL:

```
http://localhost/documents/prog_actionscript30.
pdf#search="ECMAScript edition 3"
```

We add a pound sign, and the command that we are targeting at Acrobat.

> You need to pass the search parameters in quotation marks according to the documentation.

After searching the Web for details on PDF parameters, we found "Parameters for Opening PDF Files" on the Adobe website. It is a short but useful PDF document that will assist in maximizing the use of these types of resources. When we run this example, it opens a sidebar search stating what we were looking for, and a list box with the results available to scroll through and search within the document.

Other options of what can be done may reach beyond the search done by Verity. Here is a list of the parameters, and if we find a way to use them with a database-based search, the other parameters may be of great value.

- nameddest=destination
- page=pagenum
- comment=commentID
- collab=setting
- zoom=scale | scale,left,top
- view=Fit | FitH | FitH,top | FitV | FitV,left | FitB | FitBH | FitBH,top | FitBV | FitBV,left
- viewrect=left,top,wd,ht

- pagemode=bookmarks | thumbs | none (default)
- scrollbar=1 | 0
- search=wordlist (remember to place this list in quotes)
- toolbar=1 | 0
- statusbar=1 | 0
- messages=1 | 0
- navpanes=1 | 0
- highlight=lt,rt,top,btm
- fdf=URL (Specifies an FDF file to populate form fields in the PDF file being opened. This should be a URL location, and it should be the last parameter.)

Suggestions

One of the most popular additions to search engines over the years has been the suggestion of another search that might work better. Sometimes, spelling errors, or ambiguous requests can be an issue. ColdFusion's built-in capabilities to make suggestions are exceptional. The following highlighted rows are the changes needed to add this set of features. We just add two parameters to the search tag, `status` and `suggestions`. If we want to look at the results, we can use the CFDump to see the returned value and the names of the variables.

```
<cfparam name="form.params" default="">
<cfparam name="target" default="searchVerity2">
<cfsearch
    name="foundResults"
    collection="developmentDocs"
    criteria="#form.params#"
    status="info"
    suggestions="5"
    contextPassages = "1"
    contextBytes = "300"
    maxrows = "100">
<cfinclude template="searchVerityForm.cfm">
<hr />
<h3>Search Results</h3>
This search returned a total of <cfoutput>#foundResults.recordCount#</
cfoutput> results.
<cfif info.FOUND lte 5 AND isDefined("info.SuggestedQuery")>
<br>
Did You Mean:<cfoutput>
<a href="#target#.cfm?query=#info.SuggestedQuery#">#info.
SuggestedQuery#</a>
```

```
</cfoutput>
</cfif>
<cfoutput query="foundResults">
<hr />
<p>
    File: <a href="#foundResults.URL#" target="_blank">
       <cfif len(foundResults.title) EQ 0>
               - Result -
       <cfelse>
           #foundResults.title#
       </cfif>
          </a> (score=#foundResults.score#)<br />
    Highlighted Summary: #foundResults.context#
</p>
</cfoutput>
```

Integrating Third-Party Searching

The first thing we need to ensure is that we have the legal right to use information from other search engines. We also need to realize which are open-source products, as these will be more prone to changes. This means that it is a good idea to have some sort of logging and testing to ensure that this service remains available.

We are going to be looking at the integration of Google's site search features. We have integrated the site features into a custom tag to make things easier to implement. This is just a prototype of a full-featured work that we will make available later. Check my blog for details and other works.

Google Details

The page can be found at `http://www.google.com/sitesearch` at this time. Each technology has strengths and weaknesses. One thing to consider about adding the Google Search Engine to your site is that it tends to come with additional links to other resources in the **Standard Edition**. The **Business Edition** comes with no added advertisement at this time. Here is a chart to show the comparison of the two editions available at the time this was written. Check online for updates.

	Standard Edition	Business Edition
Google.com Quality Search	Yes	Yes
Hosted by Google	Yes	Yes
Ads Alongside Search Results	Required*	None
User Interface Customization	Limited	Complete Control with XML
Google Branding	Required	Optional
Email Support	No	Yes (English Only)
Phone Support	No	Yes (For premium customers)
Cost	Free	Starts at $100 per Year

* Non-profits, schools, and government do not need to show ads.

This search gives us the ability to include links outside as well as inside our site.

Custom Search Engines (Google)

Here is an example of a CSE (custom search engine) we built to highlight our COOP technologies. Custom search engines are not the same as the site search engines that Google provides. These custom engines can be for just one website, multiple websites, or for specific web pages. It is possible to provide the search results on our websites just like the site search. At this time, this technology is still in beta.

```
http://www.google.com/coop/cse/marker
```

CSE have some universal benefits. They help our visitors find what they are looking for. They can be hooked up to AdSense (another Google service) to create a revenue stream. If you are in a business, you can purchase this service in the **Business Edition** and get extra features similar to the site search that we looked at earlier. It is also possible to get multiple people contributing to these search engines to lighten the load of management.

On-The-Fly Search Engine

This is using the same Google CSE, but the results are translated to a search on the fly for the site containing the search. Of course, if we want additional control, then we should create something a bit more detailed. As the code clip says here, if we use this technology, we are agreeing to the terms of the service as Google states.

```
<script src="http://gmodules.com/ig/ifr?url=http://www.google.com/
coop/api/003333491672643455516/cse/v0m2otbkfli/gadget&amp;synd=open&am
p;w=320&amp;h=75&amp;title=COOP&amp;border=%23ffffff%7C3px%2C1px+solid
+%23999999&amp;output=js"></script>
Current time: <cfoutput>#now()#</cfoutput>
```

We did not create this code manually. It was generated by the Google webmaster tools. (It might also be worth looking into modifying the search with Google's "Subscribed Links".) Here is what this code looks like in our browser. When we created this search, we created a search based on the COOP open-source technology. We included a number of sites that we knew would return actual information that would be of interest to someone searching for this topic.

Here is what we get if we search in this quick search for **jQuery**. We will notice that it is searching sites that are not related to our chief search of COOP but this will be much narrower than searching the entire internet.

Now, while that may be nice, it has little to do with ColdFusion. If we want to do ColdFusion, we need to do a bit more. We will be looking at using a custom tag that was built to show off the power of searching with a remote search vendor through a custom tag interface. We will see how the same custom tag can allow for multiple solutions. We will do a standard search, a search type (web, video, blog, news, image, book) search, site-restricted search, local search, and show how to enter an initial value that loads the same time as the page does.

Simple Search

The simple search is mainly an introduction to our custom tag. In practical use, we should make sure that we get a Google ID and agree to the terms of use. We should not change the search content as returned by the provider unless the license permits that usage. The initial search box will look the same in all these searches, but the results are clearly different. In this case, we encapsulate the power offered by Google in a friendlier tag!

```
<!--- Simple Search --->
<cf_googleSearch id="simpleSearch"
   label="Search results"/>
```

We can see that the search is returning the top result by default. There is a set of three tool buttons that can return ever increasing numbers of results on the same page. It should be noticed that compared to the other search result, these results are AJAXed. This means that the results on the page update without loading a new page. We can also click on **X** besides the search to clear the results and the text.

Search Types

There are different types of contents that are indexed on Google. These content types include blogs, books, images, news, and video.

```
<!--- Declaring Search Types --->
<cf_googleSearch id="contentTypeSearch"
    searchBooks="true"
    searchImages="true"
    searchNews="true"
    searchVideo="true"
    searchBlogs="true" />
```

Here, we can see that our search has returned many types of content. We get the top item for each of these content types. We get regular web search results that work just like the simple search. Then we get our video results. Notice that the video result has independent tools that match the same features as the simple search. Yet, there is one more item that looks like a little gear of sorts. This is what we see when we click on it:

Each type of content may have its own unique settings and options. We will see similar unique controls for each type of content returned.

Site Restricted

We have thought about a search that works similar to our site. What if we have three or four sites that are related, and want to be able to return content for each of those sites? This is one of the unique things we can do very simply through Google and this custom tag. We will search `RiaForge` and `CFLib` for data-oriented content.

```
<!--- Site Restrictions --->
<cf_googleSearch id="restrictedGSearch"
    siteRestriction="riaforge.org,cflib.org"
    siteRestrictionLabels="RIA Forge, CFLIB" />
```

In the case of sites, we get one search for each site, and we can name the search section as we choose. We see that there is no option for special settings and options at this time.

Local Search

The local search is very simple. We use the same attributes that we would for a simple search. But in this example, we will not create a label but let the default label that has been returned from Google to be used. This is the town where the book was written, so we will use that as our point of reference. I personally enjoy acoustic guitar, so we will use that as the focus of our search this time.

```
<!--- Local Search --->
<cf_googleSearch id="localSearch"
    searchLocal="true"
    localSearchCenterPoint="Stevensville MI 49127" />
```

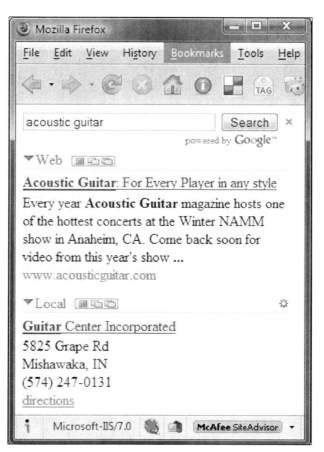

We do get a special option button for local searches. With this, we could enter into a new location, and the search will update on that location instantly.

There is one other attribute that may be useful. We can pre-populate the search that get's loaded into the browser with a default search using this attribute. We won't bother looking at a screen, but will instead look at the code.

```
<!--- Initial Value Search --->
<cf_googleSearch id="initValSearch"
    initSearchValue="RIA" />
```

Summary

In this chapter, we have covered a basic introduction to searching and have explained how to do different searches within the ColdFusion world of development. We have covered the following topics in this chapter:

- Creating Verity Search Collections
- Initializing the Verity Indexes
- Interfacing with the Indexes
- Interfacing with PDF content for more control when calling documents
- Doing simple Google searches
- Making Google searches simpler through custom tags

13
Working with Files, Email, and Images

When working with websites, there are some topics that we generally use over and over. The nature of dynamic sites includes knowing how to work with the areas of files, emails, and images. Dynamic websites do more than click from one page to another. This chapter will show how ColdFusion working with these common features will empower developers to shift web pages to web applications in very useful ways.

Working with Files

What is a file in the context of this section? We are going to focus on files the user may add to a site. These files in real world-sites could be zipped files, PDF files, images, or any other type of file. What is important here is that we learn how to let the website receive and manage what the user sends.

Uploading Files

We are going to start sending files from the user's browser to the server. Let's jump right in and look at the page code we are going to be using to select and send the file from the browser.

```
<cfset oFiles = createObject("component","file")>
<h3>File Upload Example</h3>
<cfif structKeyExists(form,"fileContents")>
    <cfset currentDirectory = getDirectoryFromPath(getCurrentTemplatep
ath())>
    <cfset fileData = oFiles.
uploadFile(destination:"#currentDirectory#testFolder\
",fileField:"fileContents")>
    File was uploaded!
    <br />
```

This is the structure that is returned when we upload a file:

```
<cfdump var="#fileData#">
<cfelse>
<form method="post" action="" name="uploadForm" enctype="multipart/
form-data">
    <input name="FileContents" type="file"><br />
    <input name="submit" type="submit" value="Upload File">
</form>
</cfif>
```

We have moved the file functions into a component called `file.cfc`. That is why the first line of our page code calls this object class and creates and instance. We then have a simple form with a file input box and a submit button. The logic inside our page looks to see if the form variable "FileContents" exists. If it does the file will be uploaded to our server. Of course on the first attempt this will not exist and the form will be displayed.

This is an example of a self-posting form page. It is common for many applications to post a form to a different page. In general, it is best to follow some administration of pages and make sure that you have an authenticated user doing any file uploading on your site. Though the concept is outside the focus of this chapter, it is important to take into consideration while we are building real-world applications. Here is the file upload page in the browser:

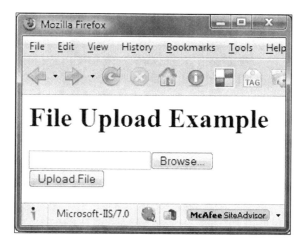

Here is the code for the file upload method that is called in the file upload page:

```
<cffunction name="uploadFile" output="false">
    <cfargument name="destination" required="true">
    <cfargument name="fileField" required="true">
    <cfargument name="accept" required="false" default="">
```

```
      <cfargument name="nameConflict" required="false"
                                      default="overWrite">

      <cfset var myReturn = ''>
      <cffile
        action = "upload"
        destination = "#arguments.destination#"
        fileField = "#arguments.fileField#"
        accept = "#arguments.accept#"
        nameConflict = "#arguments.nameConflict#"
        result = "myReturn">

      <cfreturn myReturn>
  </cffunction>
```

When we submit the file, we will get the following results. Notice all the file values that are returned. Most of what we need to know when handling uploaded files is contained in this detailed structure.

We can see that there are options that can be set for if we want a file to be overwritten or not. There are options for creating unique names, if the file exists. In the ColdFusion 8.0.1 update, there is also an option for how long it takes to timeout during the upload. Check the documents for this new feature.

Local File Control

Even after we get files into our system, we may have files that need to be edited or created in the workflow of the user interaction with the site. We will be going over an example that performs multiple functions.

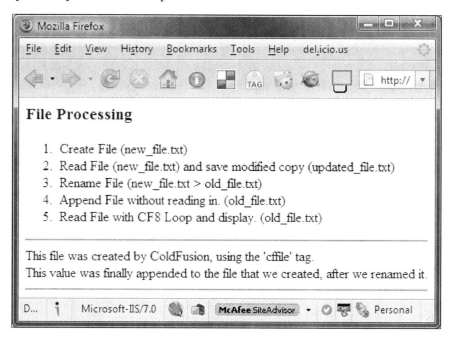

The previous screenshot shows us what we will be doing inside our code. The horizontal rule separated section at the bottom of the page is the output from item number five. Then we see an output example. Let's take a look at the code that was used to produce this sample. We could have done this all in the main template, but this is good practice in order to learn the use of CFCs. Again, remember that when we are prototyping, we may not be doing things in the same form that we would be doing in a final product. That can be reworked after we get our basic application running. One of the goals of this book is to get people to use and understand CFCs. So, we will take a liberty and place that code in an object class.

```
<cfscript>
oFiles = createObject("component","file");
// 1. Create File
```

```coldfusion
oFiles.writeFile(
    file:"#getDirectoryFromPath(getCurrentTemplatepath())#new_file.
txt",
    value:"This file was created by ColdFusion, using the 'cffile'
tag."
);
// 2. Read File Append
myFile = oFiles.readFile(
    file:"#getDirectoryFromPath(getCurrentTemplatepath())#new_file.
txt"
) & "This is extra content added inside CF before saving.";
oFiles.writeFile(
    file:"#getDirectoryFromPath(getCurrentTemplatepath())#updated_
file.txt",
    value: myFile
);
// 3. Rename File
oFiles.renameFile(
    source:"#getDirectoryFromPath(getCurrentTemplatepath())#new_file.
txt",
    destination:"old_file.txt"
);
// 4. Append File
oFiles.appendFile(
    file:'#getDirectoryFromPath(getCurrentTemplatepath())#old_file.
txt',
    value:"This value was finally appended to the file that we
created, after we renamed it."
);
</cfscript>

<h3>File Processing</h3>
<ol>
    <li>Create File (new_file.txt)</li>
    <li>Read File (new_file.txt) and save modified copy (updated_file.
txt)</li>
    <li>Rename File (new_file.txt > old_file.txt)</li>
    <li>Append File without reading in. (old_file.txt)</li>
    <li>Read File with CF8 Loop and display. (old_file.txt)</li>
</ol>
<!--- 5. Read File with CFLoop --->
<hr />
<cfloop file="#getDirectoryFromPath(getCurrentTemplatepath())#old_
file.txt" index="iLineText">
    <cfoutput>#iLineText#</cfoutput><br/>
</cfloop>
<hr />
```

Write File

This code is a bit more commented than has been done in other sections of our book. This is because we are doing many individual actions, which we will look at one at a time here. We create an instance of our file interaction CFC, and then we call a function to receive content and save it to a file. Most of these functions have more optional attributes, but we are going to look at the most basic and commonly used attributes in our examples. Here is the function in our object code:

```
<cffunction name="writeFile" output="false">
    <cfargument name="file" required="true">
    <cfargument name="value" required="true">

    <cffile
        action = "write"
        file = "#arguments.file#"
        addNewLine="yes"
        output = "#arguments.value#">
</cffunction>
```

This is the calling code:

```
oFiles.writeFile(
    file:"#getDirectoryFromPath(getCurrentTemplatepath())#new_file.
txt",
    value:"This file was created by ColdFusion, using the 'cffile'
tag."
);
```

We see two parameters that are passed both to the method and then again to the file tag. There are two standard functions that are used to get the actual current directory of the ColdFusion page that is being run. Then, we append the filename to the location where we are creating the file. This will create a file with the content of the `value` variable.

Read File

Here is the method code for the read file method. This is about as easy as it gets.

```
<cffunction name="readFile" output="false">
    <cfargument name="file" required="true">
    <cfargument name="charset" required="false" default="">

    <cfset var myReturn = ''>
    <cffile
```

```
    action = "read"
    file = "#arguments.file#"
    variable = "myReturn">
  <cfreturn myReturn>
</cffunction>
```

Here is the calling code again. We read the file from the current directory, and then immediately add additional text to the content variable. Lastly, we use the same write file function as we used previously, and then we create a file with another name.

```
myFile = oFiles.readFile(
file:"#getDirectoryFromPath(getCurrentTemplatepath())#new_file.txt"
) & "This is extra content added inside CF before saving.";
oFiles.writeFile(
file:"#getDirectoryFromPath(getCurrentTemplatepath())#updated_file.
txt",
    value: myFile
);
```

Rename File

Here is the function code for renaming our files:

```
<cffunction name="renameFile" output="false">
    <cfargument name="destination" required="true">
    <cfargument name="source" required="true">

  <cffile
    action = "rename"
    destination = "#arguments.destination#"
    source = "#arguments.source#">
</cffunction>
```

Here is the code to call the function. We follow the same process as for getting the filename for the source, but for the destination; we can assume that it is writing to the same directory. If we take the complete filename away, we get an error on our system that it couldn't write a file to that directory. If we wish to put the file in a specific directory, we could name that directory.

```
oFiles.renameFile(
source:"#getDirectoryFromPath(getCurrentTemplatepath())#new_file.txt",
destination:"old_file.txt"
);
```

Append File

Here is the function code for appending additional content to a file:

```
<cffunction name="appendFile" output="false">
   <cfargument name="file" required="true">
   <cfargument name="value" required="true">

   <cffile
     action = "append"
     file = "#arguments.file#"
     output = "#arguments.value#">
</cffunction>
```

Here is the code that we use to call and pass in the content that we want to append to our file. Again, we see the same full path is passed in.

```
oFiles.appendFile(
file:'#getDirectoryFromPath(getCurrentTemplatepath())#old_file.txt',
value:"This value was finally appended to the file that we created,
after we renamed it."
);
```

Read File via Loop

Here, we see a new feature of CFLoop where we can use a file as a source, and loop through the file based on the lines of content. Each loop it looks for a single line of code and pulls that line into the index variable. When it reaches the last line, it exits looping after that particular loop.

```
<cfloop file="#getDirectoryFromPath(getCurrentTemplatepath())#old_
file.txt" index="iLineText">
   <cfoutput>#iLineText#</cfoutput><br/>
</cfloop>
```

Working with Email

We will continue writing our code with much of our core functionality being separated into a CFC. We will look at sending a message, retrieving a list of messages, pulling back individual messages, and even deleting messages from our server. Remember that it is a real delete function. So do not delete a valuable piece of mail. Here is our base page and the code. This page lets us send email either with or without an attachment. There are a few required fields. We must fill in the fields for the server. Just fill them all in to make sure it is a good way to test for now.

```
<cfparam name="form.server" default="">
<cfparam name="form.user" default="">
<cfparam name="form.password" default="">
<cfparam name="form.to" default="">
<cfparam name="form.subject" default="">
<cfparam name="form.attach" default="">
<cfparam name="form.message" default="">

<cftry>
<cfscript>
oMail = createObject("component","mail").init(
    server:form.server,
    user:form.user,
    password:form.password
);
oFile = createObject("component","file");

if(structKeyExists(form,"submit")){
    fileStruct = structNew();
    attachment = "";
    if(len(form.attach)){
```

```
        fileStruct = oFile.uploadFile(
    destination:"#getDirectoryFromPath(getCurrentTemplatepath())#attac
hments\",
    fileField:"attach"
);
    attachment = fileStruct.serverDirectory & "\" &
      fileStruct.serverFileName & "." &
        fileStruct.serverFileExt;
}
oMail.send(
    to:form.to,
      from:form.user,
      subject:form.subject,
      message:form.message,
      attachFile:attachment,
      removeFile:true
);
}
</cfscript>

<cfoutput>
<form action="mail_out.cfm" method="post" enctype="multipart/form-
data">
    Server:<br />
     <input name="server" type="text" value="#form.server#"><br />
    User (from):<br />
     <input name="user" type="text" value="#form.user#"><br />
    Password:<br />
     <input name="password" type="password" value="#form.password#"><br
/>
To:<br />
    <input name="to" type="text" value="#form.to#"><br />
    Subject:<br />
     <input name="subject" type="text" value="#form.subject#"><br />
    Message:<br />
     <textArea name="message">#form.message#</textArea><br />
    Attachment:<br />
     <input name="attach" type="file"><br />
     <input name="submit" type="submit" value="Send Mail">
</form>
</cfoutput>

    <cfcatch>
        <cfdump var="#cfcatch#">
        <cfdump var="#form#">
    </cfcatch>
</cftry>
```

This code allows us to send email, either with or without an attachment. We also included the dump routines so that experiments can be done, and the exceptions are easier to spot. If an email does not go through, it is good to note how email works internally for the CF Server. Inside the CF directory, there is a directory called "Mail" with two sub-directories "Spool" and "Undelivr". If the mail has not yet tried to deliver, we can find it in the Spool directory. If the delivery of the mail fails, it can be found in the Undelivr folder. As of 8.0.1, you can also set a flag to delete attachments upon delivery. Remember to copy all the attachments to a directory where you aren't working with the originals. Also be cautious about attaching the same file for two users, if you are using this technique. This code is just a base to get us started. It is also key to remember that we could also include the user/password fields to give more power in order to connect to many mail servers on the fly, but we are using the settings for the default email server set in the ColdFusion Admin.

Here, we are re-using the file handler upload section, which we have discussed before. We create a variable called "attachment" that is zero length unless it gets an attachment directory placed into it. This directory is the result of a file upload from a page post. Let us look at the mail `send` method in our CFC.

```
<cffunction name="send">
    <cfargument name="to" required="true">
    <cfargument name="from" default="#variables.cfg.user#">
    <cfargument name="password" default="#variables.cfg.password#">
    <cfargument name="subject" required="true">
    <cfargument name="message" required="true">
    <cfargument name="type" default="text/HTML">
    <cfargument name="attachFile" default="">
    <cfargument name="removeFile" default="false">

    <cfmail
        to="#arguments.to#"
        from="#arguments.from#"
        password="#arguments.password#"
        server="#variables.cfg.server#"
        subject="#form.subject#"
        type="#arguments.type#"
        remove="#arguments.removeFile#">
    <cfif len(arguments.attachFile)>
        <cfmailparam
            file="#arguments.attachFile#">
    </cfif>
    #arguments.message#
    </cfmail>

</cffunction>
```

Thus, we can see that most of the arguments are just passed in but there are two special attributes that change the way the email is handled. The first is the attached file location. If this is included, then we add the attachment to our outgoing email. There is also a new attribute in CF 8.0.1 known as `remove`. This includes the information into the spooled email so as to know how to remove the attached file when it is sent. This is a great tool to assist in preventing stray files utilizing our disk space.

*** CF8 Update 1 Notes:

- The `cfmail` and `cfmailparam` tags have a `remove` attribute that tells ColdFusion to remove any attachments after successful mail delivery. If you have any mail that does not get delivered, you can look in the undelivered mail folder, and open a mail to see where the associated file for that email is located.

- The `cfmailparam` tag has a `content` attribute that allows you to send the contents of a ColdFusion variable as an attachment. You can do so by specifying the variable wrapped in # signs as the content attribute value in the following example:

  ```
  <cfmailparam file="myAttachment" content="#myContent#">
  ```

- The filename is not the file on the ColdFusion system, but the filename to be included in the mail header.

Working with Images

Historically, one of the most requested features for ColdFusion has been native graphics-processing features. It does not process photos on the level of Photoshop, but it does many things that are said to have more than a handful of wonderful features.

Let's look at our first image-handling code. We will also create each of our images before sending them to the page. It is a best practice to separate processing from display code wherever possible, and this is what we will do on this page. The next thing we will do is create a new image to work with, that is 100 by 100 pixels. We set a size attribute of 50, which we will use for all of our coding examples. Then, we set the color of our pen to black. Lastly, we draw some text on the image that we created earlier. The text is the number 1.

The next two segments of code processing are for images 2 and 3. This example pulls a graphic from a file. The image is copied for later use. Then, we set the drawing color to white, and place it on the image. The third segment of code for image 3 creates a red square of the same size as our other images. It then sets the drawing color to green, and puts a number 3 on the image.

The last processing logic in this example is when we take the copy of our image 2 and rotate it 45 degrees. We then paste this image over the copy of the red image as we did in the third step. We do have to offset the image location because the image rotates from the corner, and not from the center of the image. The drawing color is set to orange, and then we paste the text "45" with the degree mark specially coded as character "176", to show the degree symbol. Now that our processing is complete, we can move to presentation. We have simple code here to output all four of our images. The first image has an `alt` tag. This ability was added in version 8.0.1 of CF.

```
<cfscript>
attributes = structNew();
myImage = ImageNew("", 100, 100, "argb");
attributes.size = 50;
imageSetDrawingColor(myImage,"black");
imageDrawText(myImage,1,30,70,attributes);

//Process Image 2
myImage2 = ImageNew("images\shell.png");
// copy for later in code
copyImage2 = imageCopy(myImage2,0,0,100,100);
imageSetDrawingColor(myImage2,"White");
imageDrawText(myImage2,2,30,70,attributes);

//Process Image 3
myImage3 = ImageNew("", 100, 100, "argb", "ff0000");
imageSetDrawingColor(myImage3,"Green");
// copy for later in code
copyImage3 = imageCopy(myImage3,0,0,100,100);
imageDrawText(myImage3,3,30,70,attributes);

//Work with Copies
imageRotate(copyImage2,45);
imagePaste(copyImage3,copyImage2,-25,-25);
imageSetDrawingColor(copyImage3,"Orange");
imageSetAntialiasing(copyImage3,"ON");
imageDrawText(copyImage3,'45#chr(176)#',24,70,attributes);

</cfscript>
A number as an image.<br/>
<cfimage action="writetobrowser"
    alt="A number as an image."
    source="#myImage#" format="png"/><br/>
An image with number combined on it.<br/>
<cfimage action="writetobrowser"
    source="#myImage2#" format="png"/><br/>
Number as image on colored background.<br/>
<cfimage action="writetobrowser"
```

```
    source="#myImage3#" format="png"/><br/>
Same image rotated 45 degrees with text.<br/>
<cfimage action="writetobrowser"
    source="#copyImage3#" format="png"><br/>
```

Here is the screenshot from the code that shows a sample of what can be done with ColdFusion.

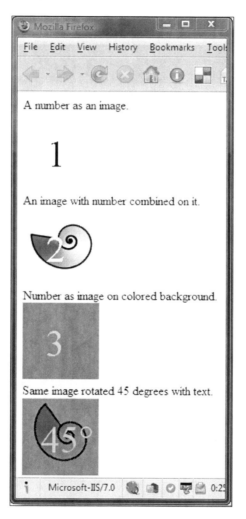

One thing worth noting is how the text of the 45 degrees looks as compared to the other text. This is because we turned the anti-aliasing on for the target object, while drawing the text in. If we want to make a site with dynamic graphics, then this would be the key to clean professional presentation. We could create custom tags for creating tabs, sidebar items, and more. They would have clean anti-aliased text on nice graphical backgrounds. We can check to see if graphics exist before generating them, and even cache the section of code to make things run faster. The point is that skinning a website could reach new levels of power by using these techniques.

Image Information

Here, we will see what we can get if we start using the image information readers in ColdFusion 8. One thing we know is that the browser is too small to display a full-resolution image. How do we know the size of an image? Let's look at two ways of getting the information. We will pull in an image of an old barn. We will then capture the metadata of the image and store that. Next, we will dump the metadata. In the dump, we see that the height and width as well as the source name are a part of the information. There is also some more specific information we can use if it is helpful to us. In our case, we are concerned about making sure that the image fits into the screen.

We should also note that after dumping the data collection to the screen, we have functions in ColdFusion that tell us the height and width of the image directly. These are some of the better ways to check if an image should be rescaled.

```
<cfscript>
myImage = ImageNew("images\Barn.jpg");
myData = imageInfo(myImage);
</cfscript>
<cfdump var="#myData#">
<cfoutput>
Width: #imageGetWidth(myImage)#<br />
Height: #imageGetHeight(myImage)#<br />
</cfoutput>
```

This is a dump of the data for the barn image file metadata.

We can tell this image is NOT going to fit inside a browser window! Well, perhaps some users actually have a computer monitor big enough to view this image. The rest of us who aren't so fortunate do not wish to hear about it! We want to learn how to automate re-sizing the image in the right-size for the browser. The server is unaware of the browser size. So we will create a size that is expected to work with most browsers. Let's figure for larger views as everyone can see an image of 640 by 480. This will allow us to have the picture and other content on the screen as well. We will not add the other content here, but we will create the code in order to manage the images well. Try some more, and see how things work.

```
<cfscript>
myImage = ImageNew("images\Barn.jpg");
imageScaleToFit(myImage,640,480);
```

```
</cfscript>
<cfimage action="writeToBrowser"
   source="#myImage#">
```

This picture happens to be of same width and height. This scale-to-fit function will translate the image to be "no bigger" than the size listed, but still the original shape of the source image should be present. This is called preserving the aspect ratio by photographers and image type professionals. With that information, we could look at a directory, pull all the images, and make thumbnails of those images. Then, we could display them on the screen. We will read the directory and then loop through the images. We will store the resized images back to the source folder, and then display them with standard HTML image tags.

```
<cfset myPath = getDirectoryFromPath(cgi.CF_TEMPLATE_PATH)>
<cfdirectory action="list"
   directory="#myPath#images"
```

```
        name="files"
        filter="*.jpg">

<cfloop query="files">
    <cfif left(files.name,3) NEQ "th_">
    <cfscript>
        thisImage = imageNew("images/#files.name#");
        imageScaleToFit(thisImage,50,50);
        imageWrite(thisImage,"images/th_#files.name#");
        </cfscript>
     <cfoutput>
         <img src="images/th_#files.name#">
         #files.name# thumbnail created.<br />
     </cfoutput>
    </cfif>
</cfloop>

Image Thumbnails Complete.
```

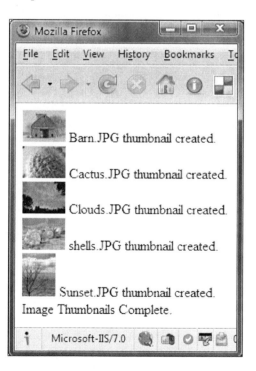

We first pull a listing of the directory where the files are located. We are only pulling in the `.jpg` files for this example, so we have filtered those files. We then loop through the listing. Each file is loaded and then scaled to no larger than 50 pixels on either axis. Next, we store the resized image as a thumbnail in the same directory. Last in our sequence is putting a copy of the file out to the screen and text to declare what is there. We see the images we get when we run the page. They are being pulled from the same directory. Now, we can get creative and make a gallery or any other thing.

Note: You can find more of my daughter's photos at:
`http://www.flickr.com/photos/susannajoy`

*** CF8 Update 1 Notes:

- When using images that store color as CMYK, the information is converted to RBG for processing. The source image is not changed.

- The `cfimage` tag and image functions now retain the `EXIF` data after operating on an image. This is the data most digital cameras store about an image and some other tools. Check out more details at `http://www.exif.org/` for more information.

- Now, there is support for `alt`, `style`, and other standard HTML attributes in the `CFImage` tag. In the first code sample for images, you can see where the `alt` tag is used.

Summary

It may not take the least number of lines to use CFCs to group common functions together as we have done in this chapter, but it does allow for separation of thought. One of the big wars among computer coders is the question of procedural coding versus pure object-oriented coding. The truth is that each set of functions that happen one after the other is procedural. The real benefit comes by putting groups of common functions into common segments where the shared features can be updated. We can see only one example in this chapter where the optional sending of an attachment with an email is partially encapsulated. It would be better encapsulated if all that logic was moved out of the base procedural code.

In this chapter, we have learned the basics of many areas of web development and the code could be re-used very easily, since it is wrapped into objects. In fact, one advantage is that with this structure we can re-use all the ColdFusion object methods inside script because the methods can be called from script where the tag-based use cannot. Thus, we are finding that objects make these resources more accessible. This also allows business logic and secondary functions such as logging to be packaged into the same methods, and universally cared for without additional code in calling pages.

Here is what we have covered in this chapter.

- File
  - ◦ Upload
  - ◦ Create
  - ◦ Read
  - ◦ Rename
  - ◦ Append

- Email
  - ◦ Send
  - ◦ Attachments
  - ◦ Deleting attachment upon send
  - ◦ Reading the list of mail on server
  - ◦ Getting an individual message
  - ◦ Deleting a message from server

- Images
  - ◦ How to get a copy of an image inside CF to work on
  - ◦ How CF can create an image
  - ◦ Writing text into an image
  - ◦ Copying an image into another image
  - ◦ Anti-aliasing text we write on image
  - ◦ Getting image metadata (width, height, and more)
  - ◦ Resizing graphics (into thumbnails)

14

Feeds, REST Services, and Web Services

The common thinking is that the Web is only about email and web pages. But today, we can see that it has become much more than that. In this chapter, we are going to look at how to reach out and become a part of the web community. We will learn the basics of interacting with other web servers and creating features on our site that will allow others to interact with us.

Collaboration

We have many ways of sharing content. We will look at these by using some of the more popular services. We will cover multiple techniques that are available in some of the more common interactive websites.

Flickr

Over the four years since its launch, this site has gathered a lot of content. The membership of Flickr, and the number of photos included in it are astounding. Flickr has a robust interface. We will start by looking at some of the feeds that it offers.

Feeds

There are several types of feeds. Different sites offer different feeds. We will cover a small variety of Flickr feeds so that we get a grasp of what can be done. Browsers send requests that are typed into the address bar to the server via a protocol called HTTP. These HTTP requests form the way in which the feeds are normally addressed.

We will get the ID of a group at http://www.flickr.com/groups/. Once you are at the group, go to the link 'feed' on the page and copy the ID for the code.

If your site hits the main site on each request from your site, it is considered an abuse and may result in Flickr blocking requests.

RSS

This is an XML-based response package technology. It is the most common feed type consumed by external users. This is proved by the number of tools that have RSS readers. Nearly every current browser and most of the current email programs now have the ability to request RSS feeds. There are many types of RSS standards. So we need to make sure that we test whether the feed is working or not.

```
http://api.flickr.com/services/feeds/groups_pool.gne?id=#flickr.
group_id#&format=cdf
```

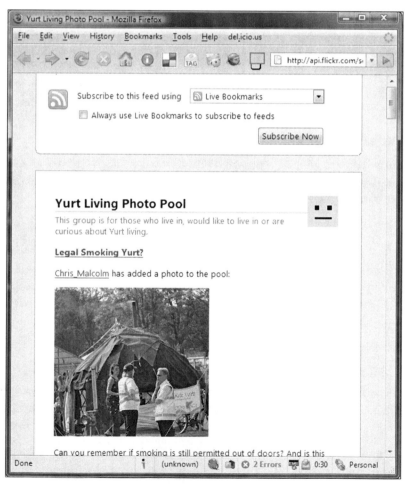

In the preceding screenshot, we can see the RSS feed and a checkbox that allows the site to be bookmarked. We can paste the feed address into any RSS tool, and it would work. The feed does not send the graphics and HTML formatted text in the way that it appears on the browser here. It is an XML file that is being translated. It is good that tools are aware of the standards and are able to translate to a user friendly presentation like this.

ColdFusion can take the XML feed and store it into a database or pass it to any other function that can be written. Let's take this same feed and translate the XML and then use it to create a custom page of our own, if we can get it written fast enough before the data of the feed gets updated. Pardon the shrinking, but it returns tons of data. This is a straight CF Dump of the converted XML structure.

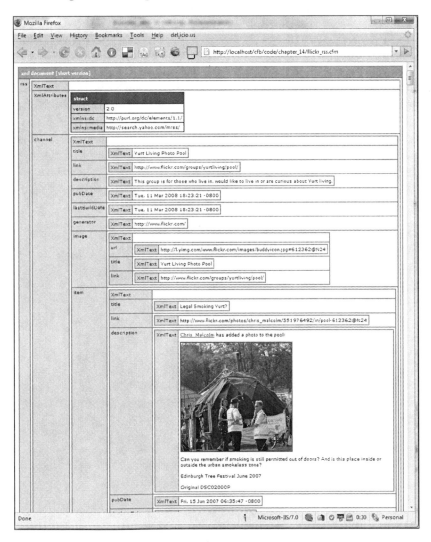

Now, we can use the structure and turn it into a ColdFusion page. We will see how we can handle it in ColdFusion. Here is the code:

```
<cfhttp url="http://api.flickr.com/services/feeds/groups_pool.
gne?id=#flickr.group_id#@N24&lang=en-us&format=rss_200">

<cfscript>
flickr_xml = cfhttp.filecontent;
feed = xmlParse(flickr_xml);
</cfscript>

<cfdump var="#feed#">
```

Did you notice that the `cfhttp` tag didn't need anything other than the URL attribute? This tag stores the content by default in a variable structure called `cfhttp`. We pull the return value coming back from the server from the variable file content inside that structure. Lastly, we convert it with the built-in XML parse function for dumping to the screen.

Now, we can build a processor to show the RSS feed in our own custom format. To comply with the Flickr standard at this time, we must make sure all pictures link back to the Flickr service page where the source photo is located at `Flickr.com`. This will be simple as that link is a part of the feed that is already formatted. There is a tag called `<cffeed />` in ColdFusion 8, but we want to pull some of the namespace content that does not get delivered with that tag. The same applies with any other XML that we need to parse. We are going to learn how to use minor XML here. This also shows the simple power of doing XML inside CF.

```
<cfhttp url="http://api.flickr.com/services/feeds/groups_pool.
gne?id=#flickr.group_id#=en-us&format=rss_200">

<cfscript>
flickr_xml = cfhttp.filecontent;
feed = xmlParse(flickr_xml);
items = xmlSearch(feed,"/rss/channel/item/");
</cfscript>
<ul>
<cfoutput>
<cfloop from="1" to="#arrayLen(items)#" index="i">
    <cfset thumb = xmlSearch(feed,"/rss/channel/item[#i#]/media:
thumbnail")>
  <li>
      <img  src="#thumb[1].xmlAttributes.url#"
          height="#thumb[1].xmlAttributes.height#"
          width="#thumb[1].xmlAttributes.width#"
          alt="#items[i].title.xmlText#"
          align="middle" vspace="3">
```

```
        <span>
          <a href="#items[i].link.xmlText#" target="_blank">
            #items[i].title.xmlText#
          </a>
        </span>
      </li>
  </cfloop>
  </cfoutput>
  </ul>
```

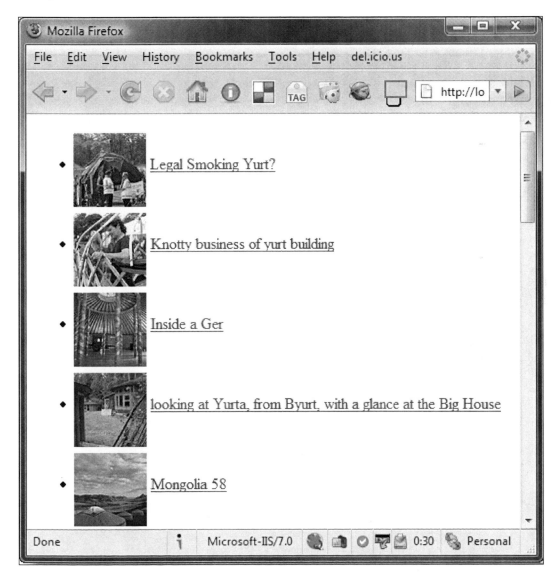

Here it is. We have a prototype of a feed repurposed through the power of ColdFusion. Note that we did our XPath searching of the content in order to pull back subsections of the structure from our XML document. When we need to pull the namespace back, we just need to extend the XPath in our search to go further into the structure and give more output than the feed tag built in. This is not something that we normally need to do. But if our XML feed includes namespace elements, then it becomes very easy to solve what could be wrongly evaluated as an impossible situation.

CDF

This is another XML-based response document. It is known as a "Channel Definition Format". We do not need to get into the history to know that it differs from the RSS in that it follows different standards and goals. Check it out. If it looks more like what is best in your use-case scenario, then choose it when it is available. There are no CDF readers available, as there are RSS readers. This feed will not appear good in browsers. It will appear as plain XML.

```
http://api.flickr.com/services/feeds/groups_pool.gne?id=612330@N24
&format=cdf
```

There are a few things that we need to do with this XML because the XML is formed differently. If we look at the code we are pulling, we will also notice that the XML has many names in caps. It is important to remember this, or else our XML XPath will not work. Notice how we have created the XPaths in our code. Further, note that we tested and had some issues with returning nested items. We resolved that by just doing a couple of extra XPath searches inside our output loop.

```
<cfhttp url="http://api.flickr.com/services/feeds/groups_pool.
gne?id=#flickr.group_id#lang=en-us&format=cdf">

<cfscript>
flickr_xml = cfhttp.filecontent;
feed = xmlParse(flickr_xml);
items = xmlSearch(feed,"/CHANNEL/ITEM/");
</cfscript>
<ul>
<cfoutput>
<cfloop from="1" to="#arrayLen(items)#" index="i">
    <cfset thumb = xmlSearch(feed,"/CHANNEL/ITEM[#i#]/LOGO")>
    <cfset title = xmlSearch(feed,"/CHANNEL/ITEM[#i#]/TITLE")>
    <li>
        <img  src="#thumb[1].xmlAttributes.href#"
              alt="#title[1].xmlText#"
              align="middle" vspace="3">
        <span>
```

```
        <a href="#items[i].xmlAttributes.HREF#" target="_blank">
          #title[1].xmlText#
        </a>
      </span>
    </li>
  </cfloop>
</cfoutput>
</ul>
```

JSON

JSON stands for JavaScript Object Notation. You can get more information about it at `http://json.org/`. ColdFusion 8 provides built-in support for JSON. There is also a CFC library that has good support located at `http://www.epiphantastic.com/cfjson/`. This library does not depend on CF8, but works with it very well. It may make some of your projects more portable.

```
http://api.flickr.com/services/feeds/groups_pool.gne?id=612330@N24
&format=json
```

Here is a view of what the returned JSON looks like. The returned value of this feed, for those familiar with JSON, is not standard JSON. The start of the feed return is `jsonFlickrFeed` (and that is not standard JSON form). We will have to deal with that at two levels. Apparently, the ColdFusion server sees this as some sort of a Java object. We will use the "`.toString()`" to translate it back to text, and then we will strip the extra characters off the front and back to make it a more universally valid JSON. It appears as though the feed is meant to be converted via JavaScript. So, we have to adjust it, as shown here:

```
jsonFlickrFeed({
     "title": "Yurt Living Photo Pool",
     "link": "http://www.flickr.com/groups/yurtliving/pool/",
     "description": "This group is for those who live in, would like
to live in or are curious about Yurt living.",
     "modified": "2008-03-12T14:52:21Z",
     "generator": "http://www.flickr.com/",
     "items": [
{
     "title": "Yurt",
     "link": "http://www.flickr.com/photos/nuritwilde/275863461/in/
pool-612362@N24",
      "media": {"m":"http://farm1.static.flickr.com/110/275863461_
fa2f97d579_m.jpg"},
     "date_taken": "2006-10-21T21:30:33-05:00",
```

```
       "description": "&lt;p&gt;&lt;a href=&quot;http://www.flickr.
com/people/nuritwilde/&quot;&gt;magnolia83912&lt;/a&gt; has added a
photo to the pool:&lt;/p&gt; &lt;p&gt;&lt;a href=&quot;http://www.
flickr.com/photos/nuritwilde/275863461/&quot; title=&quot;Yurt&quot;
&gt;&lt;img src=&quot;http://farm1.static.flickr.com/110/275863461_
fa2f97d579_m.jpg&quot; width=&quot;240&quot; height=&quot;179&quot;
alt=&quot;Yurt&quot; /&gt;&lt;/a&gt;&lt;/p&gt; &lt;p&gt;The word
yurt is originally from the Turkic word meaning &amp;quot;dwelling
place&amp;quot; in the sense of &amp;quot;homeland&amp;quot;; the term
came to be used in reference to the physical tent-like structures only
in other languages. In Russian, a yurt is called &amp;quot;yurta&amp;
quot; (юрта), and there is an obsolete term &amp;quot;kibitka&amp;qu
ot; (кибитка). From Russian, the word came into English. I took this
definition from Wikipedia. My friends have a Yurt in their back yard
which they currently rent to a young man. I have to get some photos of
the inside. It's really a great place for someone to live.&lt;/p&gt;",
       "published": "2006-10-22T04:30:33Z",
       "author": "nobody@flickr.com (magnolia83912)",
       "author_id": "38045881@N00",
       "tags": "losangeles tent tentlikestructure"
}
```

Here is our code for processing the feed so that we get output similar to what we got in our first feed (RSS) example. As there are no thumbnails, we will either have to display the pictures in a larger size, or manually force them to a smaller size. We will just leave them as they are. Notice that the ColdFusion functions are serializeJSON() and deserializeJSON(). As we have mentioned, we do some processing on the return string before we translate it into a ColdFusion structure.

```
<cfhttp url="http://api.flickr.com/services/feeds/groups_pool.
gne?id=#flickr.group_id#&lang=en-us&format=json">

<cfscript>
flickr_json = cfhttp.filecontent.toString();
myJSON = replace(flickr_json,"jsonFlickrFeed(","");
myJSON = left(myJSON,len(myJSON)-1);
feed = deserializeJSON(myJSON);
</cfscript>
<ul>
<cfoutput>
<cfloop from="1" to="#arrayLen(feed.items)#" index="i">
   <li>
      <img  src="#feed.items[i].media.m#"
         align="middle" vspace="3" />
      <span>
         <a href="#feed.items[i].link#" target="_blank">
         #feed.items[i].title#
```

```
        </a>
      </span>
   </li>
</cfloop>
</cfoutput>
</ul>
```

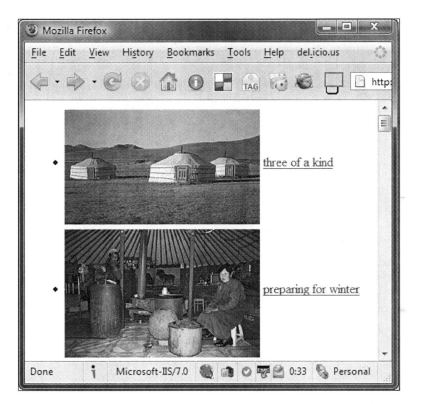

We will now show you the changes that are needed so we can use the open-source CFC JSON library. The first thing to do is to create an instance of the object. Then, we only need one more change. We can encode and decode with this library. Everything else works the same, and the output is identical. Here is the section of code we have to change:

```
<cfscript>
oJSON = createObject("component","json");
flickr_json = cfhttp.filecontent.toString();
myJSON = replace(flickr_json,"jsonFlickrFeed(","");
myJSON = left(myJSON,len(myJSON)-1);
feed = oJSON.decode(myJSON);
</cfscript>
```

SQL

This is an unusual type of feed but worth mentioning because it shows the extent to which Flickr has sought to make collaboration easier for developers. Although they deserve kudos for the effort, this approach could make a site more vulnerable to hackers if it was blindly automated into a website. However, this could still be a great way for new developers to learn some SQL basics and get things set up.

```
http://api.flickr.com/services/feeds/groups_pool.gne?id=#flickr.
group_id#&format=sql
```

Here is some of the code returned with this request:

```
CREATE TABLE IF NOT EXISTS feeds (
   guid varchar(255) NOT NULL default '',
   title varchar(255) NOT NULL default '',
   url varchar(255) NOT NULL default '',
   image_url varchar(255) NOT NULL default '',
   description text NOT NULL,
   pub_timestamp int(10) unsigned NOT NULL default '0',
   PRIMARY KEY (guid)
);

DELETE FROM feeds WHERE guid='/grouppool/612362@N24';
INSERT INTO feeds VALUES (
    '/grouppool/612362@N24',
    'Yurt Living Photo Pool',
   'http://www.flickr.com/groups/yurtliving/pool/',
   'http://l.yimg.com/www.flickr.com/images/buddyicon.jpg#612362@N24',
   'This group is for those who live in, would like to live in or are
curious about Yurt living.',
    '1205333541'
);
```

This is a unique innovation to help people in building websites based on the Flickr technology. If we look at the whole feed, we will see that the associated items table is created and managed well. Real live applications need more control than allowing external vendors to manage our updates directly. It can be a very good resource while building or prototyping a site.

Introduction to REST Services

Basically, REST services are XML-based services that work without the need for secondary standards such as SOAP. SOAP is the first broadly accepted standard for Web Services. REST has become the preferred solution to many for performing web services. It does not completely replace SOAP, but it does things in an equally stable and powerful way without any extra complexities required to do SOAP in many programming environments. REST services have been found to run much faster than SOAP. This means that it scales better and runs faster.

The REST request is made over HTTP with the same tag that we used in our earlier feed requests. A full-featured REST service will commonly support GET, HEAD, POST, PUT, and DELETE. We can actually achieve much with GET and POST considering that these are all that HTML forms support. We should be able to capture and handle the responses of REST service calls.

We will go back to the Flickr website to check out REST services. Flickr chose to build its user interface around REST rather than SOAP. On riaForge, there is great work called **CFlickr** being done by Chris Blackwell. The project homepage can be viewed at `http://cflickr.riaforge.org/`. This is a packaged work for the Flickr API. But we will still build some ourselves in order to understand the basic REST service interaction. The API for Flickr can be found at `http://www.flickr.com/services/api/`. Specifically, we will be using the test API first. All the variables would be similar to those that we would type into a URL. This is considered a "GET"-based request.

This is an 'include' file that is being used to hold the common API variables.

```
<cfscript>
flickr.api_key = "-----------------";
flickr.group_id = "--------";

yahoo.api_key = "";
</cfscript>
```

This is the actual file that will be requesting the REST service from Flickr.

```
<cfinclude template="my_api_keys.cfm">
<cfhttp url="http://api.flickr.com/services/rest/?method=flickr.test.
echo&name=value&api_key=#flickr.api_key#">

<cfdump var="#xmlParse(cfhttp.fileContent)#">
```

We will need to acquire an ID by signing up for an account on Flickr. Then, go to the tools section and look for the developers division. There will be a link to the public Flickr API. Click on that and you will find a link to the "API Keys". Websites change and things get moved around every now and then. But as we go over this material, it will remain in the same place where it was written. You will get two keys. There is an API key that we will use in these examples, as in the code sample above, and a secret key that is used for authentication. Be careful while securing the secret key. Both these keys are hidden. That is why they are not available in the code samples for the book. We all want good practice examples, don't we?

Here is a dump of the rest request to Flickr.

We used the test API to make the first call to the Flickr REST service. This was done by using the 'GET' form of request. Now, we are going to use the 'POST' form of request. Essentially, this is similar to what a browser would send if someone did a POST from a web form. Note that the `<chttppparam>` tags have an attribute `type="formfield"` to pass the variables to the request. This is another way that will prove to be useful for more complex REST requests.

```
<cfinclude template="my_api_keys.cfm">
<cfhttp url="http://api.flickr.com/services/rest/" method="post">
   <cfhttpparam name="method" value="flickr.groups.pools.getPhotos"
type="formfield">
   <cfhttpparam name="api_key" value="#flickr.api_key#"
type="formfield">
   <cfhttpparam name="group_id" value="#flickr.group_id#"
type="formfield">
   <cfhttpparam name="per_page" value="20" type="formfield">
</cfhttp>

<cfdump var="#cfhttp#" expand="false">
<cfdump var="#xmlParse(cfhttp.fileContent)#">
```

Here, we see the results of this request. Look at the structure of the returned XML and you will find a base type of rsp for the root. Under the root, we see the structure for "photos". The attributes are valuable to us. They allow us to see that this set of results is the first of seven pages. The total number of items per page is 20, and the total number of items is 120. Next, we will see the photos with their attributes. Now, this is a little different from Feeds because we would have to continue building, using the API to get additional details. Look at the API, and we will see additional methods for getting individual pictures back.

We start off by including the API keys from a different file. These are not hard-coded as we need to set up our own keys to use REST-style services. We connect to the REST service with the POST form of request. In this example, the response is converted and stored in a variable called `fl_xml`. We loop through the array of photo listings with a minor change. We take each item and create an item variable as we go. This is just to make the code easier to read. It is not required and has no benefit other than making the code easier to read. We also pop any selections up in a new window. It would also be very easy to convert this to a tool that flows through the set of data available on the server, as it returns the number of photos, pages, and the current page with the response. The API is present at the following page on Flickr:

```
http://www.flickr.com/services/api/flickr.groups.pools.getPhotos.html
```

The method name has `.html` at the end.

```
<cfinclude template="my_api_keys.cfm">
<cfhttp url="http://api.flickr.com/services/rest/" method="post">
    <cfhttpparam name="method" value="flickr.groups.pools.getPhotos"
type="formfield">
    <cfhttpparam name="api_key" value="#flickr.api_key#"
type="formfield">
    <cfhttpparam name="group_id" value="#flickr.group_id#"
type="formfield">
    <cfhttpparam name="per_page" value="20" type="formfield">
</cfhttp>
<cfscript>
fl_xml = xmlParse(cfhttp.fileContent);
photo = fl_xml.rsp.photos.photo;
</cfscript>
<cfoutput>
<ul>
<cfloop from="1" to="#arrayLen(photo)#" index="iPhoto">
    <li><cfset item = photo[iPhoto].xmlAttributes>
        <a target="_blank" href="http://www.flickr.com/photos/#item.
owner#/#item.id#/in/pool-#flickr.group_id#">
        #photo[iPhoto].xmlAttributes.title#
        </a>
    </li>
</cfloop>
</ul>
</cfoutput>
```

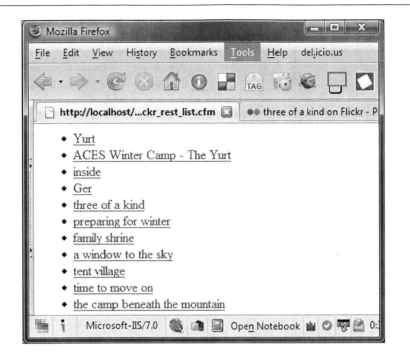

And when we click on any of the links, it brings us to the page for the photo similar to the following one. The group alias name is not available in the REST response interface. But we can use the group ID at the end of the URL as in the code segment above. This is equivalent to the Flickr server.

If we want to build a REST service, we will require to take in a URL or form variables as we would take them from a normal webpage into a `.cfm` page. A method that makes it work better is to store the variables into a common scope. This was initially made popular in ColdFusion with the Fusebox framework. It has been copied to many other frameworks. Doing this does means that you don't have to code the server to respond either to the form or to a URL because the response code is always in the same scope. In order to do this, use the `structAppend()` function, and push the form to a common structure to make sure that it exists. After that we push the URL into the structure. Now, building our own REST services became easier to code as both the forms of incoming variables are packaged in a common structure.

There are several sites that support REST. These include 37Signals, Amazon, del.icio.us, eBay, Flickr, and Yahoo. The ColdFusion community developers who learned it are not just using it. They are also promoting it as the preferred method in most scenarios.

SOAP Web Services

SOAP web services are very valuable. There are certain things offered by SOAP that are not offered by REST. One of these is the ability to interact with Flex/Flash/AIR apps along with SOAP-based services. This standard is the best standard for packing the data that goes to the Flex/Flash/AIR apps. The larger the data, the more valuable this standard becomes. It makes data five times smaller. Therefore, the larger the data packets are, the more is its impact. It is possible to support both REST and AMF requests from the same app and server if it helps to optimize.

SOAP has traditionally been a very challenging technology with which to work. If someone is using a different platform, then it may be harder for them to provide or consume the resource, than it is for us to do our connections on the ColdFusion side of the interaction. We are going to build a simple date application to tell us how many days until a special event. In this book, we will take the summer event of CFUnited as the big event. We can modify the code as we want by changing the date. When we look at `http://cfunited.com`, we see the date in 2008 will be on June 18th. The first thing that we will do is build a CFC and get it working inside a regular web page. We will do this to prototype our web service. When it starts working right, we will show how the CFC runs as a web service.

We have our CFC here. We are storing the dates as an XML local. But this would be stored either in a database, or in an external XML source once we go beyond the prototype stage. We use an XML search to get the event requested and then do a date difference in order to get the number of days until or since the conference's start date. We have set the function/method to an access type of remote right off. This is because local applications can still access the method even though it is set to remote. Without setting it to remote it cannot be accessed remotely.

```
<cfcomponent output="false">
  <cffunction name="until" access="remote" returnType="numeric">
      <cfargument name="event" required="true">
      <cfset var xml = "">
      <cfset var myEvent = "">
      <cfxml variable="xml">
      <events>
         <event name="CFUnited" start="6/18/2008" end="6/21/2008">
         10th Anniversary of the largest annual CF conference.
      </event>
         <event name="cf.Objective" start="5/1/2008" end="5/4/2008">
         Enterprise Engineering Conference for ColdFusionMX
Programmers
      </event>
      </events>
      </cfxml>
      <cfset myEvent = xmlSearch(xml,"/events/event[@name='#arguments.
event#']")>
      <cfreturn dateDiff('d',now(),myEvent[1].xmlAttributes.start)>
  </cffunction>
</cfcomponent>
```

Now, we can have a look at our test by using a ColdFusion page with a form to select the conference and return the days between the start date and the present date. Here is our testing page code. It sets up a default event variable for the form, and creates an object based on the countdown class CFC if the event variable is not blank. Then it writes the output with the use of script commands and a call from the object out to the browser. The form at the end of the page is just to complete our manual prototype interface. The following are the code and resulting screenshots:

```
<cfparam name="form.event" default="">
<cfscript>
if(form.event != ""){
    oEvent = createObject("component","countdown");
    writeOutput("
      The event (#form.event#) is in #oEvent.until(form.event)# days.
      <hr />
    ");
}
</cfscript>
<cfoutput>
<form method="post" action="getEvent.cfm">
    Event:<br/>
    <input type="text" name="Event" value="#form.event#"><br/>
    <input type="submit">
</form>
</cfoutput>

(Enter either CFUnited or cf.Objective.)
```

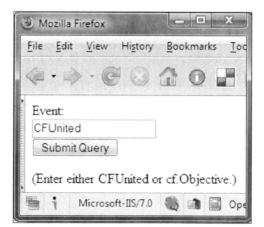

Now we see that our prototype is working. We can move to testing by calling the CFC remotely via a web service call rather than the local call as in our prototype tester. We are going to use the browser to test that WSDL is working. This stands for Web Service Description Language. This is one of the interesting features of SOAP. The WSDL gives many details of the web service. Each service can have more than one method even though ours has only one method. CFC methods that are available as a web service must have the access set to remote. Here is the URL for our test:

```
http://localhost/cfb/code/chapter_14/countdown.cfc?wsdl
```
(Your URL may differ).

There is not much benefit in reading this when we know about our CFC features. But it can be good to compare it in the future to understand web services in a better way. We will now change a line in our local test form to pull this information from the same CFC but by calling the CFC by making an additional call to the web server.

Previously this was done directly inside the same request. The results will be returned and the page will run in the same way as it did before we were connected to it as a web service. This is because web services are remote business components connected to our applications. We see a transformation that happens by a single change. The external web service is not acting like an internal object in our software.

```
<cfparam name="form.event" default="">
<cfscript>
if(form.event != ""){
   oEvent = createObject("webservice","/cfb/code/chapter_14/countdown.
cfc?wsdl");
   writeOutput("
      The event (#form.event#) is in #oEvent.until(form.event)# days.
      <hr />
   ");
}
</cfscript>
<cfoutput>
<form method="post" action="getEvent.cfm">
   Event:<br/>
   <input type="text" name="Event" value="#form.event#"><br/>
   <input type="submit">
</form>
</cfoutput>
```

(Enter either CFUnited or cf.Objective.)

Web services are very powerful, and can also be used as remote objects. There are additional tags for doing specialized SOAP features.

We will also note that the AMF interaction components for Flash-based technologies (AIR/Flash/Flex) are set up in a similar manner. The method of connecting them is outside the scope of this book. AMF features are built into ColdFusion, and at this point it is the only platform with this built-in technology.

Summary

This is a summary of what we have covered in this chapter. We hope that the content of the chapter has given everyone a broad launch into the world of collaboration. Feeds, REST, and SOAP are the primary ways in which websites interact with one another.

- Feeds
  - How to use `<cfhttp>`
  - RSS
  - CDF
  - JSON
  - Flickr JSON
  - SQL

- XML Handling
  - Parsing XML
  - XPath Searches
  - Handling Namespaces

- REST
  - URL versus form-style connections
  - Simple REST services

- SOAP Web Services
  - Prototyping
  - Setting web service access
  - WSDL checking from a browser
  - Connecting to a web service from CF Code

15
Building Dynamic Reports

Reporting is a very important aspect of software development. There are many companies that hire people to generate reports. In this chapter, we are going to cover the fundamental aspects of reporting. This chapter includes a broad introduction to ColdFusion's way of generating dynamic reports. We will also see how to create a report design that works with both current data and selections of data to present fresh views of the information.

Traditional Web Page Reporting

Firstly, we need to define traditional web page reporting. We will get our data, and then we will look at a couple of techniques that are used to display the data as we need it in an HTML-based view.

Simple Report

A simple report can be considered a formatted data dump. We will take the results from the query and place them on the screen. We will use a pre-built CFC to pull the data so that we can focus our attention on reporting features. We create an instance of our report data object and then pull back a list of the artists in the database. Then, we create the table header. Next, we use <cfoutput> to loop through the returned recordset. We will output a table row for each of the database rows.

```
<cfscript>
objReport = createObject("component","artists_reportData").init(dsn:"c
fartgallery");
myData = objReport.getArtists();
</cfscript>
<table border="1" style="cell-spacing:0;">
   <tr>
        <th>Artist</th>
```

```
          <th>City</th>
          <th>State</th>
     </tr>
     <cfoutput query="myData">
     <tr>
          <td>#myData.firstName# #myData.lastName#</td>
          <td>#myData.city#</td>
          <td>#myData.state#</td>
     </tr>
     </cfoutput>
</table>
```

Every company prefers to use its own styles and we should remember to personalize the reports with the client's custom style. Here is the output that we get from the previous code.

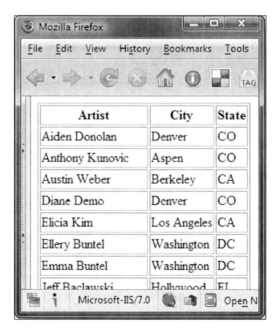

Grouped Data

It is clear that a table report can be used to create very useful information. It is also evident that it will rarely be enough. Our code example is very similar to simple data. We changed the method that was called to get a more complex grouped recordset. We added a style for this table because it makes it easier to view what is going on. If we look at the same functional line where we start output of our recordset, there is some difference. We are grouping by the `artistid` field in the data. We need to make sure our data gets to this point with the data already arranged by grouping. Otherwise it will not group correctly in our report.

Now, we create a secondary <cfoutput> with no grouping. Our code takes all the records that are in the same group and loops through them in order to process our data for the nested groups for output. We could actually have a number of layers here if we wanted. We can see in the output that this makes the report much more valuable.

```
<cfscript>
objReport = createObject("component","artists_reportData").init(dsn:"c
fartgallery");
myData = objReport.getArtistsWorks();
</cfscript>
<style>
.report th{
    color: #FFFFFF;
    background-color: #444444;
}
.report .detail {
    background-color: #DDDDDD;
}
</style>
<table border="1" class="report" style="cell-spacing:0;">
    <tr>
        <th>Artist</th>
        <th>City</th>
        <th>State</th>
    </tr>
      <cfoutput query="myData" group="artistid">
    <tr>
        <td>#myData.firstName# #myData.lastName#</td>
        <td>#myData.city#</td>
        <td>#myData.state#</td>
    </tr>
        <cfoutput>
    <tr class="detail">
        <th valign="top">Work</th>
        <td>
```

```
            <strong>#myData.artName#</strong><br />
                    (#myData.mediaType#)<br />
                    #myData.description#
            </td>
            <td valign="top" align="right">
              #dollarFormat(myData.price)#
             </td>
        </tr>
          </cfoutput>
          </cfoutput>
      </table>
```

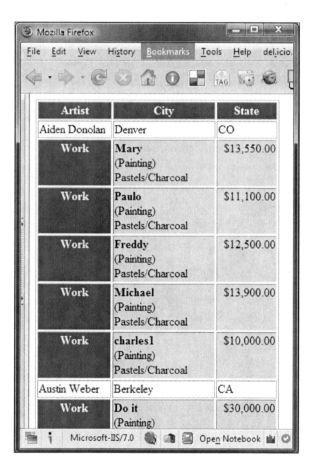

Drill-Down Reporting

Rather than loading another form and copying the data down to run that report, we could use the a concept of a drill-down report. Here, one report has a link on the page that links to another report pre-selecting the data filter. It can speed things up greatly.

Let us say we have an online shopping business. We want a report that shows the sales on a monthly basis. We would get total sales for the month and each line could have a link to drill down the sales report for the selected month. Again, in that report, we could total sales by the client and we could drill down to the clients to show individual sales. Then we could drill down to items on the sale and get information there. Each of these could have multiple links leading to different types of information.

Now, we are just going to do a basic drill-down so as to understand the concept well. We will modify both the simple data and the grouped data to show how the previous two reports can be used in a drill-down manner. In the following code, we have added a column for the works of art by each artist, and then we created a hyperlink to show those works of the artist.

```
<cfscript>
objReport = createObject("component","artists_reportData").init(dsn:"c
fartgallery");
myData = objReport.getArtists();
</cfscript>
<table border="1" style="cell-spacing:0;">
   <tr>
        <th>Artist</th>
        <th>City</th>
        <th>State</th>
        <th>ART</th>
   </tr>
    <cfoutput query="myData">
   <tr>
        <td>#myData.firstName# #myData.lastName#</td>
        <td>#myData.city#</td>
        <td>#myData.state#</td>
        <td>
        <ahref="report_drilltarget.cfm?id=#myData.artistid#">Show
                                                Works</a>
        </td>
   </tr>
    </cfoutput>
</table>
```

This works very well and we can add more than one linked column. There can be reasons to drill off in many directions here. A robust system can do statewise and artistwise sorting. Perhaps, the user wants to see all the work for a unique state or city. There could be some logic added for things such as adding link if it was a certain kind of art. This could be done if the user was looking for paintings and not photography or something else along these lines. Reporting is very flexible. In this example, we will get the result using the previous code.

Now, we will change our grouped example so we can see what happens when we click through or drill down to the artist to see his or her works of art. We are only going to show the top part of the code because the rest of the code did not change in any way. First, we need to set a default for the ID. This is good practice to prevent errors on the users' side. Next, we will pass the `artistid` into the object method as an argument. Inside our object, we have placed the query to filter if the `artistid` is not equal to zero. Therefore, we will get only the artist and the works done by that artist in our returned recordset. We can see the results below the code.

```
<cfparam name="url.id" default="0">
<cfscript>
objReport = createObject("component","artists_reportData").init(dsn:"c
fartgallery");
myData = objReport.getArtistsWorks(artistid:url.id);
</cfscript>
```

With drill-down, it might be appropriate to set the data to page and show fewer records at a time. When it comes to reporting, it usually makes sense to put all the data on the screen at the same time. This is one of the major differences between general data display in ColdFusion and reporting pages preparation.

Output Formats

Sometimes, observing data is good. Yet, often people need to pass on the data to others. This may be because the other people are not inside a company where they can access the pages that display the data or perhaps the data needs to be moved to an Excel spreadsheet where they can use it for other purposes. Let us look at how we can take the traditional HTML-oriented data and push it out in a format that fulfills the business needs of our users. Let us revisit some of the techniques and show some others for doing this for report pages. Some of the popular formats are CSV (comma-separated values), XML, PDF, JSON, and HTML.

While generating reports, we would generally want to save them offline or open them in another application. Some of the applications can open up right inside the browser depending how the user's computer is configured. We will first look at the simple changes that we have made to our code. Then, we will convert the code to show the PDF for the previous example.

PDF Output

To turn a report into PDF in ColdFusion, wrap the page in <cfdocument> tags. There are more things that can be done with this tag. One of the changes in the CF8 update was to add an evaluate-at-print item to <cfdocumentitem> tags. We are going to loop over our output a few times, so we can get additional pages and see the effect of this new attribute.

We wrap our page content with the document tag and then add a document item to the page. As this is a header, it will appear at the top of each page. We can see that the document has its own variable structure called CFDocument. We can now run on-the-fly calculations to check whether this is an even page or an odd page.

```
<cfscript>
objReport = createObject("component","artists_reportData").init(dsn:"c
fartgallery");
myData = objReport.getArtists();
</cfscript>
<cfdocument format="PDF">
    <cfdocumentitem type="header" evalAtPrint="true">
            <cfoutput>
            <cfif (CFDocument.currentPageNumber % 2 eq 0)>
                    Even Page #CFDocument.currentPageNumber#
    <cfelse>
                    Odd Page #CFDocument.currentPageNumber#
            </cfif>
            </cfoutput>
    </cfdocumentitem>
<table border="1" style="cell-spacing:0;">
    <tr>
            <th>Artist</th>
            <th>City</th>
            <th>State</th>
    </tr><cfloop from="1" to="5" index="iLoop">
    <cfoutput query="myData">
    <tr>
            <td>#myData.firstName# #myData.lastName#</td>
            <td>#myData.city#</td>
            <td>#myData.state#</td>
    </tr>
    </cfoutput></cfloop>
</table>
</cfdocument>
```

This results in the page showing either "Odd Page #", # of course being the number of the current page, or "Even Page #".

Excel Output

We start off in many output cases by making sure only the content that is explicitly declared will go to the output. This is what the `<cfsetting>` tag is used for in this template. We load the data as we have in other examples. We create a tab and a new line so Excel can recognize the structure and place the data properly into a spreadsheet. In the output section, we place a tab character between each data field, and then we place a new line at the end of each row of data. Refer to the screenshot that follows the code for the results.

```
<cfsetting enablecfoutputonly="true">
<cfscript>
objReport = createObject("component","artists_reportData").init(dsn:"c
fartgallery");
myData = objReport.getArtists();
tabChar = chr(9);
newLine = chr(13) & chr(10);
</cfscript>
<cfcontent type="application/msexcel">
<cfheader name="Content-Disposition" value="filename=Artists.xls">
<cfoutput query="myData">#myData.firstName##tabChar##myData.lastName##
tabChar##myData.city##tabChar##myData.state##newLine#</cfoutput>
```

It should be noted that `<cfcontent>` and `<cfheader>` appear before the generated content.

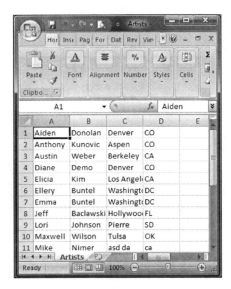

There is another way we can work with Excel. We can format our page with an HTML table, and Excel will translate that into a spreadsheet. Here is the code generating an HTML table. Excel translates it just as well. The spreadsheet looks a little different though. Just as in HTML, the general table formatting used will be actually carried right into the spreadsheet. There are many other things that you can learn to do in order to make an Excel document format without having to do it manually.

```
<cfsetting enablecfoutputonly="true">
<cfscript>
objReport = createObject("component","artists_reportData").init(dsn:"c
fartgallery");
myData = objReport.getArtists();
</cfscript>
<cfcontent type="application/msexcel">
<cfheader name="Content-Disposition" value="filename=Artists.xls">
<cfoutput><table border="1">
    <tr>
            <th>Artist</th>
            <th>City</th>
            <th>State</th>
    </tr>
</cfoutput>
<cfoutput query="myData">
    <tr>
            <td>#myData.firstName# #myData.lastName#</td>
            <td>#myData.city#</td>
            <td>#myData.state#</td>
    </tr>
</cfoutput>
```

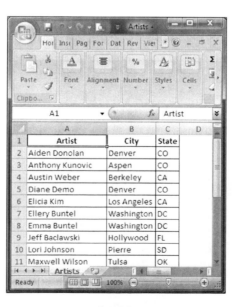

Again, we need to notice the HTML styles that are carried into the spreadsheet for column headings. This is a great way to generate dynamic stylized data for Excel users.

CVS Output

This is one output form that can be a bit difficult at times. The reason being it is possible that the data could contain a quote or comma depending on how the data was formed and then throw off the flow of the CSV file. Although there is very little that can be done about this, it still remains one of the more popular data formats over the years.

Here is our code. We see that we wrap our data output with quotes for every field and place a comma between the data fields. It is also optional to include a first line that has the same number of fields but is the names of the fields rather than the actual data. The type attribute of the content is set to text/plain.

```
<cfsetting enablecfoutputonly="true">
<cfscript>
objReport = createObject("component","artists_reportData").init(dsn:"c
fartgallery");
myData = objReport.getArtists();
newLine = chr(13) & chr(10);
</cfscript>
<cfcontent type="text/plain">
<cfheader name="Content-Disposition" value="filename=Artists.csv">
<cfoutput query="myData">"#myData.firstName#","#myData.
lastName#","#myData.city#","#myData.state#"#newLine#</cfoutput>
```

This is the text that will appear right inside the browser.

```
"Aiden","Donolan","Denver","CO"
"Anthony","Kunovic","Aspen","CO"
"Austin","Weber","Berkeley","CA"
"Diane","Demo","Denver","CO"
"Elicia","Kim","Los Angeles","CA"
"Ellery","Buntel","Washington","DC"
"Emma","Buntel","Washington","DC"
"Jeff","Baclawski","Hollywood","FL"
"Lori","Johnson","Pierre","SD"
"Maxwell","Wilson","Tulsa","OK"
"Mike","Nimer","asd da","ca"
"Paul","Trani","New York","NY"
"Raquel","Young","Atlanta","GA"
"Taylor Webb","Frazier","Santa Fe","NM"
"Viata","Trenton","New York","NY"
```

XML Output

Here, we start with a simple `text/xml` content type. We set the filename to `Artists.xml` and then output the tags as a valid XML document. We need to remember that valid XML requires a single root tag wrapping the document. This is what it takes to get the job done:

```
<cfsetting enablecfoutputonly="true">
<cfscript>
objReport = createObject("component","artists_reportData").init(dsn:"c
fartgallery");
myData = objReport.getArtists();
</cfscript>

<cfcontent type="text/xml">
<cfheader name="Content-Disposition" value="filename=Artists.xml">
<cfoutput><?xml version="1.0" encoding="utf-8"?>
<artists></cfoutput>
<cfoutput query="myData">
   <artist>
         <firstname>#myData.firstName#</firstname>
         <lastname>#myData.lastName#</lastname>
         <city>#myData.city#</city>
         <state>#myData.state#</state>
   </artist></cfoutput>
<cfoutput>
</artists>
</cfoutput>
```

JSON Output

Putting the data out as JSON is the easiest thing to do. Here, we have a plain text format. We just need to push the content out with the built-in JSON `serialize` function.

```
<cfsetting enablecfoutputonly="true">
<cfscript>
objReport = createObject("component","artists_reportData").init(dsn:"c
fartgallery");
myData = objReport.getArtists();
</cfscript>

<cfcontent type="text/plain">
<cfheader name="Content-Disposition" value="filename=Artists.json">
<cfoutput>#serializeJSON(myData)#</cfoutput>
```

Using CFReport and Report Builder

We need to install the report builder before we can start creating a report. The installation is quite simple. We need to make sure that we have the connection to our server set up correctly. We can either set up the connection when we install the application, or we can change it later as required. Once this is set up, we have a robust reporting tool that comes at no additional cost for ColdFusion. There is no per seat cost for using the report builder. The cost is in running the reports. This means that we can run the reports if we have a licensed server. If we are working on a free version of the server, it puts a watermark to allow us to build reports for the licensed server. This is very good ROI for the developers. Report builder is a Windows-only product.

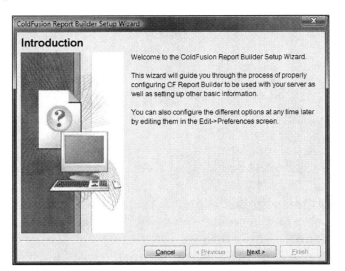

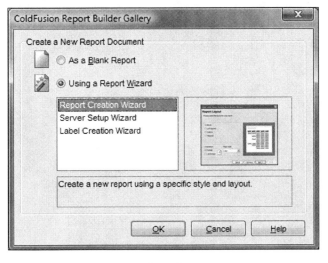

Select the **Report Creation Wizard** and click **OK**.

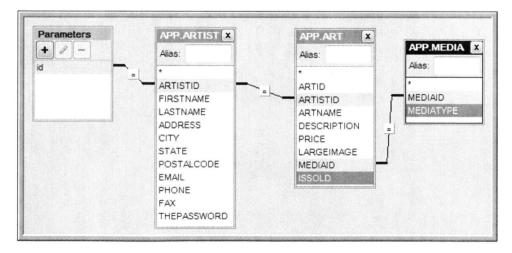

Now, we select the **Query Builder** button and get the data that is needed to model this report. Now, we will be working with the built-in Art Gallery data tables that come with the installation of ColdFusion. These are Derby database tables. We will add these three tables and an **id** parameter field that is linked to the **artistid** field of the artist table.

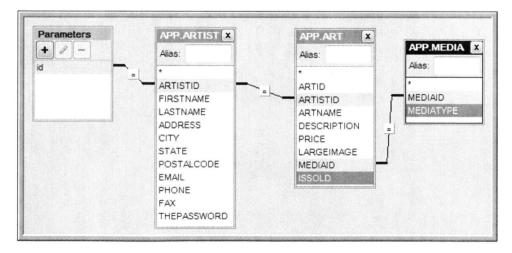

We will add the following fields to our query:

- Artists Table
    - ° artistid
    - ° firstname
    - ° lastname

- Art Table
    - ° artname
    - ° description
    - ° price

- Media Table
    - ° mediatype

Now, we will save the query by adding the firstname and lastname fields. It will actually produce the SQL for us. We could also have tested the query on the query builder screen if we wanted.

```
SELECT    ARTISTS.ARTISTID, ARTISTS.FIRSTNAME, ARTISTS.LASTNAME,
ART.ARTNAME, ART.DESCRIPTION, ART.PRICE, MEDIA.MEDIATYPE
FROM      APP.ARTISTS, APP.ART, APP.MEDIA
WHERE     APP.ARTISTS.ARTISTID = APP.ART.ARTISTID
  AND     APP.ART.MEDIAID = APP.MEDIA.MEDIAID
ORDER BY ARTISTS.FIRSTNAME, ARTISTS.LASTNAME
```

It will ask us about printed and non-printed fields. The only field that will not be printed is the **artistid** field. The following screen appears:

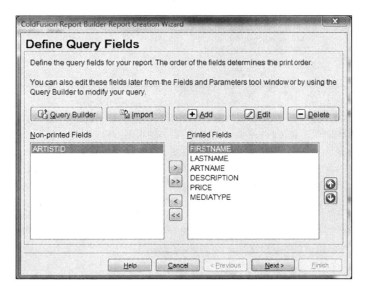

Now, we will come to a grouping screen where we will group on the basis of full name. We did not design our query to deal with this by putting the first and last name together. So, we will create two groups that will function as one field. It will also serve to emphasize how to get the totals when it is required.

The following screenshot shows the report layout. We will just follow the defaults and move on. Any of the settings can be adjusted in the report builder as this is just a wizard. Click **Next** and we will get the Report Style screen. We will select to create totals for numeric fields and leave the rest of the settings on the defaults.

Again, on the Report Theme page, we will follow the defaults. Now, we have a report name called **artists_works**. We will keep the other fields void. We will see how a report is generated and we will save it before moving further. Refer to the following screenshot now:

Now if we go to the `.cfr` file from the browser URL, we will find that the report will load and run. When we load it, there is no ID passed in. So, we will get all the artists and their works. We need to create a `.cfm` page in order to call the report and pass an artist ID to show the work of any artist. We also note that the report has a current date at the top and the page numbers at the bottom of the report. These were added to the report by the wizard.

Next, we will change the name to a concatenated field showing both the first and last name. Double-click on the last name field and put the following line into the requestor.

```
query.FIRSTNAME & ' ' & query.LASTNAME
```

Then, we can change the FIRSTNAME to NAME and delete the LASTNAME label. We also need to resize the field in the LASTNAME band by stretching it to reach the margin on the left. Now, we will remove the FIRSTNAME band contents and hide it so that it is not visible. The outer band forms the first grouping. So it works great.

Now, let us work on the detail band. We will remove the description from the report. We will then swap the position of the media type and the price. We will expand the **artname** field so it is larger towards the media type. (Do not forget to move the column header labels to match the fields below them.)

The last thing we are going to do is create a calculated field and add it to one of the bands of our report. Bands are horizontal sections of the page with the section name on the left panel. We will be working with the **Calculated Fields** option, which is present in the right panel. Right click on **Calculated Fields** and select **Add Calculated Field**. Then a requestor with that name will appear. In the **Name** field, fill in **worksTotal** and in the **Default Label Text** field, fill in **Works Total**. The **Data Type** is **Float** and the **Calculation** is **Sum**. Under **Perform Calculation On**, select **query.PRICE** with **Initial Value** as zero. Now the key points are to reset the field when the group changes. Select the **Reset Group** as **LASTNAME**. This will give us a requestor that appears as follows:

Observe the **worksTotal** field under **Calculated Fields**. We can drag-and-drop these fields onto our report bands. Firstly, we need to make sure it will insert a label and a field. This can be done by right-clicking on the field and by adding and selecting that radio button from the menu. Now we need to go into the detail band and make sure our **LASTNAME** footer band is expanded downward so that we can drag our item onto it. Let us give it a try now. We will see a label and a field. Here is the screenshot that shows how our report appears. We observe that the first name bands are not visible and we are using the last name bands. We have almost completed our report. Since we are not customizing our report, we can make modifications to it whenever it is desired.

If we run this report directly from the CFR file, the output will be as shown below. We can observe that this report was run on a dev environment by the watermark. This will not appear on a live server. So do not worry about to seeing this it when building reports.

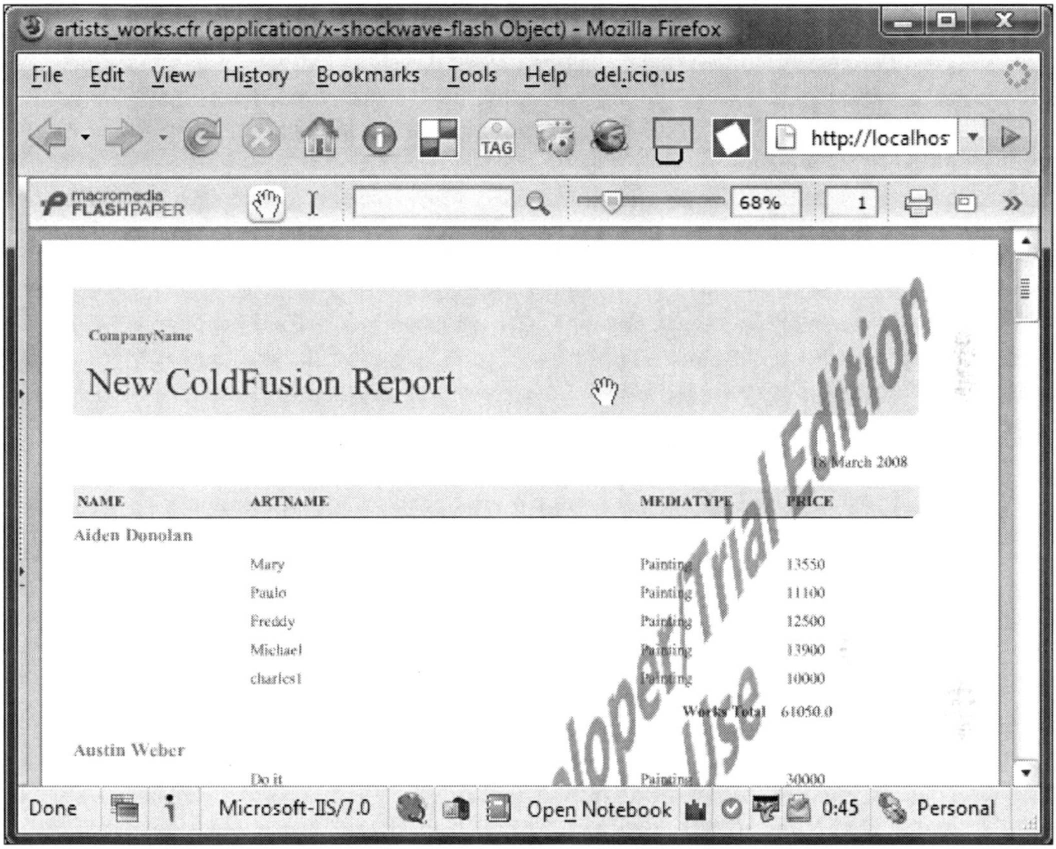

There is another aspect of reporting that will be exciting for ColdFusion developers. We can see that we have the prices for our listed works of art. Yet, we do not have them formatted as currency. Let us go back and change that. We find that all the functions that are used in ColdFusion are available to the report builder. We will change the field by double-clicking on it. If we do not know the name of the function, the bottom of this requestor will allow us to search for functions, which are grouped by categories. It also has constants, operators, and variables. This makes it a powerful report creation tool. We are going to change our value from **query.PRICE** to **dollarFormat(query.PRICE)**. We need to open our totals field and modify it in the same fashion. The date field at the top of the report and the page number at the bottom are both generated in a similar manner. They are not modifying any fields.

Now it's time to call this report from an actual ColdFusion page. There are two aspects of doing this. One aspect is to select the parameter and pass it into the report when our report already has a parameter. The other aspect is to show that we can generate our data for the report outside the report as well. This may be simple but this feature was unique to report builder in ColdFusion. Time might fly that but it was innovative to think in this manner when the feature was added. Here is our code.

```
<cfscript>
objReport = createObject("component","artists_reportData").init(dsn:"c
fartgallery");
myData = objReport.getArtistsWorks(artistid:3);
</cfscript>
<cfreport template="artists_works.cfr" format="PDF" query="myData" />
```

We see that we are generating the same code as we did in our previous examples but this time we output to the `<cfreport>` element thereby passing the data to the `artists_works.cfm` file. We can format the report in a number of ways. We choose to output all our reports as PDFs. But the reporting tool can actually output as PDF, FlashPaper, Excel, RTF, HTML, or XML. This means that if this report was generated as HTML and had a hyperlink in it, we could use it to generate drill-down reports and have access to the same functions that are built into ColdFusion. It is also possible to build custom functions inside CFR files.

We also have many powerful options for both the `<cfreport>` and the `<cfreportparam>` tag. There are nested reports, charts, passing-in styles, or CSS filenames, setting owner and user passwords for PDFs, encryption, and saving the file. The reality is that it is a very powerful reporting tool. It should also be noted that if the `<cfreport>` is embedded into a thread, it will require to be run with a filename attribute. Here is the final report as it is run in the free developer edition in our previous code. We can modify our `report_drillsource.cfm` file and pass in the ID of the selected artist if we want to make it fully automated for selection.

Summary

In this chapter, we have learned many styles and interactions for reporting in ColdFusion. Here is a list of what was covered in this chapter.

- Basic HTML reports
- Grouped data reporting
- Drill-down reporting
- Output formats (PDF, HTML, JSON, XML, Excel, and so on)
- Report builder

16
Dynamically Generated Web Presentations

The Internet has been a constant source of remarkable solutions to date. One example of this power is the `<cfpresentation>` tag inside ColdFusion. It can be used to give lecture materials that are used to share notes, presentations, stock reports and much more. The presentations can have some interesting aspects, which we will discuss as we move further.

Introduction to CFPresentation

We will start with a more basic code example to practice the features in ColdFusion 8.

We wrap everything with CFPresentation tags and then we have two elements. We have presenters and slides. We can have more than one presenter and assign them as we move from one slide to another. We can put a picture into the sidebar for the presenter as well as a logo. We can add the name of the presenter, a biography, and a contact email ID. We then put the title for each slide and the content in standard HTML. We can stylize the slide using CSS to some degree as well.

```
<cfpresentation title="Practice">
   <cfpresenter name="Joe"
     biography="Joe Goman is a skilled database manager and
               application developer.">
   <cfpresenter name="Veronica"
     biography="Veronica Dustin is a skilled HTML and CSS site
               designer.">
   <cfpresentationslide title="Introduction"
       presenter="Joe"
       duration="5">
```

```
        Welcome to the Practice CFPresentation slides.
    </cfpresentationslide>
    <cfpresentationslide title="Stump Speech"
        presenter="Veronica"
        duration="10"
        notes="This is where the notes for our presentation would go.">
        This is where I (Veronica) will sell you on some concept. Don't
         worry it won't take long.
    </cfpresentationslide>
    <cfpresentationslide title="Conclusion"
        presenter="Joe"
        duration="5">
        Isn't Veronica amazing? We will enjoy having you as a
        customer.
    </cfpresentationslide>
</cfpresentation>
```

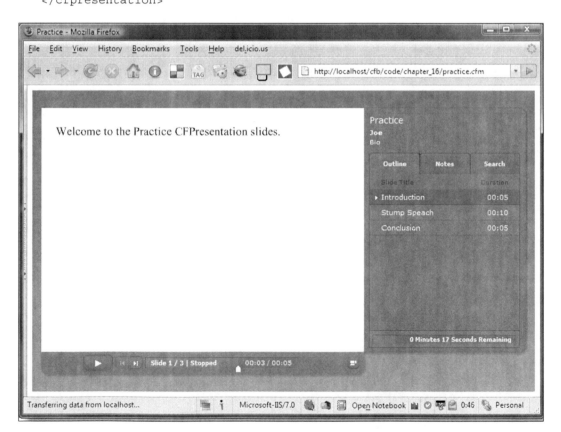

Now we can see the results of the practice example of the presentation tags. We have the main slide, the play control on the bottom of the slide, a maximize button, a show sidebar button, and the sidebar itself. The sidebar has the speaker notes, and/or video. It also has tabs for the outline, notes, and searches of the contents of the slide. There is actually a good deal of power packed into this set of three tags. Here is a view of what the screen looks like for item two in the practice presentation if we maximize it.

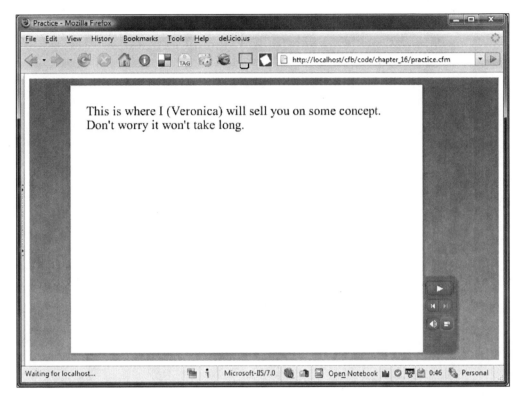

Now, the presentation is not competing with the notes, outline, or the image of the presenter. It is still available with a single click. We can still pause, play, move to the next or the previous slide, or mute audio as we choose.

Mixing in the Media

This is a web-based presentation tool and the media are an integral part. As we are learning with prototypes, we will not be looking for a polished presentation here but rather a great example as a foundation for learning.

The first thing we did was to write a gallery CFC that could be replaced by real data if we wanted to move this into production. This is a way we can prototype our application. Here is the code for creating a prototype data collection for our example.

```
<cfcomponent output="false">
  <cffunction name="getWorks">
    <cfscript>
     var works = queryNew("title,image,audio,duration,note");

      queryAddRow(works);
      querySetCell(works,"title","Barn");
      querySetCell(works,"image","Barn.JPG");
      querySetCell(works,"audio","barn.mp3");
      querySetCell(works,"duration",7);
      querySetCell(works,"note","This is an old barn on our block
                where we live.");

      queryAddRow(works);
      querySetCell(works,"title","Cactus");
      querySetCell(works,"image","Cactus.JPG");
      querySetCell(works,"audio","cactus.mp3");
      querySetCell(works,"duration",7);
      querySetCell(works,"note","This is a cactus we keep in our
                house to survive the winter.");

      queryAddRow(works);
      querySetCell(works,"title","Clouds");
      querySetCell(works,"image","Clouds.JPG");
      querySetCell(works,"audio","clouds.mp3");
      querySetCell(works,"duration",7);
      querySetCell(works,"note","These are the clouds over Lake
                Michigan from the other side of Chicago.");

      queryAddRow(works);
      querySetCell(works,"title","Shells");
      querySetCell(works,"image","shells.JPG");
      querySetCell(works,"audio","shells.mp3");
      querySetCell(works,"duration",7);
      querySetCell(works,"note","These are some shells my siblings
                collected.");

      queryAddRow(works);
      querySetCell(works,"title","Sunset");
      querySetCell(works,"image","Sunset.JPG");
      querySetCell(works,"audio","sunset.mp3");
      querySetCell(works,"duration",7);
      querySetCell(works,"note","We will end our exhibit with a
                sunset over Lake Michigan.");
```

```
            return works;
         </cfscript>
      </cffunction>
   </cfcomponent>
```

We create a query type recordset and then create several rows for it. We return the recordset back to the calling program. Again in a real application rather than a prototype like this, we would normally be pulling this from a database.

The next thing we will do is build a page that calls the recordset and uses it in an application. This shows us that we can have dynamic data inserted into our current presentation thereby building dynamic presentations. Another point of interest here is that we will be using structures to set the attributes for our tags in some cases rather than set them manually inside the tags. This is done with a single attribute called **attributesCollection**. The following code illustrates how to use it. We create a structure, which is named `preso`, and then assign the attribute variables to the structure to be passed in all at once. We should also note that we are setting many attributes for customization. Along with colors, we are setting the controls to appear on the left panel rather than the default right panel. Here is a screenshot of the first page that pulls its content from an external HTML page.

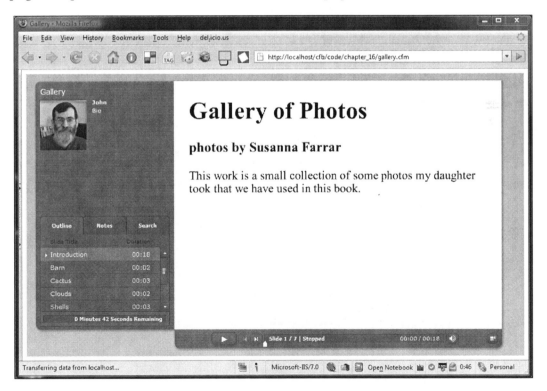

We do a similar thing for the slides to pass in the attributes on the photo slides. The audio in the slides is prototyped. This means it is not intended to be a final work but a complete concept. It is evident that the presentation looks much better with some photographs along with the plain text. Take time to make real presentations. It still needs the same basic fundamentals that any successful presentation would require. In the last slide, see the animated SWF file at the upper left. We had some issues with this until we saved it as Flash 7. The main window did not seem to have the same issues when we loaded content but it tended to skew the graphics until we made it an older version.

```
<cfscript>
preso=structNew();
preso.title = "Gallery";
preso.controlLocation = "Left";
preso.backgroundColor = "##C8C0B0";
preso.glowColor = "##A8AFBF";
preso.lightColor = "##A8A8BF";
preso.primaryColor = "##78788F";
preso.shadowColor = "##58586F";

oGallery = createObject("component","gallery");
rsWorks = oGallery.getWorks();
works = structNew();
works.presenter = "Susanna";
works.advance = "auto";
</cfscript>
<cfpresentation attributeCollection="#preso#">
    <cfpresenter name="John"
        image="media/john.JPG"
        biography="John Farrar is a the author of this book."/>
    <cfpresenter name="Susanna"
        biography="Susanna Farrar is photographer for this exibit."/>
    <cfpresentationslide title="Introduction"
        presenter="John"
        notes="This is our presentation."
        audio="media/introduction.mp3"
        src="gallery_intro.htm"/>

    <cfloop query="rsWorks">
        <cfscript>
            works.title = rsWorks.title;
            works.notes = rsWorks.note;
            works.audio = "media/#rsWorks.audio#";
        </cfscript>
    <cfpresentationslide attributeCollection="#works#">
        <cfoutput><div align="center">
            <h1>#rsWorks.title#</h1>
            <img src="media/#rsWorks.image#">
```

```
            </div>
         </cfoutput>
      </cfpresentationslide>
   </cfloop>
      <cfpresentationslide title="Conclusion"
            presenter="John"
            duration="10"
            video="media/anim.swf">
            You can please some of the people all of the time,<br>
            You can please all of the people some of the time,<br>
            But you can never please all of the people all of the time.
         <hr />
         (Note: On the side pannel there is a flash swf file.)
      </cfpresentationslide>
   </cfpresentation>
```

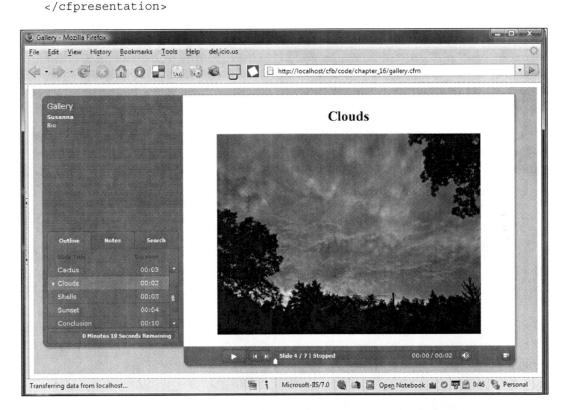

This results in a great presentation. We did learn a few tips along the way. If we add audio to the file and the time duration in the slide, it will play the audio until the end of the clip and then it will pause in the current version at the end of the audio clip. Therefore, we should not put an audio clip and the time duration on the same slide. We can also scale the content if necessary, and this can give us additional control as needed.

Another technique that can be used is to set a `.src` file for the slide. This could be HTML content, or it could contain a `cfchart`, or it can call a remote web page and can even call a `.swf` file directly. This did not seem to have the same issues as the scaling issues that were available in the sidebar. In other words, the current Flash versions worked here.

We will also find that we can click on the search tab and search through a presentation for words in the notes or in the text of the main page. Well, it will search for text notes but not text that has been converted to a graphic or an SWF file.

Caching the Contents

This is a powerful feature, but it takes a bit of machine power to create these presentations. One solution to this would be to cache the presentation. In order to do that, we have to set the directory attribute in the main presentation tag. This can be either a full path or a path relative to the current location. We choose the relative path because the same data will work for both paths and directory references that way. We also need to reference the created file to show it once we cache it. We create a directory called **cachme**, if it is not already created to put the files in.

We can use charts on dynamically created pages. Here is a page that we have created as the first page of our presentation with a 3D pie chart. Again, this is a presentation prototype. So do not try to get the accurate number from the pie chart.

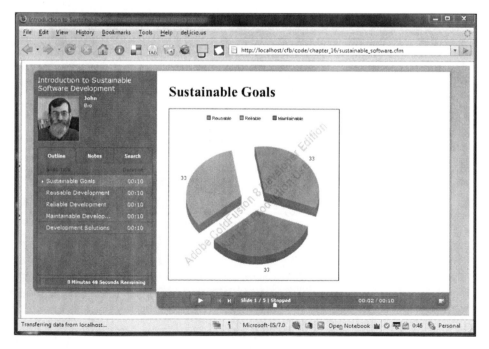

This code starts off with the same basic style as our previous example with the exception of the added directory attribute. We also check to see if the directory exists, and if it does not, then we create it.

```
<cfscript>
preso=structNew();
preso.title = "Introduction to Sustainable Software Development";
preso.controlLocation = "Left";
preso.backgroundColor = "##C8C0B0";
preso.glowColor = "##A8AFBF";
preso.lightColor = "##A8A8BF";
preso.primaryColor = "##78788F";
preso.shadowColor = "##58586F";
preso.directory = "cacheme";
</cfscript>
<cfif not directoryExists(preso.directory)>
<cfdirectory action="create" directory="#preso.directory#">
</cfif>
```

Next, we make the presentation as we would expect apart from one exception. We found that when the presentation was cached on our system, an exception error was thrown. To handle this, we wrapped the presentation code in a try-catch method and search for a unique exception. This means that if there is a different exception, it will appear on the screen. If the code has been cached, it will just move on.

```
<cftry>
<cfpresentation attributeCollection="#preso#">
    <!--- Presenters --->
    <cfpresenter name="John"
        image="media/john.JPG"
        biography="John Farrar is a the author of this book."/>
    <!--- GOALS --->
    <cfpresentationslide title="Sustainable Goals"
        presenter="John">
        <h1>Sustainable Goals</h1>
        <cfchart format="png"
            showborder="true"
            chartHeight="400"
            chartWidth="400"
            pieslicestyle="sliced"
            show3d="true">
        <cfchartseries type="pie">
        <cfchartdata item="Reusable" value="33" />
        <cfchartdata item="Reliable" value="33" />
        <cfchartdata item="Maintainable" value="33" />
```

```
        </cfchartseries>
        </cfchart>
    </cfpresentationslide>

    <!--- Reusable --->
    <cfpresentationslide title="Reusable Development"
        presenter="John">
        <h1>Reusable Development</h1>

    <ul>
            <li>Deployment</li>
            <li>Compatibility</li>
            <li>Encapsulation</li>
            <li>Libraries</li>
    </ul>

    </cfpresentationslide>

    <!--- Reusable --->
    <cfpresentationslide title="Reliable Development"
        presenter="John">
        <h1>Reliable Development</h1>

    <ul>
            <li>Parts and Tools</li>
            <li>Implementation</li>
            <li>Libraries</li>
            <li>Testing</li>
    </ul>

    </cfpresentationslide>

    <!--- Reusable --->
    <cfpresentationslide title="Maintainable Development"
        presenter="John">
        <h1>Maintainable Development</h1>

    <ul>
            <li>Lifecycle</li>
            <li>Integration</li>
            <li>Customization</li>
            <li>Time and Resources</li>
    </ul>

    </cfpresentationslide>

    <!--- Reusable --->
    <cfpresentationslide title="Development Solutions"
        presenter="John">
        <h1>Development Solutions</h1>

    <ul>
            <li>Open Source</li>
            <li>Libraries (tested)</li>
            <li>IDEs</li>
```

```
            <li>Generators</li>
            <li>Modular (Integration)</li>
            <li>Configurable</li>
            <li>Skinable</li>
        </ul>
        </cfpresentationslide>

    </cfpresentation>
        <cfcatch>
            <!--- do nothing but catch if already exists --->
        <cfif not findNoCase("Unable to create file",cfCatch.Message)>
            <cfdump var="#cfcatch#">
            <cfabort>
        </cfif>
        </cfcatch>
    </cftry>
```

The last thing we need to add to our code is the steps to take the cached version of our presentation and put it out on the screen. This is quite simple as shown in the following code. We make it a point to set the browser title to match the presentation by passing in the same variable as in our presentation. We also use the same relative paths. We also need to remember to wrap it with CFOutput so that the variables get converted.

```
<cfoutput>
<!DOCTYPE HTML PUBLIC "-//W3C//DTD HTML 4.0 Transitional//EN">
<html>
    <head>
        <meta http-equiv="Content-Type" content="text/html;
        charset=utf-8">
        <title>#preso.title#</title>
        <script type="text/javascript" language="JavaScript"
         src="#preso.directory#/loadflash.js" >
        </script>
    </head>
    <body>
        <script type="text/javascript" language="JavaScript">
        showFlash("#preso.directory#/viewer.swf", '100%', '100%',
            </script>
    </body>
</html>
</cfoutput>
```

We now have a complete cached presentation. Normally, presentations are cached to a `temp` directory. In this case, we get a real copy that can be moved to a disk, zipped up, emailed, and more. This creates a file called `index.htm` in the root of the cache directory. If we do not want to let an outsider know about the directories and try and load them, we could easily remove that file with some ColdFusion commands. All the images and assets are loaded into that directory. It also has a few XML files and an SWF file for every slide. These are stored in a `data` directory under the `cache` directory. Refer to the following screenshot:

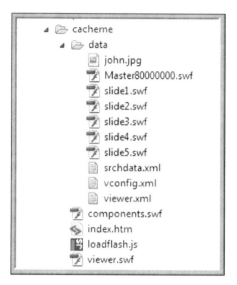

Dynamic Benefits

Here is a point of interest that sets this apart from some other solutions. Let us have a look at a few scenarios. We will not be actually building each of these. Instead, we will look at some unique solutions that would make it one of the best presentation products. Each of them shows some specific areas where this software proves to be beneficial.

Scenario 1: Sales Force

Business Requirements: This will be an application that presents a sales representative and the product lines. It would have a standard voice over, or if provided, a custom voice over from the sales representative for each of the products. It would either assemble this presentation on the fly, or cache the content.

Outline

- Selected introduction to company (site owners)
- Introduction of sales representatives
- Show the products that will be promoted by the sales representatives.

Scenario 2: Client-Specific Presentations

Business Requirements: This will be an application that provides each of the site customers with a customized presentation of both the products and sales representatives. By using the database, it can pull out the assigned sales representatives and the products that a particular site wants to present to its specific customer.

Outline

- Selected introduction to company (site owners)
- Introduction of presenters (the assigned sales representatives)
- Using representatives' recorded audio on products deliver targeted product slides
- Have primary account representative for customer slide to close

Scenario 3: Live Audience Sensitive Content

Business Requirement: This application will allow the speaker to ask a couple of questions at the start of his or her talk and will then generate a live on-the-fly presentation with the content suitable to the audience on hand. (This can also be used online or as a sales pitch.)

Outline

- The speaker takes a verbal survey of audience or uses some other method and then quickly selects the information from a check list.
- The server only generates the relevant slides live, on the fly.

Summary

Presentations are now available for both static and dynamic content. In this chapter, we have covered how we can cache the content and zip it up for delivery when required. Here is a recap of our introduction to CFPresentation.

- Features of the created presentation
    - Main slide
    - Sidebar presenter details
    - Video in sidebar
    - Tabs
        - Outline
        - Notes
        - Search
    - Maximize or Show Control Sidebar
- Manually created content
- HTML or SWF Content
- Dynamic content
- Caching content and generated files
- Extended unique advantages of CFPresentation over other solutions

A
Getting Your System Ready for Development

There are a number of things that we can do in order to be more productive, and to help us to enjoy our work. In this appendix, we will cover some ideals for setting up a development environment that will help us achieve these goals.

Tools

If you run into a veteran CF developer who has been using ColdFusion since the 'Old Days', you will probably hear him or her praise CFStudio. This migrated to a rewrite of HomeSite that shared a common codebase. It is known as HomeSite+. Adobe still provides the language updates for ColdFusion 8. Dreamweaver was chosen to fill the need for a full IDE tool and had an uneven start, but the later versions have shown great improvements.

Adobe has also done much to support an Open Source CFEclipse project. These are the two primary IDE solutions for CF Development at this time. There has been a public consideration with no promise from Adobe to kick-start the CF IDE and come up with a solution. This does not mean the solutions now do not work; it just means that developers recognize there is always more that can be offered to help them do a better job. Here is a list of features that different IDEs could or may have.

- Automatic update notification
- Code hinting
- Comparison tools (comparing two files, to find the differences between them)
- Data Interaction (Code Generation) Tools
- Debugging tools (to pause running code and check variables while code is running as well as stepping, or step through the code.)

- File (Local and Remote) Management
- Help Files (Tags, Functions, and so on.)
- Layout Customization (IDE layout)
- Macros (Record, Edit and Playback)
- Menus (Sensitive to current edit type and much more)
- Plug-Ins (Extensions)
- Project Management (Team features are also great)
- Synchronization Tools (Information of what changed and at which location)
- Snippets (Local and network available libraries)
- Source Control Tools (SVN is the current best choice)
- Toolbars (Context sensitive)
- Unit Test Integration
- Wizards (Pop-Up editors)

Here are the current popular IDEs for ColdFusion.

- **Dreamweaver**

  `http://www.adobe.com/products/dreamweaver/`

  Dreamweaver is an increasingly-valid option for doing CF development. It does not have some of the resources that are available to some of the Eclipse products, yet, it does make for a nice single point of entry programming solution enjoyed by a great number of CF developers. It has all of the basic tools needed to build CF-based sites. Primarily, this tool was created to support a designer's view point. It still does a good job while working with a developer because it is highly customizable. Also, there are a number of plug-ins available for Dreamweaver. This tool also has workflow integration with other Adobe products. This feature depends on the developer's style of coding and is the most important reason to consider.

- **Eclipse Stand-Alone Products**

  A number of tools are built on this base. Each of these tools can be mixed in as a plug-in. Moreover, many of them have their own stand alone solution that can be used with the other Eclipse products such as plug-ins.

  - **Aptana Studio**

    `http://aptana.com/`

    Aptana Studio is a powerful IDE for the Ajax development environment that runs standalone or within other Eclipse solutions.

There are editors for HTML, CSS,and JavaScript. It has debuggers
and additional plug-ins. It supports prototype, dojo, jQuery, ExtJS,
MooTools, and so on. There is a free version, and an extended version
available at a premium. One of the plug-ins that may be of interest
would be the plug-in for building the JavaScript based AIR applications. (This will be required to add in the ColdFusion plug-ins.)

- **Flex Builder**

  http://www.adobe.com/products/flex/

  Flex is a highly productive, free, open-source framework for building
  and maintaining expressive web applications that deploy consistently
  on all major browsers, desktops, and operating systems. Although
  Flex applications can be built using only the free Flex SDK software,
  developers can use the Adobe Flex Builder 3 software to dramatically
  accelerate the development. This software can build both AIR and
  Flex based applications. (This will be required to add in the
  ColdFusion plug-ins.)

- **MyEclipse**

  http://www.myeclipseide.com/

  This package was built primarily for Java developers. Some CF
  developers take time to interact with Java so this could be a better
  tool for them. It includes features such as a JavaScript debugger and
  editor, Swing Designer, NetBeans, UML, database support for Microsoft SQL, mySQL, Oracle and Sybase, Java image editor, Ajax tools,
  myEclipse Reports, Visual Web Designer, XML Editor, Toplink tool,
  Hibernate tool, Spring tools, Struts designer, JSF Designer, CSS and
  much more. (This will have to be added in ColdFusion plug-ins.)

- **Eclipse Plug-Ins**

  The standalone tools listed above are also available as plug-ins. So if we
  install any of the above tools, the others will plug into our preferred platform.

  - **Adobe ColdFusion Plug-In**

    http://www.adobe.com/support/coldfusion/downloads.html

    On the current version of this page, there is a link called
    "ColdFusion 8 Developer Tools". Under this section, you can find
    "ColdFusion 8 Extensions for Eclipse" This will include a debugger,
    code wizards, RDS, and so on.

- ○ **CFEclipse**

  http://cfeclipse.org/

  CFEclipse was released in February 2004. The goal of the CFEclipse project is to create a plugin for the Eclipse platform that provides a professional quality IDE for CFML developers. CFEclipse offers most of the features that are found in a traditional CFML, and also offers some more unique features. It allows the developers to take advantage of the wealth of other Eclipse plugins, CFEclipse comes with a developer-friendly price tag: It is free!

  http://www.adobe.com/devnet/coldfusion/articles/cfe-clipse.html

- ○ **Subclipse**

  http://subclipse.tigris.org/

  Subclipse is an Eclipse Team Provider plug-in that provides support for Subversion within the Eclipse IDE.

These tools are very effective. Consider finding a local user group, developers in online forums and bloggers who blogs on these topics and get some research which tools that will best match your development style.

AJAX

AJAX adds RIA to HTML pages. There are some special AJAX tools that allows Flex pages to interact with HTML pages. These are the tools that help in bringing new and exciting ways. View the sites and demonstrations and select a suitable one for your projects and customers.

- • **EXTJS**

  http://extjs.com/

  This is a powerful library, and some of its technology actually drives the features of AJAX inside ColdFusion 8! The library has advanced to version 2 since the release of CF and that is expected to follow the CF update cycle.

- • **jQuery**

  http://www.jquery.com

  This is perhaps the most popular in terms of library growth and ease of use libraries in the market today. It seems like this library has captured more of the who's who of developers in the industry.

- **MooTools**

  `http://mootools.net/`

  MooTools is an excellent AJAX library with proven features and delighted users.

- **Prototype or Scriptaculous**

  `http://script.aculo.us/`

  We can find links to Prototype from this page. The best information about the status of the supporting project is also on this page so we will only offer this link. Today, this is a well-used technology.

- **Spry**

  `http://labs.adobe.com/technologies/spry/home.html`

  This is a technology that has been included in ColdFusion, DreamWeaver, and is used by sites all around the world. Technically, it is still in beta test at this time but that is not final yet, considering how it is being used even by its creators. This is a proven AJAX technology with a loyal following and full feature set also.

Ant

This is a major topic to be covered in an appendix. It is on the rise in popularity inside the CF community. Ant allows automation of routine tasks. This can be, including synchronizing the SVN repository, FTP transfer of files to Unit Testing. My suggestion to you to getting this until you have a working understanding of ColdFusion. However, it is something that should definitely be revisited. A great resource on Ant can be found at `http://www.thecrumb.com/wiki/ant`.

Database Engines

Databases are one of the most important elements of many dynamic websites. These electronic filling cabinets are what makes these websites dynamic. They allow selective and interactive retrieval of narrow information, based on software constraints and user selections. Here are engines common to ColdFusion.

- **Access**

  `http://office.microsoft.com/en-us/access/default.aspx`

  This is a product that should be passed over for developing websites. It is a stable solution, but has a number of down-sides. The greatest down-side is that MS that owns SQL Server has now made the platform work as a scalable solution for servers. We would not go as far as to say DON'T USE IT, although you will find that is the practice mostly adopted at this time. Consider one of the other data platforms first.

  Some of your clients may already be using Access and may be accustomed to that environment. It can be easier to migrate from Access applications for some clients if they can still have access to the data through an "Access" interface. This means 'DO NOT store the data in Access but let the client connect to the data if that lets them feel better about moving in a new direction'.

- **Derby**

  `http://db.apache.org/derby/`

  Derby is an open-source powerhouse that has been created under the Apache project initiative. This database can run on all ColdFusion platforms. This version is automatically included as a part of ColdFusion.

- **mySQL**

  `http://mysql.com/`

  This is probably the most broadly-used database across all platforms at this time. Recently, this has become part of the Sun's product offerings. It is a robust and featured offering that has full features since version 5.

- **MSSQL**

  `http://www.microsoft.com/sql/default.mspx`

  This is Microsoft's SQL solution. It is a very powerful and scalable option for enterprise usage.

  - **Compact**

    `http://www.microsoft.com/sql/editions/compact/default.mspx`

  - **Express**

    `http://www.microsoft.com/sql/editions/express/default.mspx`

- **Oracle**

  http://www.oracle.com/index.html

  This is Oracle's enterprise data solution. It is also a lead for being able for scaling in the enterprise.

Database Tools

- **mySQL Query Browser**

  http://mysql.com/products/tools/query-browser/

  For many years, mySQL has been the mostly used cross-platform database. Recently, they were acquired by SUN.

- **Navicat**

  http://www.navicat.com/index.html

  This is a great mySQL developer tool with versions for Windows, Mac, and Linux.

- **RazorSQL**

  http://www.razorsql.com/

  This tool supports every database that will be crossed in any ColdFusion application. This includes the new internal database in ColdFusion, and Derby.

- **SQLYog**

  http://www.webyog.com/en/

  This is one of the popular SQL developer tools for mySQL. It is used widely and a product that is suggested by the mySQL users.

Media Tools

There are four basic types of graphics that will be considered here. These include still, vector, motion, and animation. Some of these programs will take up a specialized section within this scope and others will specialize in a way that covers multiple sections. In the previous generation, the need to know about video was not significant. Today, if this is not being considered, then it shows a lack of understanding of the platform of Internet. We will be discussing about audio before starting with graphics.

Audio Software

- **Soundbooth**

  http://www.adobe.com/products/soundbooth/

  Would you like to clean up fuzzy background sound, on a cell phone call from audio files? This tool changes the volume and much more. It is valuable for presenting a quality end-product in terms of audio.

Image Software

- **Acrobat Professional**

  http://www.adobe.com/products/creativesuite/acrobatpro/

  Acrobat is a tool that creates and displays PDF files. Now, PDF forms can be created with this or with the help of the LiveCycle designer. With the latest version of ColdFusion, PDF and the Server have become more connected to each other.

- **Aperture**

  http://www.apple.com/aperture/

  This can be used if you are a Mac user and you intend to have the digital photography package written by Apple.

- **Fireworks**

  http://www.adobe.com/products/photoshop/family/

  Fireworks is a great graphics editor and a creation tool when you are not looking to perform high level of photo manipulation. If you are looking to create composite designs for websites, there are some new special tools that can speed this process.

- **Photoshop**

  http://www.adobe.com/products/photoshop/family/

  This would include Photoshop and Lightroom. Each of these tools are unique in power and extension. If you are trying to include digital photography, then Lightroom should be considered. If bitmap editing of photos with higher power is the goal, then Photoshop goes beyond any digital camera editing package. Both Photoshop and Lightroom have strengths and work well with each other.

Video Software

- **Final Cut Studio**

  http://www.apple.com/finalcutstudio/

  This is one of Apple's success products that perform well in the real business world. If you own a Mac, this would be worthy to consider for your video production tool kit.

- **OnLocation**

  http://www.adobe.com/products/premiere/onlocation/

  This is one of the best products for moving projects from concept to success. This tool can change the project quality by creating a better foundation. The foundation of any video project is the source video. If you are not a movie producer with deep pockets, this could be your favourite tool of all your production tools.

- **Premiere**

  http://www.adobe.com/products/premiere/

  This is one of the longest running business video solutions on the market. One of the greatest features is the seamless integration into the workflow of the other Creative Suite products by Adobe. Combine this with the power of tools like After Effects, and it creates good quality video material.

- **Ultra**

  http://www.adobe.com/products/creativesuite/production/ultra/

  Chroma color keying is not an area in which it is traditionally easy to achieve success. Ultra is a powerhouse money-saver tool if this is an area of video you are considering. This is one of the products acquired from Serious Magic, where the way we think about the video production costs and features have changed. This tool contains animated sets, foregrounds, backgrounds, and loads of features and controls.

  This is a Windows-only tool.

- **Visual Communicator**

  http://www.adobe.com/products/visualcommunicator/

  This is an all in one simple but professional, video recording, and production tool. It can be used for everything from video blogging to preparing quality documents. The available effects and simplified user interface makes it a top scoring solution.

Reporting

Here is the link to acquire ColdFusion's Report Builder. This is a free offering for Windows users. The reports will run on any platform but the generation tool only runs on Windows. This is a powerful tool worth learning and using.

```
http://www.adobe.com/support/coldfusion/downloads.html
```

SVN

Historically speaking, there have been many good choices for version control, including Microsoft Source Control and CVS. Currently, the choice of almost all CF developers is SVN. This can be integrated with Ant tools also for automation. This will allow the developers to keep a track of all the changes in software.

- **SVN 1-Click Setup**

  ```
  http://svn1clicksetup.tigris.org/
  ```

  The goal of this project is to simplify the process of setting up a Subversion repository on a Windows-based computer. SVN 1-Click Setup takes you through the necessary steps to install the Subversion command-line utilities and TortoiseSVN, as well as to create a repository and initial project.

- **Subversion**

  ```
  http://subversion.tigris.org/
  ```

  The goal of the Subversion project is to build a version-control system that requires a compelling replacement for CVS in the open source community.

Unit Testing

There are three testing platforms with support inside the CFEclipse. These are CFUnit, CFCUnit, and MXUnit. Unit testing should be used by all the developers. We expect our cell phones to work. We expect our cars to be safe to drive down highways. Our clients and customers expect the software that runs their websites to also work. This is what Unit Testing is about. Some people might think that Unit Testing is just to test the exceptions that come up. This is not the most ideal use but far better than no testing at all. Unit Testing also allows new updates and exception fixes to be tested against older tests to makes sure fixes and updates aren't breaking things again.

- **CFUnit**

  `http://cfunit.sourceforge.net/`

  This was the first widely-accepted solution in the ColdFusion community and it made us to understand the concept well. The current version of CFEclipse has support for this built-in testing.

- **CFCUnit**

  `http://www.cfcunit.org/cfcunit/`

  This was another step forward in features and it became the most popular Unit Test tool in the community for a long season. Sean Corfield has a download on his blog at `http://corfield.org/blog/index.cfm`, and it is located in the sidebar under "software". This is only for the façade that allows CFCUnit to be used with the CFEclipse internally.

- **MXUnit**

  `http://mxunit.org/`

  This is the tool that we suggest to the CF Developers for use. It has better support and more output options. It allows running of individual tests or directories of tests. It has more features and more power. It is very easy to use. This toolkit is one of the recent ones but it is growing to be the most popular test environments at this time.

- **JSUnit**

  `http://www.jsunit.net/`

  This is a unit test technology solution for testing JavaScript libraries.

Conclusions

- We need the following items to be as productive as possible:
  - Good IDE
  - Handy Docs (See Appendix B for reference links)
  - SQL IDE for our platforms
- We benefit by using the libraries that are tested. It does not profit any of us to have people that create the same thing all over again.
- Make sure that the user interface looks good, and is not just technically correct and high with Web 2.0.
- Unit Testing makes a reliable software.
- ANT will allow automation that improves software reliability through testing, version control, deployment, and much more.
- Almost every library such as `jQuery` has ColdFusion developers involved in it.

B

Resources to Build Your Skills

The web is a growing community. The ability to collaborate is essential for the success of most sites. The links and resources in this appendix are aimed at giving us a good starting base of information that we can build upon by using what we have learned in this book. The libraries will continue to improve. So, obtain a good base of knowledge and then build on it. It would be beneficial for us to develop modular and reusable sites, so we can adjust to the changing world around us more easily.

Blogs

Blogs influence the community by sharing opinions and discoveries online. Each has a special outlook, and we hope that they are helpful to everyone.

- **Charlie Arehart**

  http://carehart.org/blog/client/index.cfm

  Charlie was one of the guys who has served our community in many offices. His skill and understanding makes him a high-value commodity of read when he puts something out for us to read.

- **Ray Camden**

  http://www.coldfusionjedi.com/

  Ray is the open source king of ColdFusion. He has done much more for the open source community than anyone else has, till date. He has written multiple free products and has run some of the most visited CF sites.

- **Sean Corfield**

  http://www.corfield.org/blog/

  Sean is a stand-up guy. He is an intelligent and insightful software engineer and contributes much to the ColdFusion community.

- **Mark Drew**

  http://www.markdrew.co.uk/blog/

  Mark is the person who has worked a lot on CFEclipse. This is his prevailing Free IDE for ColdFusion.

- **Ben Forta**

  http://www.forta.com/blog/

  Ben is the long-standing evangelist for ColdFusion. He has worked with Allaire and Macromedia before Adobe owned the language. He is a community leader and is well-versed in the product and the ColdFusion market.

ColdFusion Conferences

Conferences help us to gather information and meet the people who are driving the communities of technology. It would also be good to get outside the box where people challenge what we think, so we can either answer fresh questions, or gain insight into things we wouldn't find in our own sheltered domain.

- **CF Conference Central**

  http://www.cfconf.org/

  This is not a conference. It is a site dedicated to listing CF Conferences.

- **CFObjective**

  http://www.cfobjective.com/

  This conference is for those who like to think in terms of Pure OO, Design Patterns, and Enterprise.

- **CFUnited**

  http://cfunited.com/

  This is a general conference held every year. Now, European and smaller regional conferences called CFUnited Express are also held. The US conference is the largest conference on ColdFusion in the world, and is celebrating its 10th year in 2008.

- **MAX**

  http://www.adobe.com/events/max/

  Adobe is the company that owns the product called ColdFusion. This conference always has things of interest to ColdFusion developers.

- **Spring
**

  http://www.sbconference.com/

- **WebDU**

  http://www.webdu.com.au/

  You don't have to be in America to find big conferences. This is a great show. So if you live in the region, or just need an excuse to take a vacation down under, this is worth considering.

Coding Frameworks

Frameworks are collections of techniques and packaged code that make programming easier, more structured, and also offer other advantages. Methodologies are styles of coding. Some frameworks facilitate programming using one methodology while others work across multiple methodologies. Here are a few methodologies that will make larger projects and/or projects with multiple developers easier to manage.

- **ColdBox**

  http://www.coldboxframework.com/

  This seems to be recently-formed but one of the most exciting MVC OO focused frameworks for ColdFusion. The core site is good, and is worth visiting.

- **COOP**

  http://www.sosensible.com/index.cfm/product/coop

  COOP is a hybrid combination of the things that make ColdFusion important. It is a mixture of custom tags and CFCs that may make MVC simpler. This provides a number of advantages including preDOM coding.

- **FarCry**

  http://www.farcrycms.org/

  FarCry is one of the oldest and the most respected open-source frameworks. It is particularly focussed on CMS and is designed for a longer period.

- **Fusebox**

  http://www.fusebox.org

  This is an existing and widely-used ColdFusion application framework. Fusebox allows a broad range of programming styles and is supported by books, websites, and a large active community. The latest version allows you to program with, or without using XML.

- **Mach-II**

  http://www.mach-ii.com/

  Mach-II is a powerful, object-oriented, open-source MVC framework for ColdFusion that focuses on simplifying software development and maintenance. Mach-II was the first object-oriented framework for ColdFusion and continues to innovate with new features designed to help ColdFusion developers build and maintain large-scale applications more easily.

- **Model-Glue**

  http://www.model-glue.org/

  Model-Glue is an easy-to-learn MVC framework for ColdFusion that makes use of implicit invocation for application flexibility.

    - **Event Guard**

      http://eventguard.riaforge.org/

      Event Guard is a small Action Pack for Model Glue 2 that allows you to protect your event-handlers from unauthorized access. Event Guard checks whether the user is logged in, and then redirects them to a defined login event-handler by defining which events are locked, and which ones are open. This Action Pack does not do the actual login for you; it simply checks that the user is authorized.

    - **Event Validation**

      http://eventvalidation.riaforge.org/

      Event Validation is an Action Pack for Model Glue that allows you to validate input from a form or URL (or anything else that is in the event object) against a set of guidelines. It will generate an ErrorCollection object that you can then use to obtain and display the errors to the user. Other features include taglibs, which you can use to set up your form for all the required validations, as well as perform client-side validation using AJAX.

- **(SOS) Community**

  http://www.sosensible.com/index.cfm/product/sos

  This is a framework that allows multiple coding methodologies to run on the same site, in parallel. This provides a slightly more robust API for development, and is currently going into beta testing for version 5.

General ColdFusion Sites

- **CF Docs**

  http://cfdocs.org/

  This site has a full reference to the ColdFusion documents for tags and functions.

- **CF Quick Docs**

  http://cfquickdocs.com/

  This is one of the most popular search resources.

- **ColdFusion Cookbook**

  http://www.coldfusioncookbook.com/

  This site helps people solve common programming difficulties as they learn to use ColdFusion and connect ColdFusion with the outside world.

- **ColdFusion Community**

  http://www.coldfusioncommunity.org/

  This is a leading social website that is built around the ColdFusion community. It includes groups, personal pages, chat, community news, mailing list, forum, and much more. Members can also create links to other members. This allows us to find out what the people we associate with online look like, and what their interests are.

- **ColdFusion Meetup**

  http://coldfusion.meetup.com/17/

  This site is used to manage online meetings. ColdFusion libraries and technologies can be presented to people across the world at the same time through conferencing software. This site only does not include conferencing software, and works as a way to keep the community informed of upcoming meetings.

- **EasyCFM.com**

  http://easycfm.com/

  We all have areas where we are strong and areas where we are not. This site is full of resources and links to strengthen our weaker areas.

- **cfFrameWorks**

  http://cfframeworks.com/

  This is a site dedicated to help other developers in exploring ColdFusion-based frameworks.

- **LearnCF.com**

  `http://learncf.com/`

  This is one of the newer sites in the community, and has tutorials for learning ColdFusion.

- **RiaForge**

  `http://www.riaforge.org/`

  This is an open-source library that supports SVN, WIKI, main file download for a project, ticketing, and forums. It is the site most often used for Open Source ColdFusion libraries.

- **Yahoo ColdFusion Developer Center**

  `http://developer.yahoo.com/coldfusion/`

  Whoot! (or rather... Yahoo!) We have a site segment on one of the giant sites now.

Libraries and Tools

Libraries are collections of similar items. The following are some items grouped into common classifications which makes them easier to locate and a brief description of their benefits.

Aspect or IoC or DI

This is a design-pattern-oriented concept where you pass a postage handler into an object rather than have the object handle pull another object manually. This allows us to swap out the postage handlers without rewriting the object that uses its functions. There are many more advantages to it, but this one concept is sufficient to explain its use.

- **ColdSpring**

  `http://www.coldspringframework.org/`

  ColdSpring's core focus is to make the configuration and dependencies of your CFCs easy to manage. ColdSpring uses the 'inversion-of-control' pattern to 'wire' your CFCs together.

- **Lightwire**

  `http://lightwire.riaforge.org/`

  This is a lightweight DI or IoC framework. You can use the code for XML configurations.

Content Handling/Generation

We see content on websites. There are many ways to present the content but the following ones make the task of handling content and content packaging easier and standardized for delivery.

- **Chorus**

  `http://chorus.riaforge.org/`

  Dynamic sharing as a remote service site for HTML pages.

- **sosContent**

  `http://soscontent.riaforge.org/`

  sosContent will help you manage things such as JavaScript code blocks and imports, and CSS inline style blocks and imports. This is a shared component of COOP and CFish libraries.

- **microformats**

  `http://microformats.riaforge.org/`

  These CFCs help you in creating your own valid microformats: hCards, hCals, and hReviews. These CFCs will also parse out the same kind of data from other sites.

Database

The following libraries will make it easier to interact with databases. There are many common features of database interaction that should not be entirely manual. Each of these tools has different approaches, with different benefits, to automating interaction with our data layers.

- **CFCDataMapper**

  `http://cfcdatamapper.riaforge.org/`

  CFCDataMapper is a tool that allows you to map data from one database to another database without writing any SQL query.

- **Coldfusion Random Data Generator**

  `http://coldfusiondatagenerator.riaforge.org/`

  This creates highly random, highly readable data.

- **DataMGR**

  `http://datamgr.riaforge.org/`

  This is a data-access layer component that simplifies CRUD actions. It also has the ability to help port the data from one platform to another.

- **Derby**

  `http://db.apache.org/derby/`

  This database that comes packaged with ColdFusion. It replaces the Access databases and provides a universal data platform standard for all distributions of CF on smaller simple sites. It also works well for example application code data.

- **Dynamic Bean**

  `http://dynamicbean.riaforge.org/`

  The dynamic bean simplifies the creation of a bean with generic access (using the setter and getter methods) by automatically creating the access in the memory at runtime. This is done by using the method `OnMissingMethod()` that is provided with ColdFusion 8.

- **Reactor**

  `http://www.alagad.com/go/products-and-projects/`
  `reactor-for-coldfusion`

  Reactor is an Object-Relational Modeling tool that generates database abstractions as quickly as needed. Reactor is sometimes called an "Inline Dynamic Database Abstraction" API.

- **Squidhead**

  `http://squidhead.riaforge.org/`

  An application generator for CF and MSSQL that generates applications using stored procedures.

- **sqlCFC**

  `http://sqlcfc.riaforge.org/`

  CRUD Statements made easy.

- **Transfer**

  `http://transfer.riaforge.org/`

  This is an **ORM** (Object Relational Mapper) for Coldfusion. This is the lead ORM solution for ColdFusion.

- **Transfer Config**

  `http://transferconfig.riaforge.org/`

  This application introspects a database by using the ColdFusion tag `cfdbinfo`, and creates the Transfer ORM configuration file based on settings that you specify in the `environment.xml` file and the UI.

- **Validat**

  http://www.alagad.com/go/products-and-projects/validat-data-validation-engine

  Validat is a data validation engine developed in ColdFusion, that can be dropped into any application with a minimal amount of customization, and will perform any required data validation for that application.

JavaScript

Web developers make sites dynamic by sending pages back to the server and modifying them. This may be great for the developer, but it is not so good for the user. These libraries are changing things by making it much easier for the server-side developer to perform browser-side software development:

- **DOJO**

  http://dojotoolkit.org/

  The core supports AJAX, events, packages, CSS-based query, animations, JSON, language utilities, and much more.

  - **CFWidgets**

    http://cfwidgets.riaforge.org/

    A set of custom tags that wrap some of the Dojo functionalities in order to create rich AJAX interfaces without writing JavaScript.

- **EXT JS**

  http://extjs.com/

  CF8 contains EXT JS 1.1, but the most recent version being used is 2.x. The following frameworks try to extend the same technology:

  - **CFExt**

    http://cfext.riaforge.org/

    It is a ColdFusion wrapper for the Ext JavaScript Framework.

  - **ColdExt**

    http://coldext.riaforge.org/

    ColdExt is a tag library for ColdFusion based on the JavaScript Library, Ext JS.

- **jQuery**

  `http://jquery.com/`

  jQuery is a fast, concise, JavaScript Library that simplifies how you can traverse HTML documents, handle events, perform animations, and add AJAX interactions to your webpages. jQuery is designed to change the manner in which you write JavaScript.

    ◦ **CFJS (ColdFusion JavaScript for jQuery)**

      `http://cfjs.riaforge.org/`

      JavaScript equivalents of useful ColdFusion functions.

    ◦ **CF_jQuery**

      `http://cf_jquery.riaforge.org/`

      Widgets and custom tags based on the jQuery library.

    ◦ **jQuery ICE**

      `http://coop.riaforge.org/wiki/index.cfm/index.`
      `cfm?event=Main&path=DOCS.ICE&redirectedfrom=ICE`

      This is a growing jQuery library that runs with COOP.

- **MooTools**

  `http://mootools.net/`

  MooTools is a compact, modular, object-oriented JavaScript framework designed for the intermediate-to-advanced JavaScript developer. It allows you to write powerful, flexible, cross-browser code with its elegant, well-documented, and coherent API.

- **Prototype or Scriptaculous**

  `http://prototypejs.org/`

  Prototype is a JavaScript Framework that eases the development of dynamic web applications.

  `http://script.aculo.us/`

  The `script.aculo.us` provides us with easy-to-use, cross-browser user interface JavaScript libraries to speed up your web sites and web applications.

Project Management

The greater the number of tasks, events, and people we have involved in a project, the more benefit we gain by creating a shared planning and organization interface. The following tools prove to be great resources:

- **Lighthouse**

  http://lighthousepro.riaforge.org/

  This is Ray Camden's issue-tracking software.

- **Project 6**

  http://project6.riaforge.org/

  This is a project tracker that is a mixture of Flex and CF mixture.

- **Project Tracker**

  http://projecttracker.riaforge.org/

  This is one of the most important project management tools. It is simple and has many features. It has milestones, tickets, messages, issues tracking, files, svn integration, rss feeds, and a great graphical user interface.

- **Skweegee**

  http://skweegee.riaforge.org/

  This is a full-featured project manager. It has issue-management, a wiki, and an SVN browser built in.

Script

Script was the domain of all the other languages during most of the ColdFusion years. ColdFusion was about doing things using tags. CF developers found themselves becoming familiar with scripted code with the help of JavaScript (due to AJAX) and ActionScript in Flex, Flash, and AIR. Script has been supported more fully in ColdFusion. There are many functions that do not exist, but they can be created to extend features that are built into tags. The following libraries can help in making the integration simpler:

- **ScriptCFC**

  http://scriptcfc.riaforge.org/

  This component provides some standard tag functions missing in CFCs. Most of the times we do not use Script because the functionality is not available natively in Script. Since this is a packaged solution, it can be plugged in and extended.

- **Scripting for ColdFusion 8**

    http://scripting.riaforge.org/

    This is collection of custom tags and libraries that allow you to run a variety of scripting languages, such as PHP, Ruby, and so on, inside ColdFusion.

- **scriptaGulous**

    http://scriptagulous.riaforge.org/

    This is a library of functions for every CF tag, with the intention that it should be community-driven, but without CF8 tags.

Search

One of the most common things that people search for on the internet is content. Here are a couple of libraries that can help you.

- **AmazonCFC**

    http://amazoncfc.riaforge.org/

    This is a CFC for using the Amazon web service item search.

- **Seeker**

    http://seeker.riaforge.org/

    This is a wrapper for 'Lucerne's search engine code.

Site Integration APIs

Communities are becoming more central to what the internet is about. They provide the networking side of the internet. The following libraries are for popular sites that have created community interfaces to allow others to interact with their services.

- **Amazon**

    http://www.amazon.com/

    ○ **Amazon SQS CFC**

    http://sqscfc.riaforge.org/

    This is a ColdFusion component for accessing the Amazon Simple Queue Service (SQS) API.

- **AOL**

  `http://www.aol.com/`

  ○ **AOL APIs**

    `http://aolpictures.riaforge.org/`

    Provides access to AOL Pictures, Truveo, XDrive, and OpenAuth APIs.

- **Authorize.net**

  `http://authorize.net/`

- **Recurring Billing API CFC**

  `http://authorizenetrecurring.riaforge.org/`

  This CFC is used for accessing Authorize.net's recurring billing API.

- **Basecamp**

  `http://www.basecamphq.com/`

  ○ **BasecampCFC**

    `http://basecampcfc.riaforge.org/`

    This is a ColdFusion Interface to the Basecamp API.

- **Connect**

  `http://www.adobe.com/go/gntray_prod_acrobat_connect_pro_home`

  ○ **ConnectAPIcfc**

    `http://connectapicfc.riaforge.org/`

    This supports 27 different functions, supported by Breeze 5, that generally relate to obtaining reporting information from Breeze. The API functions for creating, editing, or removing accounts and meetings have not been built. However, if you examine the code, you will see that much of the work of calling functions within the API has already been built. So, adding new functions is just a matter of building a parameter structure and passing that to the pre-built functions for creating XML, and sending the request.

- **Constant Contact**

  `http://www.constantcontact.com/`

  ○ **Constant Contact CFC**

    `http://constantcontact.riaforge.org/`

    This is a simple CFC that allows you to send information to your permanent account to add, modify, and remove subscribers with ease.

- **Delicious**

  `http://del.icio.us/`

  ◦ **DeliciousCFC**

    `http://deliciouscfc.riaforge.org/`

- **digg**

  `http://digg.com/`

  ◦ **DiggCFC**

    `http://diggcfc.riaforge.org/`

    This is an Interaction with the Digg API.

- **Facebook**

  `http://www.facebook.com/`

  ◦ **Facebook REST Client**

    `http://facebookclient.riaforge.org/`

    This is a simple ColdFusion client library for the `facebook.com` API.

- **FeedBurner**

  `http://www.feedburner.com/`

  ◦ **Feedburner API**

    `http://feedburnerapi.riaforge.org/`

    This is an API for managing feeds on feedburner.

- **Flickr**

  `http://flickr.com/`

  ◦ **CFlickr**

    `http://cflickr.riaforge.org/`

    This is a ColdFusion wrapper for Flickr's REST API.

- **Google**

  `http://www.google.com/`

  ◦ **Cf_googleMap**

    `http://cfgooglemap.riaforge.org/`

    This is a custom tag for integrating a custom Google map into your page.

  ◦ **CheckoutCFC**

    `http://checkoutcfc.riaforge.org/`

    This is a Coldfusion Checkout CFC for Google Checkout.

- ○ **Google Geocode**

  `http://googlegeocode.riaforge.org/`

  This component provides an interface to the Google Geocoding service.

- ○ **Google Maps Tag**

  `http://googlemapstag.riaforge.org/`

  This is a Google Maps ColdFusion tag.

- ○ **GoogleCal**

  `http://googlecal.riaforge.org/`

  This is an an API to Google's Calendar.

- ○ **GoogleCalendarCFC**

  `http://googlecalendarcfc.riaforge.org/`

  This returns a query containing data from a given Google Calendar feed URL.

- **SimpleGeocode**

  `http://simplegeocode.riaforge.org/`

  This is a Simple Google Geocode.

- **JangoMail**

  `http://jangomail.com/`

  - ○ **JangoMail CFC**

    `http://jangomailcfc.riaforge.org/`

    This is a CFC for communicating with the JangoMail API.

- **JFree Chart**

  `http://www.jfree.org/jfreechart/`

  - ○ **JFree Chart Custom Tag**

    `http://jfreechart.riaforge.org/`

- **Open Social**

  `http://code.google.com/apis/opensocial/`

  - ○ **cfOpenSocial**

    `http://opensocial.riaforge.org/`

    This is an Open Social API Tool.

- **PicasaCFC**

  http://picasa.google.com/

  ○ **cfLightCasa**

    http://cflightcasa.riaforge.org/

    This is a combination of CF, LightBox, and Picasa.

  ○ **cfPicasa**

    http://cfpicasa.riaforge.org/

    This is a CFC to personalize your Picasa Web Album.

  ○ **picasaCFC**

    http://picasacfc.riaforge.org/

    This reads RSS feeds from Picasa Web Albums.

- **Sales Force**

  http://www.salesforce.com/

  ○ **salesForceCFC**

    http://salesforcecfc.riaforge.org/

    This integrates CF with the SalesForce.com API via SOAP.

- **riaForge**

  http://www.riaforge.org/

  ○ **riaForge Updater**

    http://riaforgeupdater.riaforge.org/

    This is a small CFC that allows programming updates to your RIAForge Project.

  ○ **riaForgeCFC**

    http://riaforgecfc.riaforge.org/

    This is a component used for retrieving your project data from RIAForge.

- **Twitter**

  http://twitter.com/

  ○ **twitterCFC**

    http://twittercfc.riaforge.org/

    This makes calls to Twitter via the use of a CF component.

- **UPS**
  - ○ **ColdFusion UPS Package**

    `http://cfups.riaforge.org/`

    The ColdFusion UPS Package is a set of components that make it easy to work with the various UPS services. Recently, support for Address Verification, Shipment Tracking, and Service Rates has been added.

- **Yahoo!**

  `http://www.yahoo.com/`

  - ○ **ColdFusion Yahoo Package**

    `http://cfyahoo.riaforge.org/`

    The ColdFusion Yahoo Package is a set of components that make it easy to work with the various Yahoo services. Currently there is support for Answers, Traffic, Weather, Search, Geocoding, Maps, Term Extraction, News Search, Contextual Search, Related Search Suggestions, Spelling Suggestions, Image Search, Podcast Search, Artist, Album or Song Search, and Local Search.

  - ○ **Yahoo Word Extraction CFC**

    `http://yahoowordextractioncfc.riaforge.org/`

    Using Yahoo's word extraction API, you can pass a body of content to this CFC and receive a query of keywords in return.

- **YouTube**

  `http://www.youtube.com/`

  - ○ **YouTube CFC**

    `http://youtubecfc.riaforge.org/`

    This CFC provides integration with YouTube's REST API. Functions include the ability to perform various searches, and return profile and video information.

- **Miscellaneous**
  - ○ **cfPayment**

    `http://cfpayment.riaforge.org/`

    This is a generalized API for interfacing to payment gateways for processing credit cards, and other forms of payment.

      °   **ISBNdbCFC**

        `http://isbndbcfc.riaforge.org/`

        ISBNdb.com's remote-access Application Programming Interface (API) is designed to allow other websites and standalone applications to use the vast library of data collected by `ISBNdb.com` since 2003.

      °   **SnipEx**

        `http://snipex.riaforge.org/`

        SnipEx is an XML-based service that allows CFEclipse users to susbcribe to snippet servers and submit their own snippets to the SnipEx servers. You can install a SnipEx server on your local network for easy sharing of snippets.

Unit Testing or Debugging

One of the most important skills that a developer can possess is the ability to debug. (This includes the developer's own code, and not just the code of others.) The following library tools help improve our ability to create robust code in less time, and with less effort:

- **CFUnit**

  `http://cfunit.sourceforge.net/`

  CFUnit is a unit testing framework for ColdFusion (CFML), modeled after the popular JUnit framework.

- **CFCUnit**

  `http://www.cfcunit.org/cfcunit/`

  CFCUnit is a full-fledged framework for unit testing ColdFusion code.

- **ColdFire**

  `http://coldfire.riaforge.org/`

  ColdFire is an extension to FireBug. It provides debug information in a FireBug tab and not at the bottom of the page. This helps you debug and keep your site layout intact, since ColdFusion's built-in debug information can sometimes interfere with your site's layout. ColdFire currently supports debugging information for general information, templates, queries, CFTRACE, CFTIMER, variables, and trace.

- **MXUnit**

  `http://mxunit.riaforge.org/`

  This is a Unit Test framework for CFMX components.

- **QueryParam Scanner**

  http://qpscanner.riaforge.org/

  qpScanner is a simple tool that scans your codebase, searching for queries. For every query found, it checks for ColdFusion variables in the query, that do not contain a cfqueryparam tag.

- **RocketUnit**

  http://rocketunit.riaforge.org/

  This is a very lightweight unit testing Unit Test framework for ColdFusion.

- **Stubbie**

  http://stubbie.riaforge.org/

  Stubbie creates a set of "test stub" objects, which can be used in your unit tests Unit Tests, based on your project's CFCs.

- **varScoper**

  http://varscoper.riaforge.org/

  varScoper is a CFC, and there are corresponding views designed to identify variables created within a CF function that does not have a corresponding (cfset var) statement.

XML Tools and Products

XML has become a business fundamental for shared solutions, configuration files, and much more. Yet managing XML documents visually can be an overwhelming task. The following tools help you with many aspects of this:

- **ALTOVA Products**

  http://www.altova.com/

  This company carries a premium set of tools for working with XML. These include xmlspy, mapforce, stylevision, diffdog, schemagent, and the free authentic.

- **Better XML**

  http://betterxml.riaforge.org/

  This is a set of two components that extends the ColdFusion XML Doc object. They simplify and accelerate XML operations for CF6.1 and 7, utilizing the XPath more effectively. This is performed by using a Java XPath API.

- **EditiX**

  http://www.editix.com/

  This company provides a premium editor with support for XML, XSLT, XSL-FO, DTD, Schema, Open XML, XML Diff, and much more.

- **Google Sitemap XML Generator**

  http://googlesitemapxmlgenerator.riaforge.org/

  Google Sitemap XML Generator creates an XML file for the Sitemap protocol (http://www.sitemaps.org) used by several search engines such as Google, MSN, and Yahoo. It follows the links and gathers information to create a site navigation tree in query format or XML sitemap format.

- **OXYGEN**

  http://www.oxygenxml.com/

  This is company provides a premium editor that works on XML, schema, XSL or XSLT, XQuery, XML Databases, with SVN, and more.

- **sosXML**

  http://sosxml.riaforge.org/

  If you would like working with XML to be simplified further, then this object class can be really helpful. You can also learn how to work with XML, if you want to do some interesting coding for your own applications.

- **Stylus Studio**

  http://www.stylusstudio.com/

  This is a commercial tool that performs XML editing, XQuery, XSL, or XSLT, EDI, XML Pipeline, XML Publishing, XML Schema, XSL-FO, DTD, XPath, and much more.

- **XMLBuddy**

  http://www.xmlbuddy.com/

  This is an Eclipse plug-in for those who want to perform some basic XML editing.

- **XmlToStruct**

  http://xml2struct.riaforge.org/

  This converts complex XML in to a ColdFusion structure.

Other Notable Works

The following groups of libaries are very significant, though the categories are not very common:

- **AntFarm**

  http://antfarm.riaforge.org/

  This is the ColdFusion-Based Build Manager.

- **CodeCop**

  http://codecop.riaforge.org/

  CodeCop is a ColdFusion code checker. It selects code on the local system, and reports all possible issues. It is fully configurable, and you can choose the rules it will use to determine any possible issues, or you can even make your own rules, or even import rules packages that others have created. It can run in the ColdFusion administrator, or in the CFMX 6.1 and above. It can be installed on any database supported by DataMgr.

- **ColdFISH**

  http://coldfish.riaforge.org/

  ColdFish is a syntax highlighter used within the ColdFusion applications. It is fast, efficient, easy to use, and allows for easy customization of the color palette. It supports ColdFusion Tags, CFScript, HTML tags, Javascript, as well as comments in all these languages.

- **ColdFusion Event Dispatcher**

  http://eventdispatcher.riaforge.org/

  In ActionScript 3, the EventDispatcher is a core class that implements the Subject side of the Observer pattern. Extending it allows you to create classes that can dispatch events as well as have event listeners registered, removed, or managed. This code mimics the AS3 IEventDispatcher interface as closely as possible.

- **CF Gen**

  http://cfgen.riaforge.org/

  CF Gen is a complete application generator that allows you to generate any kind of application using template-based code generation.

- **CF Library**

  http://cflibrary.riaforge.org/

  CF Library is a simple framework for implementing a persistent library of functions and components on ColdFusion and compatible servers.

- **CF Template**

  http://cftemplate.riaforge.org/

  CF Template is a pattern of the ColdFusion language that allows you to use the control of ColdFusion to generate anything from documentation to ColdFusion code in Ruby, Java, or XML. It allows you to use any valid ColdFusion code within your templates, and any type of the following data, recordset, iterating business object, XML, and so on.

- **Concurrency**

  http://cfconcurrency.riaforge.org/

  It Concurrency is inspired by Java 5's concurrency package. Concurrency for CFMX wraps the Asynchronous CFML Event Gateway to provide a simple syntax for performing asynchronous method calls on the CFCs, where you can easily receive the results back.

- **OAuth**

  http://oauth.riaforge.org/

  OAuth is a ColdFusion implementation of the OAuth protocol. (http://oauth.net).

Index

A

AJAX 344
AJAX tools
  EXTJS 344
  jQuery 344
  MooTools 345
  Prototype/Scriptaculous 345
  Spry 345
ANT 345
Application.cfc object
  about 79
  code flow 80
  methods 79
application variables
  about 82
  applicationTimeout 82
  clientManagement 82
  clientStorage 82
  loginStorage 83
  Name 82
  scriptProtect 83
  secureJSON 83
  secureJSONPrefix 83
  sessionManagement 83
  sessionTimeout 83
  setClientCookies 83
  setDomainCookies 83
  welcomeFilelist 84
Aspect or IoC or DI
  about 358
  ColdSpring 358
  lightwire 358
authentication
  about 138
  advanced authentication 142-144
  authentication data model 139-141

B

benefits, CFPresentation
  client specific presentations 339
  live audience sensitive content 339
  sales force 338
binding
  CFC binding 200, 202
  event based 204
  extra binding notes 205
  forms 199
  JavaScript binding 202
  on page binding 200
  URL binding 203, 204
Blogs
  about 353
  Ben Forta 354
  Charlie Arehart 353
  Mark Drew 354
  Ray Camden 353
  Sean Corfield 353
browser side applications
  about 148
  flash 148
  Javascript 148
built-in debugging
  about 215
  auto-wired AJAX links 218
  CFAjax data, sending via post 221
  customization 217
  JSON features 220
  logging features 216, 217
  onLoad JavaScript function,
    triggering 219, 220
  tag attribute list 218

C

CDF 288
CF AJAX forms
  <cfgrid /> tag 172
  <cfinput /> tag 181
  <cfselect /> tag 187, 188
  <cftextarea /> tag 190, 191
  <cftree /> tag 192, 193
  about 171
  auto suggest box 185, 186
  CFinput example 182, 183
  data requestor 184
  directory tree 194-196
  grid deletes 178
  grid paging 173, 174
  grid updates 176, 177
  linked grids 179
  page elements, binding 181, 182
CF AJAX programming
  about 199
  binding 199
  built-in debugging 215
  CFAJAXProxy 206
  CFAJAXProxy binding 207
  CFAJAXProxy class objects 208-212
  client debugging 213
  Firebug 213, 214
  multiple raio buttons/check boxes
      binding 206
  spry binding 206
CFAJAXProxy 206
CFAJAXProxy binding 207
CFAJAXProxy class objects 208
CFC methods
  access, protecting 60
CFCs
  about 37
  basic data object concept 53-56
  data, returning from CFC 47, 49
  database, connecting to 45, 47
  first object 38
  object 38
  object classes, creating 41
  object class instances 41
  object constructor 42, 43
  object method access control 56

  product 38
  query variable structure 50-52
CFPresentation
  about 327, 329
  benefits 338
  content, caching 334-338
  dynamic content, iniserting 331
  gallery CFC, writing 330
  main slide 329
  photo slides 332
  prototype data collection 330
  sidebar presentation details 329
CGI variable structure 16
client debugging 213
coding frameworks
  about 355
  ColdBox 355
  COOP 355
  event guard, Model-Glue 356
  event validation, Model-Glue 356
  FarCry 355
  Fusebox 355
  Mach-II 356
  Model-Glue 356
  SOS community 356
ColdFusion
  <cfIf> tag 32
  <cfSwitch> tag 35
  Application.cfc object 79
  application mappings, setting 93
  arrays 29, 30
  Blogs 353
  CFC file, creating 38
  CFCs 37, 96
  cfIf statement 32
  CFPresentation 327, 329
  cfSwitch statement 35
  CGI variable structure 16
  code reuse, different forms 95
  coding frameworks 355
  conditional processing, with If 32, 33
  conditional processing, with switch 35, 36
  custom authentication 138
  custom tag paths per application, setting 93
  custom tags 96
  database searching 241
  debugging tool 16

debugging window 215
default variables, setting for pages 23-26
email, working with 270
exception handling 20
files, working with 263
form structure 62
get, common structures 62
Google map, integrating with 121-127
HTML pages, turning into dynamic web
    pages 7-11
image information 277-281
images, working with 274
key permissions functions 133, 134
lists 27
loops 27
output formats 311
PDF, creating 223
PDF pages, generating 223
permissions 133-137
post, common structures 62
practical application 92
report builder, installing 317-324
search abilities, building 241
simple variables 11
structures 16
Thickbox library, wrapping 116-120
tools 341
unit testing 350
URL variable structure 18-22
verity search solutions 241
web forms 61
ColdFusion AJAX
  <cfdiv />, layout 149
  <cfdiv />layout 150
  <cflayout />, layout 151
  <cfmenu /> 163, 164, 165
  <cfpod />, layout 157
  <cftooltip /> 166, 167, 168
  <cfwindow />, layout 158-162
  about 149
  border example, <cflayout /> 151-153
  HBox/VBox example, <cflayout /> 153-155
  layout 149
  styling notes 168
  tab example, <cflayout /> 155
  tips 168

ColdFusion Components. *See* CFCs
ColdFusion Conferences
  CF Conference central 354
  CFObjective 354
  CFUnited 354
  MAX 354
  Spring
 355
  WebDU 355
ColdFusion JavaScript
  about 127
  fancy form tag 130-132
  multiple state elements 128, 129
ColdFusion Report Builder 350
content handling/generation
  about 359
  chorus 359
  microformats 359
  sosContent 359
CSE
  about 253
  Google CSE 253
  on the fly search engine 253, 255
  simple search 256
custom search engines. *See* CSE
custom tags
  about 96
  CFInclude 96
  CFInclude, integrating with 106-109
  CFModule tag 110
  custom header/footer tags 98, 100
  first custom tag 97, 98
  managing 110
  nested tags 101-106
  tag library approach 111
  website, skinnning 109, 110

D

data
  editing 65-68
  saving 68-70
Database
  about 359
  CFCDataMapper 359
  Coldfusion Random Data generator 359
  DataMGR 359
  Derby 360

Dynamic Bean 360
Reactor 360
sqlCFC 360
Squidhead 360
Transfer ORM 360
Transfer ORM Config 360
Validat 361
Database engines
about 345
Access 346
Derby 346
MSSQL 346
mySQL 346
Oracle 347
Database tools
mySQL Query Browser 347
Navicat 347
RazorSQL 347
SQLYog 347
debugging tool 16
Dreamweaver 342

E

Eclipse plug-ins
about 343
Adobe ColdFusion plug-In 343
CFEclipse 344
subclipse 344
Eclipse Stand Alone Products
about 342
Aptana Studio 342
Flex Builder 343
MyEclipse 343
email
individual messages, getting 270-274
list of messages, retrieving 270-274
message, sending 270-274
messages, deleting from server 270-274
working with 270
end methods
about 87
application end method 88
onError method 89
request end method 88
session end method 88
exception handling 20

F

features, CF AJAX forms
CFGrid 172
CFInput 181
CFSelect 187
CFTextArea 190
CFTree 192
feeds
about 283
CDF 288
JSON 289
RSS feeds 284, 285
SQL 292
file
appending 270
example 266, 267
local file control 266
reading 268, 269
reading, via loop 270
renaming 269
uploading 263-266
working with 263
writing 268
Firebug 213
Flickr 283

G

general ColdFusion sites
CF docs 357
cfFrameworks 357
CF quick docs 357
ColdFusion community 357
ColdFusion cookbook 357
ColdFusion meetup 357
easyCFM.com 357
learnCF.com 358
RiaForge 358
Yahoo ColdFusion developer center 358
Google map
integrating 121
Google site search features
Google details 252
integrating 252
local search 260, 261
searching, through custom tag 259
search types 257

I

IDE
  Dreamweaver 342
  Eclipse plug-ins 343
  Eclipse Stand Alone Products 342
  features 341
images
  image handling code 274
  working with 274-277

J

JavaScript
  about 361
  CF_jQuery 362
  CFExt, EXT JS 361
  CFJS, jQuery 362
  ColdExt, EXT JS 361
  Dojo 361
  EXT JS 361
  jQuery 362
  jQuery ICE 362
  MooTools 362
  Prototype or Scriptaculous 362
JSON 289, 290

L

libraries
  AntFarm 373
  CF Gen 373
  CF Library 373
  CF Template 374
  CodeCop 373
  ColdFish 373
  ColdFusion event dispatcher 373
  concurrency 374
  OAuth 374
life expectancy 77

M

media tools
  about 347
  Acrobat Professional, image software 348
  Aperture, image software 348
  audio software 348
    Final Cut Studio, video software 349
    Fireworks, image software 348
    image software 348
    Onlocation, video software 349
    Photoshop, image software 348
    Premiere, video software 349
    Soundbooth, audio software 348
    Ultra, video software 349
    video software 349
    Visual Communicator, video software 349
methods, Application.cfc object
  onApplicationEnd 79
  onApplicationStart 79
  onError 79
  onRequest 79
  onRequestEnd 79
  onRequestStart 79
  onSessionEnd 79
  onSessionStart 79
multiple raio buttons/check boxes
        binding 206

O

object, CFCs
  attributes 38
  constructing 39
  getter method, adding 39
  methods 39
  setter method, adding 39
  standard Coldfusion page, creating 40
object constructor 42
object method access control
  package 56
  private 56
  public 56
  remote 56
output formats
  CVS output 315
  Excel output 313-315
  JSON output 316
  PDF output 312, 313
  XML output 316

P

page flow
  improving 71

PDF 223
PDFdocuments
  encrypting 235
  manipulating 234
  merging 234
  pages, deleting 235
  permissions, setting 238
  printing, from server 228, 229
  thumbnails, generating 236
  watermarks, adding 237
PDF forms
  data, reading from 233
  populating, with data 230-233
  working with 230
PDF pages, generating
  bookmarks, adding 227
  first PDF page conversion 223, 224
  footers, adding 225
  headers, adding 225
  page breaks, adding 226, 227
  PDF documents, saving 228
  sections, creating 224, 225
  variables, adding 225-227
power CFC 59
product
  attributes 38
  method 39
product data
  managing 64
project management
  about 363
  Lighthouse 363
  project 6 363
  project tracker 363
  Skweegee 363

R

report builder
  installing 317-324
request scope
  about 78
REST services
  about 292-297
  Flickr REST service 294
RSS feeds
  about 284-288

S

scopes
  life expectancies 78
scope visibilty
  about 89
  examples 90, 91
Script
  about 363
  scriptaGulous 364
  ScriptCFC 363
  scripting for ColdFusion 8 364
search
  AmazonCFC 364
  Seeker 364
search abilities
  building 242
search abilities, building
  collection, creating 242, 243
  collection, indexing 244, 245
  collection, searching 245
  parameters 250
  PDF, linking to searches 250
  search form, building 246
  search techniques 248, 249
  suggestions 251, 252
simple variables, ColdFusion
  Boolean variables, types 12
  date and time variables, types 12
  decimal based numbers 14
  guidelines, for naming variables 12
  INTEGERS class 12
  numeric variables, types 12
  strings variables, types 12
  types 11
site integration APIs
  Amazon 364
  Amazon SQS CFC 364
  AOL 365
  AOL APIs 365
  Basecamp 365
  BasecampCFC 365
  Cf_googleMap, Google 366
  CFlickr 366
  cfLightCasa, PicasaCFC 368
  cfOpen Social 367
  cfpayment, misc./other 369

cfPicasa, PicasaCFC 368
CheckoutCFC, Google 366
ColdFusion UPS package 369
ColdFusion Yahoo! package 369
connect 365
ConnectAPIcfc 365
constant contact 365
constant contact CFC 365
delicious 366
deliciousCFC 366
digg 366
DiggCFC 366
Facebook 366
Facebook REST client 366
FeedBurner 366
FeedBurner API 366
Flickr 366
Google 366
GoogleCal 367
GoogleCalendarCFC 367
Google Geocode 367
Google Maps Tag 367
ISBNdbCFC, misc./other 370
JangoMail 367
JangoMail CFC 367
JFree Chart 367
JFree Chart Custom Tag 367
misc./other 369
Open Social 367
PicasaCFC 368
picasaCFC 368
recurring billing API CFC,
    Authorize.net 365
riaForge 368
riaForgeCFC 368
riaForge updater 368
sales force 368
SalesForceCFC 368
Simple Goolge Geocode 367
SnipEx, misc./other 370
twitter 368
twitterCFC 368
UPS 369
Yahoo! 369
Yahoo word extraction CFC 369
Youtube 369
Youtube CFC 369

SOAP web services
    about 298, 302
    prototyping 300
    WSDL, checking from browser 301
spaghetti code 59
SQL 292
start methods
    about 85
    application start method 85
    request start method 87
    session start method 86
SVN
    about 350
    Subversion 350
    SVN 1 Cllick Setup 350

T

technologies
    about 147
    browser side applications 148
    HTML-based websites 147
    server side languages 148
Thickbox library HTML style 114-116
traditional webpage reporting
    about 305
    drill down reporting 309, 310
    grouped data 307
    simple report 305

U

unit testing
    CFCUnit 370
    CFUnit 370
    ColdFire 370
    MXUnit 370
    QueryParam scanner 371
    RocketUnit 371
    Stubbie 371
    varScoper 371
unit testing platforms
    CFCUnit 351
    CFUnit 351
    JSUnit 351
    MXUnit 351
URL variable structure 18

V

verity
 built-in search engine 242

W

web form page
 data, editing 65
 data, saving 68
 new record, adding 72, 74
 page flow, improving 71
 product data, managing 64
web forms
 about 61
 description box 63
 form data 63
 form method 63

X

XML tools
 ALTOVA products 371
 better XML 371
 EditiX 372
 Google Sitemap XML Generator 372
 OXYGEN 372
 sosXML 372
 Stylus studio 372
 XMLBuddy 372
 XmlToStruct 372

About Packt Publishing

Packt, pronounced 'packed', published its first book "*Mastering phpMyAdmin for Effective MySQL Management*" in April 2004 and subsequently continued to specialize in publishing highly focused books on specific technologies and solutions.

Our books and publications share the experiences of your fellow IT professionals in adapting and customizing today's systems, applications, and frameworks. Our solution based books give you the knowledge and power to customize the software and technologies you're using to get the job done. Packt books are more specific and less general than the IT books you have seen in the past. Our unique business model allows us to bring you more focused information, giving you more of what you need to know, and less of what you don't.

Packt is a modern, yet unique publishing company, which focuses on producing quality, cutting-edge books for communities of developers, administrators, and newbies alike. For more information, please visit our website: www.packtpub.com.

Writing for Packt

We welcome all inquiries from people who are interested in authoring. Book proposals should be sent to authors@packtpub.com. If your book idea is still at an early stage and you would like to discuss it first before writing a formal book proposal, contact us; one of our commissioning editors will get in touch with you.

We're not just looking for published authors; if you have strong technical skills but no writing experience, our experienced editors can help you develop a writing career, or simply get some additional reward for your expertise.

Learning the Yahoo! User Interface library

ISBN: 978-1-847192-32-5   Paperback: 380 pages

Develop your next generation web applications with the YUI JavaScript development library

1. Improve your coding and productivity with the YUI Library

2. Gain a thorough understanding of the YUI tools

3. Learn from detailed examples for common tasks

jQuery Reference Guide

ISBN: 978-1-847193-81-0   Paperback: 225 pages

A Comprehensive Exploration of the Popular JavaScript Library

1. Organized menu to every method, function, and selector in the jQuery library

2. Quickly look up features of the jQuery library

3. Understand the anatomy of a jQuery script

4. Extend jQuery's built-in capabilities with plug-ins, and even write your own

Please check **www.PacktPub.com** for information on our titles

Printed in the United States
204615BV00003B/272/P